DISCARDED

P9-DFW-993

APR 2008

smile when you're lying

smile when you're lying

confessions of a rogue travel writer

. . .

CHUCK THOMPSON

A HOLT PAPERBACK

NEW YORK

Holt Paperbacks
Henry Holt and Company, LLC
Publishers since 1866
175 Fifth Avenue
New York, New York 10010
www.henryholt.com

Henry Holt® and ⑰® are registered trademarks of
Henry Holt and Company, LLC.

Copyright © 2007 by Chuck Thompson
All rights reserved.
Distributed in Canada by H. B. Fenn and Company Ltd.

Library of Congress Cataloging-in-Publication Data
Thompson, Chuck.
    Smile when you're lying : confessions of a rogue travel writer /
Chuck Thompson.—1st ed.
        p.   cm.
    ISBN-13: 978-0-8050-8209-8
    ISBN-10: 0-8050-8209-3
    1. Thompson, Chuck—Travel.   2. Voyages and travels.
3. Travel writing.   I. Title.
    G465.T59 2007
    910.4—dc22   2007006600

Henry Holt books are available for special promotions and
premiums. For details contact: Director, Special Markets.

First Edition 2007

Designed by Kelly Too

Printed in the United States of America
1   3   5   7   9   10   8   6   4   2

Contents

• • •

smile when you're lying

• • •

Introduction: You Deserve Better

After somewhere between ten and fifteen visits, this is my favorite anecdote from Bangkok. Every word true.

We're in a small, dark bar, an Aussie expat hangout. Across the table is my good friend Shanghai Bob, American expat and Old Asia Hand of distinguished order. To the right, a pair of astonishingly wasted guys in ridiculous bush hats (are there any other kind?) are sparking up what is certainly not the first joint of the evening. To the left, a young Thai girl is giving a rapid-fire, beneath-the-table hand job to a poker-faced German. Throughout the event, the German swigs his beer with a nonchalance that suggests he's back in Bielefeld with his loving Schnuckelputz and adorable rug rats Klaus and Liesl frolicking at his feet.

The German looks like he's in for the long haul and sometime during the girl's indefatigable ministrations a door opens near the rear of the bar. Out spills a porcine gent, half a century old if he's a day, accompanied by a slightly disheveled teenager modestly hitching up her bright orange halter top. Behind the door one can see into a narrow room, the primary features of which are a naked lightbulb swinging from the ceiling and a stained mattress on the floor.

It's at this point that Shanghai Bob looks at me and says, with utter sincerity, with complete lack of irony, "You want to get another beer here or go someplace kind of sleazy?"

Though I've spent the last decade writing about travel for national magazines, this is the first time one of my priceless Shanghai Bob anecdotes has ever appeared in print. If you're surprised that a veteran of the travel trade wouldn't have exploited this sort of golden material more often, it's probably because you don't possess the keen insight that enables you to determine instantly that stories about colorful Aussies in bush hats surrounded by drugs, booze, and Thai whores (to say nothing of Shanghai Bobs) are considered absolutely off-limits by all but a handful of travel publications. Whereas stories about colorful Aussies sporting bush hats and delightful accents, surrounded by koalas and 'roos, and perhaps sipping one genteel glass of Foster's—enjoyed at sunset overlooking the enchanting opera house on the last perfect day of your magical visit to Sydney—are considered absolutely on the money.

This book is for those who understand that, no matter what they read in the travel press, no matter what they expect to encounter once they plunge into the Byzantine world of international tourism, there's nothing genteel, ever, about Foster's, bush hats, or Australian accents. And that even koalas will bite when properly provoked.

In 1995, non–travel writer Sallie Tisdale wrote an incendiary article titled, "Never Let the Locals See Your Map: Why Most Travel Writers Should Stay Home." Published in *Harper's*, the piece was an unsparing evisceration of the travel-writing racket. "The modern reader," Tisdale wrote, "has the misfortune of living in a time when travel literature is booming and good travel writers are few and far between." Warming up to her theme, Tisdale proceeded to savage travel writers as self-important nihilists who put themselves at the center of their stories, ignored anything of genuine interest to readers, and contrived "trips taken largely to be written about, to create stories where none existed before."

With her arch tone and unsympathetic opinions, Tisdale upset a fair number of people in the travel industry, but her story was of particular interest to me inasmuch as it was published at roughly the time I was stumbling into the business. A magazine had flown me to New York to produce a feel-good feature on a group of Russian classical musicians who'd fled the chaos of Moscow and formed a successful orchestra in the shadow of the Statue of Liberty. While I was in New York, the magazine asked me to drop by the newly opened Rose Museum inside Carnegie Hall, as well as a highly regarded Indian restaurant somewhere in the East Village. I wrote a feature about the musicians and short blurbs on the museum and restaurant. The magazine ended up liking the blurbs more than the feature. Would I have any interest, they asked, in reviewing a recently remodeled four-star restaurant in Toronto?

Since then, I've traveled on assignment in more than

thirty-five countries, written two guidebooks, edited two others, worked as an editor at four magazines—including a year as editor in chief of Travelocity.com's short-lived newsstand magazine, at the end of which I was drop-kicked out the door—and been involved as writer, editor, or photographer in a conservative count of two thousand travel stories. I've hunkered down with airline execs, watched marketing campaigns being slicked up, looked behind the curtains of some of the world's largest airports, schmoozed with resort managers, and been badgered by publicists to produce reams of favorable copy. In other words, I've watched the travel world spin from more angles than most people know it has. Travel writing has changed in the decade or so since Tisdale's attempted wake-up call. But not for the better. Bright patches excepted, it's instead settled into a period of weary decline.

The point was driven home some years back by a University of Pennsylvania–sponsored travel-writing conference. Bright-eyed hopefuls expecting to attend edifying lectures, hear war stories from industry heavyweights, make contacts, and generally advance their careers were treated instead to lectures from several presenters—British author Colin Thubron, travel editors from newspapers such as the *Philadelphia Inquirer*—who expressed the opinion that most travel writers were not talented enough to write for "real" publications. They were press junketeers, starved of original thought, incapable of ending any sentence without a phone number, Web address, or other transparent plug for whatever tourist board happened to be picking up the tab for their latest vacation—"talentless freeloaders" who inhabited "the last refuge of the hack" from which they produced "journalistic tiramisu." From a convention of Mississippi Baptists mulling over gay marriage, OK. But it's not a good sign for your profession when this sort of vitriol comes out of a gathering of peers presumably intended to profit those in attendance.

If the concept of "journalistic tiramisu" seems vague, pick up any travel magazine and flip through the pages. I recently did just this at the Safeway down the street from my house. Thinking I might need five or ten minutes to find some genuine turd of an example, I picked up a basket at the door and tossed in a bag of chips and some apples, just so I wouldn't look like one of those social deviants for whom they post the "Do Not Read the Magazines!" sign.

I needn't have worried. I hit tiramisu pay dirt with the first magazine I lifted off the shelf, a special issue of *Outside* devoted to travel. Opening to a random page, here's the first piece of copy that caught my eye:

> Renaissance funhogs, brace yourselves: This trip, combining three days of mountain biking with five days of whitewater rafting on the Colorado River, may be the tastiest pairing since chocolate and cabernet. It takes you straight into the heart of Canyonlands' high-desert rock garden, defined by the goose-necking canyons of Green and Colorado rivers and an almost hallucinogenic symphony of spires, buttes, mesas, hoodoos, fins, arches, and slickrock.

Outside is a very successful, award-winning magazine, but any way you define it, that's just piss-poor writing. The breathless cheerleading (F-U-N-H-O-G-S, what does it spell?), hackneyed comparison (please, talentless scribes,

let's all stop using "delicious" and "tasty" to describe anything other than food), and insufferable hyperbole (it's a
canyon, not an acid trip)—it's enough to stop a Renais-
sance funhog dead in his tracks.

But it's not out of the ordinary. This kind of chirpy
discourse pretty much defines contemporary travel
writing. Coming across it so quickly was like tossing out
the first cast of the day and pulling in an undersized
tuna. Or an elderly flounder. A decent catch, though
nothing the world hadn't seen before.

When the brilliant social critic Joe Queenan—whose
caustic stories played a minor role in my getting fired
from *Travelocity* magazine—sat down to take his first
crack at a travel book in 2004, he was so mortified at the
possibility of being mistaken for a travel writer that he
included in the first chapter this Judas-like disclaimer:
"The narrative that follows embodies the confessions of
a reluctant Anglophile. It is not a travel book per se, as
travel books are dull."

Queenan then commenced with 240 pages of travel
narrative about England. Highly entertaining, but travel
narrative all the same.

The biggest reason travel writing is dull, as Queenan
correctly pointed out, is that most of it is devoid of anything approaching an authentic point of view. On those
rare occasions when travel writers are allowed to express an actual opinion, it must be a completely harm-
less one that's also shared by the travel industry at large.
These are usually offered as hard-hitting commentaries
describing how "quaint" a hotel room is, how "mind-
blowing" a nature park is, or how "mouthwatering" a

chef's specialty is. Everything is superlative. Like being a sports fan, one of the best things about being a traveler is complaining about the parts you don't like— hating the Dallas Cowboys not only doesn't make me any less a football fan, it probably makes me a more avid one. This is a concept the travel industry has never embraced.

Beyond copy softened by corporate considerations, published scrutiny of travel and life abroad is limited even more egregiously by the merciless hammer of political correctness. The writer who dares make anything other than holistically supportive judgments of any foreign culture (not counting Arab) risks career suicide. Add the contemporary media's increasingly polemic I'm-right-you're-an-asshole style of analysis, and it's nearly impossible to generate any frank assessment of foreign cultures and experience. Easier just to fall back on clichés and fawning descriptions of rooms, views, and meals.

Applied to an activity as presumably frivolous as tourism, this may all seem trivial, but it's not. In terms of revenue and head count, travel/leisure is now the world's second-largest commercial enterprise. In a good year, according to some, it surpasses even oil and petroleum exports as the world's largest industry. Over the past fifty years, vast regions of the world have supplicated themselves to tourism. Like my hometown of Juneau, Alaska, entire countries have mortgaged their economies to the whims of traveling strangers, altering, sometimes even desecrating, their cultures and landscapes forever. At the very least, travel and tourism deserve open and thoughtful public examination, a discussion that moves beyond the prevailing pap.

This is especially true because the business is in such dramatic flux. A golden age of international tourism may be drawing to a close. Flights across the Atlantic for pocket change? Weekend fishing safaris in South America? A market that supports entire guidebooks covering Central Pacific islands you never heard of? These basics of travel that Americans take for granted aren't gone, but they're shifting.

Skyrocketing fuel prices. Unmanageable airline budgets. A declining U.S. dollar. International instability and America's increasingly dismal reputation abroad. The new age of travel is about more than waiting in line so that a sixty-year-old TSA biddy can wave a security wand in front of your crotch. In coming years, the way we travel will change significantly. Where all of this leaves travel writing is an open question, but one thing is certain: the overly sentimental, cautious, and commercial tenor of travel writing is satisfying to almost no one beyond the navel gazers who write it and the "hospitality" advertisers who sponsor it.

After more than a decade in the business, I've grown tired of coming home from the intoxicating hell of the road and leaving the most interesting material on the cutting-room floor. The stories my friends actually pay attention to never seem to interest editors, most of them emasculated by demands to portray travel as an unbroken fantasy of on-time departures, courteous flunkies, sugar-white beaches, fascinating cities, charming locals, first-class hotels, golden days, purple nights, and, of course, "an exotic blend of the ancient and the modern." The most memorable experiences—getting laid, sick, lost, home—always seem "too negative," "too graphic," or "too over the heads of our readers" to find their ways into print. Inside information on the vagaries of the travel industry itself borders on sedition.

I bring up Tisdale and *Outside* and Queenan—and many others throughout this book—not to belittle but to commiserate. And to add to the list my own frustration with interpreting "rich and ancient cultures" for readers back home. These frustrations perhaps had something to do with my limitations as a writer, but since I'm inclined to pass around blame whenever possible, I began taking long, hard looks at the demands placed on me by the editors, publicists, marketers, executives, and various snake-oil merchants who run the travel trade. And I began taking notes.

Those reflections piled up in notebooks and those notebooks eventually led to a dog-eared epiphany. I wanted to write about travel the way I experienced it, not the way the travel business wants readers, wants you, to imagine it is. The presumption that readers have the intellectual curiosity of a squirrel monkey and the moral range of an Amish yam farmer has worn thin. This book is a small effort to correct the travel industry's bias against candor and honesty. Or at least a way to pay it back for both the good times and the trouble it's given me.

To do the job, I'll need to start off with a few stories of the sort travel writers almost never get to write. At least not for the kinds of publications that actually pay for copy. Call it my revenge. Or what my future bosses would call the first steps in the wrong direction.

PART I
Aisle →

1

. . .

"Welcome to Thailand,
Ulysses S. Grant!"

"Would you like to see a picture of me?"

A picture I didn't need. The surroundings were clear enough. Gulf of Thailand. Dinky island. Single-room, dirt-floor hut. Palm-thatched ceiling. Two chairs, table, bed. Through the smoky darkness, a kerosene lantern flickering shadows across the room at my companion, an aged, somewhat leathery Thai bar girl. Well, whore, if you must. But retired. And me, taking dictation.

Before I could answer, she shoved a creased plastic Polaroid into my hand. It was her all right. Only in the photo she was sitting on a chair. Naked. Not just naked. Leaning back on the chair, legs open, waiting-for-the-Miranda-Rights-spread-eagle naked.

The pose was intended to accentuate the usual feminine attributes, but time had not been a friend. A pair of mournful breasts wandered across her belly, putting one in mind of *National Geographic*. Or a lactating goat. Only by the fat, dark nose cones on the ends was it possible to determine where precisely the crenellated zeppelins ended. Partially concealed beneath them, several rolls of blubber spilled toward the edges of the picture. Yet none of this was enough to distract the eye from a fantastically ungroomed hedge of pubic hair. For all this, the woman in the photograph, the woman standing in front of me, wore a lottery winner's smile. As has been noted elsewhere, the Thais are the nicest people money can buy.

"See anything you like?" she inquired, somewhat daintily given the circumstances.

Fresh off a mind-numbing year teaching English to thoroughly disinterested brutes in Japan ("This is a pen. That is a pencil." Six days a week. Fifty weeks.), I searched a weary mind, desperate to divert the course of a rapidly deteriorating evening.

"Where'd you learn to speak English so well?" I asked, brimming with professional curiosity.

"In the bar. American guy. Australian guy. Swedish guy."

The contemplative Swedes, of course, speak better English than your average American teenager. I made a mental note to look into her unorthodox method of ESL acquisition. It might assist some of my more promising Japanese chipmunks.

In the meantime, the woman had retreated across the room. Crouching on the floor, ass tilted in my direction, she reached beneath the dusty frame of the bamboo bed and pulled out a platter upon which clumps of moist leaves were piled in a large mound. On top, like a garnish, tidy green kabobs were stacked in the shape of a little log cabin, all tied up nice and neat.

She set the platter in front of me. Next, like a priceless heirloom, she presented a red plastic bong.

"You smoke?" she asked, running a surprisingly soft hand across my sweaty forearm.

Steel-toed visions suddenly began kicking at the side of my head. Cops bursting into room. Two pounds of pot on table. Wrinkly whore in act of disrobing. See me there? I'm the one being handcuffed and hauled away. I'd seen the signs at customs in Malaysia: "Possession of drugs punishable by death." True, this was Thailand, but Malaysia was just across the border and there were a lot of Muslims in this part of the country. Somehow, in the midst of this nightmare, the woman had inserted herself squarely between me and the door.

I first heard about Thailand in jail. This was in Juneau, Alaska, in the mid-1980s. I grew up in Juneau and so naturally did a lot of stupid things there, including drinking a shitload of beer and doing the requisite amount of driving on icy roads. Combined, these activities are almost always fated to enrich a young man's life, and when I was nineteen (legal age in the days before insurance companies were writing federal legislation), I was slapped with a DWI. I blew .181 into the Breathalyzer, a score I'm told can kill a good-sized beaver.

Alaska has the highest alcoholism rate in the country—as my friend Anthony Barnack used to say, "There are two things to do in Juneau, drink and get drunk"—so they tend to be tough on teenage boozers. I ended up with a monstrous fine and a three-day sentence in the crossbar Hilton. Though it's the state capital and loaded with tourists in summer, Juneau's a small town. The only jail is an imposing maximum-security lockup called Lemon Creek Correctional Center. Here are housed hard cases from around the state—drug dealers, armed robbers, rapists, murderers. Tall, concrete walls. Watchtowers. Razor wire. Heavy, clanging doors. Gloomy cell blocks. You've seen the place a hundred times in the movies.

Goody-two-shoed short-timers were housed in a cell apart from the main prison population. This was for DWIs, petty thieves, and, like me, the soft-spoken and wrongfully accused. The cell had eight bunks. Problem was, for the seventy-two-hour duration of my incarceration, fourteen guys were packed inside. Only a few were short-timers. Most were authentic war daddies waiting for space to open in the main blocks so they could be rotated into their new homes.

There was a half-Tlingit guy in for his fourth stretch. He'd violated parole by stealing cash from the till at the pet store where he'd been working. When the owners called the cops, he beat up both of them—the cops, not the owners. Then he set fire to the pet shop. Guys like me did a lot of deferring to guys like him. Fourteen guys, eight bunks. I slept on the floor. Concrete. Happy to do it. You fellas chilly? Here, take my blanket. I find it a bit itchy, anyway.

Most of the time in jail I spent playing hearts, rolling cigarettes for my cellmates, laughing amiably—though nervously—at being called College Boy, and, as the only toilet was a stark squatter in the corner of the cell with no protective walls around it, trying desperately to not take any dumps. The most interesting guy inside was a short, wiry, intensely gabby Californian named Dan, who'd stabbed his girlfriend with a broken-off car antenna. Undaunted in the face of being told to shut the fuck up every two minutes by the larger animals in the

cell, Dan rambled on and on about things like the uncon-
stitutionality of the federal tax code and how secret articles of the Kellogg-Briand Pact were actually written to
facilitate Hitler's rise to power. I've always had trouble
disengaging from chatterboxes, a trait guys like California
Dan, to borrow from Fitzgerald, have a near mystical
knack for detecting and attaching themselves to.

Dan knew a lot about a lot of things, but his favorite
topic was Thailand. During those moments when violent arguments over trump suits and the questionable
accumulation of matchsticks had subsided, Dan regaled
the cell with tales of this bewitching land. Beaches with
sand as white as cocaine flake, sunshine year-round,
and, most important, legions of thin, hairless women,
with skin as smooth as polished teak, open smiles, and
nipples like Hershey's Kisses. Promised Dan, this army
of honey brown nymphettes was just waiting to bestow
foot rubs, blow jobs, and curry dinners on any guy with
enough chutzpah to land up-country with a few twenties in his pocket.

Dan claimed he'd smoked the best bud on the highest volcano in Maui. He'd slept with an actress in L.A.,
whom I won't name but who was quite popular at the
time. He hadn't paid taxes for eight years. Still, it was
Thailand that danced in his dreams. Thailand, where
he'd be heading just as soon as he got out of the slam
and that bitch out on Mendenhall Boulevard coughed
up the $750 she owed him. He had a lawyer somewhere
working on her sorry ass.

"College Boy, a young guy like you'd be an asshole
not to get his dick out to Bangkok as soon as fucking
possible," he told me after our third straight dinner of
hot dogs and Jell-O. "That's paradise for a guy like you."

For a recidivist girl beater, California Dan had a tender side. I'd revealed nothing that might've given him a glimpse of my idea of paradise, but I nodded in agreement, prudently not mentioning the sixty-some liberal arts credits to go before I could possibly experience this sexual Valhalla for myself. He wasn't Tim Robbins, I wasn't Morgan Freeman, and Bangkok wasn't Zihuatanejo. But California Dan's stories stayed with me.

Several years passed between the trauma of the Juneau hoosegow and my first visit to Thailand. I was a university graduate coming off an extremely lonely, difficult, but profitable year teaching English in the Japan Alps. Did you know there are Alps in Japan? Don't feel badly. No one else can find them on a map, either. Japanese included.

As a reward for the privations of the year abroad, fellow Japan sufferer Morgan Rodd and I had purchased tickets and made plans for ten days of R & R in Thailand. The day before our flight, however, Morgan came down with a terrible affliction. It figures that he'd meet Anime Dream Girl the week before we were set to leave the Land of the Rising Blood Pressure. He simply couldn't tear himself away from the wondrous Yumiko. He said, "Sorry, man." I said I understood, and decided to head for Thailand alone.

Just down the street from the famed 150-foot-long reclining Buddha, the magnificent Wat Phra Keo is Bangkok's primary tourist magnet. Wandering amid the temple's golden domes and intricate mosaics, I was approached by four plain-faced young women, all dressed modestly—pants, long sleeves, hair bonnets—despite the fact that in Bangkok just then it was 140 degrees in the shade, 180 inside the tuk tuks.

All four were English majors at a nearby university. The one who spoke the best English was Bit. Bit was the tallest of the group, the most mature. She had sharp, black eyes, thick ankles, and bad teeth. She said the group would like to offer me a free tour of Wat Phra Keo. For me, this would provide an opportunity to learn the secrets of a unique world treasure, and for them, a rare chance to converse with a native English speaker. The pitch was a little wooden, but as I'd been in country for two days, spent the first navigating Bangkok's maddening array of misnumbered buses, and hadn't spoken to anyone since hotel reception, I agreed to a tour.

There are two kinds of girls you have sex with in Thailand. Those you pay and those you marry. These young women were clearly not among the first set. Which was fine. Despite being a former convict, confidant of California Dan, and veteran of the usual collegiate debaucheries, I yet retained some sense of heartland morality, not to mention a genuine interest in regional history. Temples, not tits, filled my Thai checklist.

After the obligatory laps around Wat Phra Keo, Bit asked if I cared to join her classmates for dinner back at student housing. Throughout the day I'd sensed from these go-getters a few glassy-eyed hints at some Bible-thumping evangelism on the horizon. This worried me, as glassy-eyed Bible thumping is something I loathe. The Born Agains have hijacked Christianity and given it a terrible name, and it infuriates me to see them in action.

> When thou prayest, thou shalt not be as the hypocrites are: For they love to pray standing in the synagogues and in the corners of the streets, that they may be seen of men. . . . When thou prayest, enter thy closet, pray to thy father which is in secret; and thy father which seeth in secret shall reward thee openly.

You can quote Matthew (6:5–6 for those needing ammunition) to proselytizing zombies from Karachi to Kentucky, but they'll still interpret the message to mean homos will burn in hell, Muslims here on earth. I'm not sure what happened to old-fashioned Christian humility. People like to bash the Catholics, but when was the last time one knocked on your door?

Evangelical motive or not, there was no denying the bond forged that afternoon between local studentia and wandering *farang*. As I had very little going on, I said dinner sounded swell. We took a long bus ride through the sweltering, stinking, impoverished maze of Bangkok's mean back alleys to a place I couldn't find again with a time machine and squad of bloodhounds.

"Student housing" turned out to be an appalling slum of ramshackle apartments, each accommodating about ten kids, which meant eight more than they were designed to hold. The rooms made Lemon Creek Correctional Center look like the W Hotel in midtown Manhattan. The food was lousy. The concrete stoop I sat on throughout the night was covered with a pulpy, purple stain, residue from a thousand cockroaches squashed beneath the rubber slippers of nimble-footed freshmen.

Yet the evening turned into one of those golden travel experiences, something that actually makes you believe in all that hands-across-the-sea twaddle that cross-cultural consultants, NGO do-gooders, and ESL teachers love to spew. Fifteen or twenty students showed up—boys and girls—to shake my hand, try out their earnest but feeble English, listen to bad Thai pop music, and chew on chicken necks with their friends. A light rain cooled the searing temperatures. Bangkok's ever-present aroma of open sewer magically dissolved. Communication was difficult with all but a few, but the relaxed atmosphere and easy smiles put me in such an expansive mood that I decided right then to change my travel plans.

The itinerary Morgan and I had drawn up in Japan called for several days of decompressing and beer drinking in Bangkok, followed by a train ride south to Phuket, a California Dan "got to fucking go" beach destination. Time permitting, we'd head north to the mountain city of Chiang Mai, famed headland of the Golden Triangle, poppy growers, and rustic tribesmen.

My new pals frowned. It was the rainy season on the western side of Thailand, they said. Everything along the Andaman Sea, especially Phuket, was under a storm cloud—better to head for Ko Samet in the Gulf of Thailand.

"*Ko*" means island in Thai. I still don't know what "*Samet*" means, but few foreigners were said to venture there. Just some cheap beach huts. First-rate snorkeling. No massage parlors or peeler bars. I could see California Dan rolling in his prison bunk, but this was my paradise.

Thus it was decided. The next morning, Bit and the girls from Wat Phra Keo would accompany me to Ko Samet. Taking care of bus transfers, ferry tickets, and various logistics, they would be invaluable in a part of Thailand where my English would be as useful as baht in Bakersfield. In exchange I'd pay for their bus tickets and lodging. Forty or fifty bucks total for guide service from four young women was small beer to a fat-cat ESL teacher whose wallet was bulging with 1980s Japanese yen.

Were this story being written for your favorite travel magazine, it would probably end here. It's currently about standard feature length, three thousand words, give or take. More important, it's imbued with the residual glow of the impromptu dinner at the student compound. Travel writers are always on the prowl for emblematic episodes to serve as uplifting finales for their stories. Anecdotes that suggest the writer undertook his or her contrived trek for reasons other than simply money or a byline ("For years, my deepest desire had been to swim among the native carp of Yap. . . .") and that the magazine printing the innocuous recap did so for motives involving more than simply selling a full-page, full-rate ad to Thai Airways. For example, here's the final graph of a story about a trip to the Philippines I once wrote for *Islands* magazine:

> As the six of us walked in the rain, no friendship ever felt as easy, no chance encounter so special. In the sky a new thunderhead was forming over the rising breakers, bringing a promise of bad weather we barely noticed.

Not wretched. But sappy. A bit manufactured. Lolling there on the page like an old dog, the words don't embarrass me enough to delete them, though I admit to feeling about them the way I might were I to clog the host's toilet at a dinner party. Sometimes you just gotta bow your head and ask for the plunger.

When the great Spalding Gray (who helped ruin Thailand forever; more on that in a minute) wrote about Thailand, he obsessed over having a Perfect Moment, his version of an emblematic finale. "I hadn't had a Perfect Moment yet, and I always like to have one before I leave an exotic place," he wrote. "They're a good way of bringing things to an end."

The trouble with Perfect Moments is that they never come at the end of the trip. They come somewhere in the middle. Or the beginning. As a travel writer, you get to cheat. Rearrange chronology. Take your Day Two dinner with the college kids and turn it into the last paragraph, your final hurrah. It's fake, of course, but so is a lot of travel writing, so what's the difference?

Actual travelers don't have this luxury. Actual travelers exist in real time and have to deal with the kinds of troubles that don't end up as body copy between splashy photos of a beach at dawn and coconut-encrusted prawns in honey-melon-okra dipping sauce at cocktail hour. Actual travelers have to deal with actual travel. Often, this leads to the kind of trouble the travel industry would just as soon pretend doesn't exist.

Ko Samet was just OK. The beach was pebbly. The water murky. Unwashed *Lonely Planet* backpacker riffraff in white-boy dreads and Jamaican colors were scattered around the clumps of thatch huts that dotted the shore. Nothing really wrong with the scene, but after a day on a dusty bus—the shrill depredations of Chuck Norris shrieking from a TV mounted above the driver—and a bumpy ferry ride to the island, I'd been hoping for more.

We arrived early in the evening and checked into a low-rent bungalow duplex near the beach. A pair of tiny thatch rooms that shared a porch but were otherwise separate. The four girls took one side. They'd sleep two to a bed. I had the other side to myself.

The overland trip hadn't added much polish to the new friendship. By dinner, the girls were strangely quiet. It might have been simple Chuck Norris fatigue— as all Thai bus passengers know, the man has a way of sucking the marrow from your bones. But there was an edge of dissatisfaction in their mute smiles. Whatever the reason, the girls finished dinner and abruptly announced their bedtime. Eight o'clock. They pressed their hands together in that poetic Thai way, bowed just so, and disappeared. I stayed on the beach, ordering Singha beers and chatting up various potheads until finally crawling back to the hut well past midnight with a nagging concern about how I was going to entertain four teetotaling virgins for the next two days.

I woke early the next morning. With the sun rising above the waterline, a swim in the Gulf of Siam seemed like an excellent way to clear the alcoholic blur from my eyes. Spalding Gray found his Perfect Moment in the waves of the Indian Ocean, just across the peninsula, near Phuket: "My body had blended with the ocean. And there was just this round, smiling-ear-to-ear pumpkin-head perceiver on top, bobbing up and down."

I didn't have an out-of-body experience off Ko Samet, but the water was warm and it jostled me around in a therapeutic way. I stayed out long enough to banish any lingering threat of a hangover.

What happened next is difficult to describe without discussing my testicles. And the way these normally co-operative pieces of my anatomy began pushing through the body cavity—the position into which they typically recede in times of stress—rising into my abdomen, picking up steam like atoms shot through a particle accelerator and, finally, rampaging like a Khmer war party into my throat. Here they lodged and began suffocating me with a sudden, goiterlike swelling. Revolting, yes, but this is mostly what I recall of my reaction upon returning to my room and discovering that my money—all of it, cash, twelve hundred dollars in Japanese yen—was missing. While I'd been out doing hydrotherapy on my hangover, a thief had gotten into my room and made off with what amounted to almost the entire liquid wealth I'd managed to amass thus far in life.

The stages of grieving flew by in a one-minute blur. Denial. "No fucking way!" Anger. "This is bullshit! This is BULLshit!" Bargaining. "Holy God, maker of heaven and earth, of all that is seen and unseen . . ." Depression. (Speech impossible.) Acceptance. "I am totally fucked."

Nothing else had been taken. Passport, camera, even the wallet. All there. For this I was thankful, like the guy who loses only one limb in the car-bomb explosion. But my cash was gone, and I was at a point in life when traveler's checks and credit cards were the mystical domain of men more canny than I.

I rushed next door and banged hard. Surely the girls

had seen something. Knock knock. Heard something. KNOCK KNOCK! Where the hell were they?

Where they were, the owners of the beach huts told me, was on the morning ferry for the mainland, just now pulling away from the dock down the beach.

"They check out," the old lady told me. "There." She pointed to the sea. A lumbering, single-level ferry belching clouds of black smoke into a washed-out gray sky wobbled a hundred yards offshore.

"All of them checked out?" I demanded.

"They go back Bangkok."

One of the most harrowing travel articles I ever read was published in the late 1990s in British *Esquire* (for reasons to be explained later, the best travel stories usually appear in non-travel magazines). The writer was a poor sod named Stephen Leather, who, stripped of all personal dignity, laid bare his soul in recounting his own spleen-wrenching Thailand epic. Over the course of a year, Leather had been conned out of a small fortune by a Thai prostitute, with whom he'd naturally fallen pathetically in love. "Ying was going to be different. . . ."

Leather had narrowly avoided the typical horror story. Following marriage, the little stunners customarily swindle their unsuspecting foreign hubbies out of houses, property, and life savings before divorcing them. In Leather's case, throughout their relationship and unknown to him, Ying had been turning over his gifts and money to various ne'er-do-wells. My favorite part was the photograph Leather received from a private investigator he'd hired to tail his now fiancée after growing suspicious of her increasingly secretive behavior. The picture showed Ying at home. With her Thai husband! The guy was wearing one of Leather's denim shirts, one he'd presented to Ying as a gift following a morning of postcoital bliss. What guy doesn't love a woman wearing his shirt? *Esquire* probably paid Leather a couple thousand bucks to reveal his story to the British public. Which, to be fair, is better than most of us get after being jilted.

My fall wasn't quite so inglorious, but it still wasn't going to play well with the crowd at home. Still in my "lovin'-life" hibiscus-print swim trunks, I sprinted the length of the beach and tore into the surf, flailing at the water like a terrified chimp.

I am not a fast swimmer. But I was playing with adrenaline and incentive, and the boat was still picking up speed in the shallow water. My panicked strokes caught the attention of the crew, who figured I must be a surprisingly determined doper who'd happened to miss his ride. They cut the engines. Passengers gathered along the gunwales. A quarter mile from shore, I heard applause as a pair of grinning Thai deckhands hauled me aboard.

The passengers were entertained, but a wild-eyed, hyperventilating lunatic isn't someone you normally want to pull over for in the Gulf of Siam. Storming the passenger deck, I found Bit and the girls near the bow. Elastic strands of drool swinging from my lips, the initial greeting went something like "GIVE ME BACK MY FUCKING MONEY!" Mel Gibson later reprised the moment with his "Give me back my son!" ejaculation in the 1996 film *Ransom*. The girls remained at ease.

"We changed our minds and decided to go home this

morning," Bit explained. "We're sorry we didn't say good-bye."

The ship captain appeared behind me. He grabbed my arm and told me to calm down. The guy was about five foot four, with arms as thin as telephone wires, yet I've never felt a stronger grip. In his eyes I saw a man who, unlike myself, appeared comfortable with the idea of getting punched in the face once in a while. It seemed like a good time to take a step back. Over the girls' bitter denials, I explained the situation. A real show for the passengers.

The captain searched the girls' bags. Nothing. No money. He shrugged at me. His expression said, "Sorry, Whitey, but you come out here with four local chicks in tow, what do you expect to happen?" To this guy, I was about as original as a dog taking a leak on a fire hydrant.

I pleaded my case. It was impossible that the girls were innocent. After more indecipherable Thai debate—girls getting angry, passengers taking sides—the captain picked up his radio.

"Police on other side of island," he told me. "I take you and girls back. You stay beach. Wait for police."

The captain dumped us on the beach and took off for the mainland. The cops arrived on tiny motor scooters. They were inspiringly officious. Not the way I usually like my cops, but given the circumstances, my mood brightened.

The police commandeered a beach hut. The interrogation dragged through the morning and into the blazing heat of afternoon. They interviewed the girls individually. Then together. They tore apart their bags. After several hours a husky woman arrived to conduct body searches.

The cops knew the girls took the money. I knew it. Everyone knew it. Didn't they? There seemed to be some debate. But all of it in Thai. For all I knew the girls had by now paid off everyone and were simply completing the ruse by playing out an elaborate string. Twelve hundred bucks buys a lot of graft in Southeast Asia.

I sat in the sand, helpless, angry, ignorant to the alien babble. Sometime after noon Bit emerged from the interrogation hut.

"We were kind to you," she said. "We could never do what you accuse us of. You are a bad man to treat us like criminals."

Then she added, "You drank a lot of beer last night. Maybe it makes you crazy." The worst kind of Christian rebuke is the kind you can't quite put a finger on.

I told her she had to agree it looked suspicious. She told me the girls had simply reconsidered the wisdom of traveling with a strange man and decided for appearance's sake to go home. She was sorry they hadn't said good-bye, but I'd been out swimming, and they were anxious to catch the morning ferry. As we'd exchanged addresses the day before, she said she had intended to send me a letter from Bangkok.

"Now I don't write you letter," she sneered. Little daggers flew out of her eyes.

I stared into her face, but it was like popping the hood and gaping at a dead engine on the side of the highway. I'd seen all the parts before, but I couldn't figure out what any of them meant. Was her explanation plausible? Maybe this was how people behaved in Thailand. I told Bit that I still believed she had my money, but that if she didn't, then I was genuinely sorry about what had happened here. It was a strange sort of apology. I couldn't imagine the girls weren't guilty, but a thread of doubt had established itself in my mind.

Finally, one of the cops pulled me aside.

"We have nothing," he said in that happens-all-the-time way they must teach on the first day in cop schools worldwide. "We have no choice but to allow these girls to leave Ko Samet on the three o'clock boat."

So, the girls left. But not me. I had no money. And the boat captain, returning on the afternoon run, had a strict rule. No one gets to the mainland without a ticket. Especially dipshit *farangs* who roll through his territory with four local girls on the payroll.

I'd been broke before. The summer I was seventeen, I bought a 1973 Ford Torino for four hundred dollars with the idea of driving it across country and back. I made it halfway across, then only as far back as Salt Lake City, where my money ran out, and I crashed at the apartment of some friends who were even worse off than I. For three weeks we hung out in the mall around Pizza Hut, swooping in on leftover slices and crust bones before the wait staff came to clear the greasy trays left behind by paying customers. Or we talked the McDonald's and Wendy's clerks into giving us handfuls of promotional game cards, which yielded not the promised speedboats or Caribbean getaways, but life-sustaining consolation prizes, such as medium Cokes and small fries.

Dead broke and starving later that year in Honolulu—well, Ewa Beach, but only locals will know the shameful difference—I got involved in a poorly planned scheme to buy a small amount of pot, cut it with parsley and catnip, and resell it for huge profits to the marines coming into port from long deployments on aircraft carriers. The trouble was, a fourteen-year-old kid named Kimo we met behind a donut shop stiffed us for a hundred-dollar bag of shake. We couldn't decide who we were more afraid of—pissed-off jarheads or Kimo's four-hundred-pound Samoan bodyguards. Thus began and ended my career as white drug lord. We got our money back the next day by cutting out pictures of Jerry Lewis from *TV Guide*, pasting them to a dressed-up can of Foster's lager, and going door-to-door as volunteer collectors for Jerry's Kids, the annual Labor Day telethon that weekend fortuitously in full swing. We took in seventy-five dollars and used the cash to buy steaks and more Foster's.

Being broke on a remote island in Thailand was different. The isolation was oppressive. The lack of options stunning. There were no telethons to poach, no marines to swindle. There weren't even any phones. Travel was a lot more adventurous before cell phones. How Columbus made it across the Atlantic without checking in with the missus every forty-five minutes remains a mystery for the ages.

After my money was stolen, Thailand changed for me completely. The whole sweltering sump pit got about ten degrees hotter. The temples a few shades dingier. The mosquitoes—fat with malaria each one—more aggressive. The smiles, now that the money was gone, a whole lot tighter.

The old couple who owned the hut where I'd been

robbed declared their profound Buddhist sorrow for my misfortune, and they did cook me lunch on the house. Still, though they deeply regretted the incident, they simply couldn't accommodate my groveling by comping me an extra night in their grimy hut. Which was like being told your résumé looked great and the interview went well, but they still feel you're not quite right for the job at Applebee's.

The first day on Ko Samet passed in a white haze. I staggered around the beach, dragging my belongings with me, trying to drum up sympathy from the hippies, but they were almost as broke as I was and weed was all they could offer as a means out of my torment. At some point I simply curled up in the sand beneath a palm tree, thinking I'd ride out the night in communion with nature. But even the tropics get cold after sundown. By 3:00 AM, I was shivering on the damp ground with arms tucked inside my T-shirt.

The next afternoon I was still sitting in the sand wondering if it was on Ko Samet that my journey through this world would come to its unlikely close, when a smiling Thai woman approached from down the beach. She walked with the kind of sway that suggests invisible sacks of potatoes tied to each hip. She wore faded yellow shorts, a loose tank top, and had the kind of long, dry hair you get when you spend a lot of time outdoors without conditioner. She looked about forty.

"I heard about your troubles," she said.

I mumbled something, and she confirmed that Ko Samet was a small island and word got around pretty quick among the locals.

"Are you hungry?" she asked.

As I hadn't eaten in twenty-four hours, I would have

swallowed old cat droppings had any been available. She plopped down in the sand beside me.

"Let's make a deal," she said. "I'll buy you dinner, and you can stay at my house until you find a way to leave Ko Samet."

My good upbringing normally would have obligated me to make a show of grateful but apologetic rejection— "Oh, gosh, no, couldn't put you out," etc.—but circumstances were extraordinary. I listened.

"In return, all you have to do is write a letter for me," she continued.

The woman explained that she had a boyfriend in Australia. Though she could speak English, she was unable to read or write it. What she wanted me to do was copy exactly what she told me, then write his name and address on an envelope so that she might mail the letter to her one true love.

Rarely in life are we presented with opportunities that shine the spotlight so precisely on our own particular talents. I felt like the doctor on a plane when a woman is going into labor. As an undernourished man of letters, I told my new friend that I was not only eager but uniquely qualified for the assignment.

After inhaling copious amounts of curry at a little beach restaurant, the two of us walked a narrow jungle trail to her place. This turned out to be a slightly glorified version of the beach hut where I'd recently been robbed and evicted. I noted with apprehension the existence of just a single bed, but otherwise the situation seemed solid. The woman liked me, she wasn't bad company, she wasn't going to let me starve. After seating me at a table and striking a match to a pair of old hurricane lanterns—if Herman Melville had rolled out of the cupboard I wouldn't have been surprised—she produced a tablet, pen, and envelope with canceled Australian stamps and a carefully folded letter inside. The letter was from a guy named Derek who drove a taxi in Melbourne.

Thailand superexpats Richard Ehrlich and Dave Walker have many distinguished lines on their résumés, though none quite so noteworthy as *Hello My Big Big Honey!*, their anthology of love letters written to Bangkok bar girls by men of all nationalities, who, once back in the lands of dowdy, nagging women, strip malls, and other nine-to-five drudgery, can't seem to get the exotic vacation trollops of Thailand out of their minds. Derek's letter pretty much followed the sweet, surprisingly restrained, yet still creepy formula chronicled by Ehrlich and Walker.

> My Dearest Poon: My body is in Australia, but my heart is in Thailand. Every day I look at your picture and remember our last night together. I'll never forget making love to you on the beach under a full moon. Was it put there just for us? I am making plans to get back to you and Thailand as soon as possible. In the meantime, I am sending $300 to your account at Bangkok Bank so that you can continue your schooling. . . .

I finished Derek's letter, hoisted pen and paper, and told his girlfriend to fire away. She began conventionally enough. ("Hello my big, big Honey!") I faithfully scribbled down her thoughts regarding her reciprocal affection for Derek, pursuant chastity, strong distaste for black-hearted Thai men, resounding strides as a nursing student, and general pleasantries concerning life on the island. ("It's very hot here!" To which I barely resisted adding, "No shit!")

As the darkness outside became complete and the flickering lanterns gasped for more kerosene, she dragged her chair next to mine, practically resting her chin on my shoulder as she looked over my arm at the words magically appearing on the page as she spoke them. For Derek's benefit, she returned to the scene of their climactic moonlit tumble on the beach. I learned more about Derek. What powerful arms he had. What a good kisser he was. The way his wavy blond hair felt so soft in her fingers. After a bit more of this, she dropped the veil of decorum altogether.

"Derek, I want to suck your big, fat cock and have you come in my mouth," she breathed into my ear.

My pen quivered. I coughed. A gentle, social cough. A lamb choking on a blade of grass in a foggy meadow. She slid an arm across my back. In addition to everything else, crossing the Rubicon here would now include a betrayal of Derek, whom I'd sort of grown to like. Worse, I imagined a thousand unsuspecting Dereks lured into this den exactly as I'd been.

"My wet pussy wants to be fucked so hard," she moaned again into my ear, emphasizing "pussy" and "hard" with exaggerated breaths.

She knew I had no money, so what we had here was an experienced sexual athlete with a genuine appetite for intercourse. It's these single-guy-fantasy situations that find me at my smoothest with women. My response went something like, "Ah, hmm, yes, heh-heh, you don't say?"

She replied by producing the naked Polaroid picture of herself, then crawling to the bed and returning with an enormous platter of Thai stick. I'd already decided against screwing a Thai prostitute, but even if I'd been tempted, I owed it to myself to make sure she was better looking than my eighth-grade math teacher, Mrs. Steinbrenner.

It'd been a grand evening, I assured her, but it was late and I really needed to be getting back to my patch of dirt on the other end of the island. There was some back-and-forth of the "Oh, you can stay for one more cappuccino" variety, but in the end I fled into the night, still broke, but with a belly full of curry and my honor more or less intact. As I hurried down the moonlit trail, I heard a succession of wails behind me, but whether these were curses or cries of masturbatory release I'm pleased to say I'll never know.

I spent another hellish night outside, but made it off Ko Samet the following day thanks to a mop-topped young Kiwi en route to a year in China who'd heard my sad story and loaned me a hundred dollars, to be repaid upon my return to Japan. I've ever since kept a soft place in my heart for New Zealand, despite the fact that going there from the States is like traveling sixty-five hundred miles to see a junior-varsity version of the Pacific Northwest. Only with lousy food. Nevertheless, as I later did with a large donation to Jerry Lewis's telethon, I repaid the loan as soon as I was able, and to this day count meeting that Good Samaritan as one of the luckiest breaks of my life. No matter how compromising the situation, a guy can't hold out against Thai stick and wet pussy forever.

I spent my last days in Thailand hoarding my meager financial reserves amid the cheap restaurants and flophouses along Bangkok's Khao Sanh Road that catered to "backpackers," that charming euphemism for the transient community of burnouts and slackers that, then as now, polluted Thailand (though the trendsetters have since moved on to Laos and Cambodia). To this squalid quarter were drawn the unwashed canaille from all corners of Europe and North America, low-rent pseudohippies who gathered to buy Bob Marley T-shirts, consult their *Lonely Planet* guidebooks, and watch free videos at outdoor cafés. The videos were actually a good deal for those of us short on cash. For two dollars, I nursed three beers through *Good Morning, Vietnam* and actually enjoyed the movie, though when I saw it years later, I realized it was terrible. It must have been either the beer or the being lonely and defeated among the castoffs of my generation that made me so sentimental at the time.

I stayed in a room the size of a phone booth for ten dollars a night and began compiling notes for a scathing commentary on this crowd of phony nonconformists who seemed to be doing little more than smoking pot, leaving trash, and not spending any money across Thailand. Having been penniless myself a few times, and stinging from the misadventure on Ko Samet, my notes were on the angry side. Groups like this believe they're rubbing shoulders with the "real" version of whatever country they're blighting. They assume that by being poor—or at least appearing to be poor—they forge an immediate brotherhood with the locals, earning a kind of authentic "experience" the privileged scum in the five-star, air-conned hotels up on the hill can never understand. The locals, of course, are too polite to point out to the temporary bohemians that their idea of travel as *pax orbis* is as bogus as the guy at the Raffles Hotel bar ordering his third Singapore Sling, now shamelessly pumped from a premix.

What these travelers don't get is that what the Third World loves most about America, about Europe for that matter, is its staggering wealth. Its big cars, fine clothes, dependable ostentation. Seeing a young American down on his heels does nothing for a down-on-his-heels Thai or Costa Rican or Indian, who wants to go to America only to get rich. And if America must come to him, he'd prefer that it do so loaded to the gills with ready cash.

Tirades like this laced my notebook, which I eventually turned into a book manuscript that, justifiably, no publisher was ever convinced to buy. Several years later, young Alex Garland became a sensation for writing *The Beach*, a fictitious examination of Thailand's deranged expat culture. Though it was miles better than my version of the scene, *The Beach* wasn't very good, and for a while it pissed me off that someone else had gotten famous on my idea. Only later when I saw the film starring Leonardo DiCaprio was I satisfied not to have had anything to do with it.

As my experiences on Ko Samet had led me to the brink of Thai vice, I decided to spend my last night in Bangkok checking out the real thing. After the Vietnam War, Thailand's thriving though not yet world-infamous prostitute community was relocated along narrow Patpong Road. Patpong soon became synonymous with the kind of good times that could be known only in a world where widespread fear of AIDS and the Global Commission on Women's Health did not yet exist.

The golden age of Patpong ran roughly from the years 1975 to 1987, the former being the fall of Saigon, the latter date marking the film release of Spalding Gray's *Swimming to Cambodia*. Gray introduced the masses to such rituals as the Thai body-body massage, in which a heavily lathered professional girl "hops on top of you and goes swiggle-swiggle-swiggle, body-body-body, and you slide together like two very wet bars of soap." Gray laid it on thick, which bummed out all the old-timers, who knew the good days would be over once the masses got their fingers in the pie.

Basically, Gray's was a slightly more erudite version of the stories told by California Dan. Guys hear this stuff and they come running—not guys in tie-dye with no money either—and that's exactly what they've been doing ever since. If you go to Patpong today, the whores and johns—from slick-haired Western financiers to every pudgy fifth cousin of Arab royalty—are still there, but so is McDonald's, as well as thousands of yammering Japanese and Chinese tourists safely quarantined from the diseased action behind tour-bus windows.

I made it to Patpong just in time to see the legendary boulevard of reprobate corruption before it morphed into a mere street of crass commercialism. The bars there had names like Super Pussy and Pussy Alive and Snatch Happy and so on. The most famous one was King's Castle, and I'll never forget walking through its doors for the first time.

Like all guys my age, I'd spent a fair amount of time standing in the hallways, kitchens, and corners of otherwise dull parties, staring through the smoky air at the prettiest girl in the room, wondering how I might possibly weasel my way into her life, if only for a night. At King's Castle, they were *all* the prettiest girl in the room, but they were all staring at *me*, wondering how they might possibly weasel their way into *my* life, if only for a night. True, the economics were different, but that's not what you think about when a topless bint guides you through a darkened room to a table surrounded by go-go dancers gyrating to Metallica being played through a jet turbine.

After the hostess settled me in, a caramel-skinned nymph in a neon green bikini materialized to take my order. She rested a breast on my shoulder—that thing did look heavy—while I lingered over the decision. Singha or Tiger? Singha or Tiger? The music blasted. Women came by like pieces of sushi on a conveyor belt, each better looking than the last.

"So many choices you're bound to make the wrong one," some sunken-eyed Brit leaned over and coughed at me, California Dan–style.

In retrospect, it might have been divine intervention that my money had been filched on Ko Samet and I was in this place only by the grace of limited Kiwi largesse. AIDS may not yet have been on everyone's lips, but it was surely running through the bloodstream. And I'm not made of iron.

My money troubles, alas, made me a gawker who couldn't even afford the ladies drinks—ten dollars a Coke and she'll sit on your lap and pump her hips while she pretends to drink it. The working girls ID'd me as a dry well pretty quick, and once I stopped being the most popular guy at the party, it wasn't quite as fun.

I walked down the street, passing the cheerless shops featuring rows of girls in the windows with numbers pinned to their dresses. Somewhere along the way, I allowed a rather aggressive tout to steer me up a narrow flight of stairs for a show he promised I wouldn't soon forget. I was escorted to a booth by an extremely attractive young woman, who made herself comfortable on my lap as soon as I sat down. She began stroking me through my flimsy cotton shorts. A second girl with blunt-cut pixie hair and snake-charmer eyes approached with a clipboard.

"Write down you name!" As everywhere in Bangkok, the music was offensively loud, but I got the impression this girl would have yelled anyway.

"Write down my what?"

"You name! Write down you name!" She pushed the clipboard into my face.

The odds were thin against my ever running for public office, but the place was quite obviously full of Republican eyes. I refused to provide my name.

"Write down you name!"

Slightly put off, the girl on my lap wandered away, but clipboard pixie remained committed to her work. We went back and forth a few times—"Write down you name!" "No, really, prefer not to, thanks, anyway"— until I realized that neither lap girl nor any of her friends were going to return until I appeased this pint-sized witch. I smiled, took the clipboard and pen, and, with a defiant flourish, wrote "Ulysses S. Grant." She took the clipboard, nodded, and walked away.

Once again my lack of ready capital was red flagged,

so the bar girls more or less left me alone to enjoy the show. The details of these programs have been written about before; nevertheless they do make an impression on the novice. After a pointless introduction by an oily emcee, various girls trotted onto a small round stage to perform a highly specialized array of tricks for the enjoyment of a hundred pie-eyed men seated around the miniature coliseum. The first performer sat on the floor, reared onto her back, cupped her thighs in her palms, and from a straw that protruded from her vagina shot darts at balloons hanging from the ceiling. I didn't get the stat sheet, but she was at least as accurate as the average NBA point guard at the free-throw line. The next girl shoved fluorescent markers into her cooch, then hovered over the naked bodies of other girls to create not amateurish body paintings. My favorite used her female musculature to mount a flute and whistle out a few bars of "The Star Spangled Banner." Most imaginative was the girl who "drank" a bottle of Coke into her vaginal vault, held it there while she danced a quick number, then discharged the fluid back into the original bottle, whereupon a second girl arrived to put the bottle to her lips and drink the entire contents in the more conventional manner. Between these sensational displays, the clientele was kept entertained by an ongoing though somewhat uninspired string of faux lesbian action on the side.

I more than felt I'd gotten my money's worth and was ready to call it a night. Settling my meager tab, I made a move for the door but was soon stopped. Screaming pixie was back in my face.

"Fifty dollah!" she shrieked. "You owe fifty dollah!"

"No, no," I yelled back. "I had two beers. No touch girl. Nothing."

"Fifty dollah!" Her nipples were shooting out of her bikini top like lit firecrackers.

She wasn't taking no for an answer. Neither were the two thugs behind her. Before I could mount an argument, she unfurled a piece of green poster paper. On the sheet, which she thrust in front of me with both hands like a royal decree, written in large, black cursive letters, was the inscription, "Welcome to Thailand, Ulysses S. Grant!"

"Genuine pussy writing!" the pixie screamed. "You order this one! Fifty dollah for genuine pussy writing!"

I recognized the handwriting. Or pussy writing, as it were. It was the girl from the show who'd jammed Sharpies into her moneybox and drawn pictures. You can end a lot of showdowns in Asia with laughter. So I laughed. Pixie laughed with me.

"OK, for you, nice guy, twenty-five dollah!" she said, though no less insistently.

The goons behind her wore complicated smiles, somewhere on a scale between celebrating international fellowship and we fist fuck guys like you for kicks. I was being bamboozled. Just like with Bit and the girls and the cops on Ko Samet. They knew it and I knew it and they knew I knew it. But so what, it was Thailand, and I was stuck in a joint where I probably shouldn't have been in the first place. And, after a year of slogging on an ESL galley in Japan, I really did appreciate the proper punctuation on the poster.

"How about fifteen dollars?" I offered.

The pussy-writing poster turned out to be the most

expensive souvenir I brought back from Thailand. It sat in my closet for several weeks before I finally figured out what to do with it. Morgan called the day he got it in the mail.

"Welcome to Thailand, Ulysses S. Grant?" he said over the phone. "Did I miss something good?"

2

· · ·

Baked Alaska: How Drugs, Tourism, and Petroleum Tamed the Last Frontier

Few things are more depressing than watching the titans fall. Willie Mays stumbling around centerfield in a Mets uniform. Johnny Carson becoming a recluse. Aretha Franklin dueting with Kid Rock. It's why even though I've got no problem with guys shooting guns, I can't stand hunting magazines—all those dead grizzlies.

So it's good that on the last New Year's Eve in the life of Juneau's old Red Dog Saloon, I'm not yet aware that I'm watching a beautiful thing die. Perspective often makes things worse, and the night is already going badly enough. Without an end-of-the-year party to crash, my large-living, gap-toothed friend Randy and I have defaulted to the Dead Dog, planning only to ring in 1984 with a few rounds of Rainiers and another installment in our ongoing discussion about how we need to get the fuck out of this town and meet some Down South chicks—Down South to people in Alaska meaning Seattle as much as anywhere else.

Dark, wet, windy conditions keep Juneau tourist free in winter, so the bar is filled with the usual crowd: Gor-Texed locals, emotionally bankrupt state-worker clones, recently imported granola crunchers from Oregon, and a table of flannel-wrapped miners—good Juneau guys, the kind who take their showers after work, not before. Primed for the approach of midnight, the partying miners are anchored by a mastodon-bearded and spectacularly foul-mouthed Viking monster whose menacing laughter and constant demands for more booze lend the night the kind of edge most often associated with Premier League hooliganism. Even scaling back for inevitable exaggeration, I put the guy at six five, 250 pounds. Trim another inch and 30 pounds off him if you must, but on the foul-mouthed point I claim perfect memory. You don't easily forget the evening you become acquainted with the term "felching" or listen to a rogue Norseman repeatedly refer to his own mother as a cunt. Wife or pregnant daughter, cunt, sure. I'd grown up around fishermen and hunters, not Trappist monks. But this guy was trouble, even by Last Frontier standards.

Eleven forty-five hits. Behind the bar, the harried waitress begins prepping bottles of Cold Duck or Andre or whatever other sugar-saturated crap makes people at weddings and bad New Year's Eve parties think they hate champagne. That's right, Rainier beer, flannel shirts, and unwed teen mothers, and I can still find room to be a champagne snob. Who among us isn't a walking contradiction?

Eleven fifty. The Viking stands, balances more adroitly on a tippy chair than you'd expect, points to his watch, and begins the countdown. "One minute till midnight, motherfuckers!" A moment of confusion while drinkers around the bar check their wrists and look at the deer-antler clock on the wall. Grunts of protest arise from a few nitpickers seated at the bar. "Hey, asshole, check your watch. It ain't midnight yet." No matter. The Viking's eyes have rolled too far into the back of his head to see anything. Miraculously, his mouth keeps moving.

"Forty-five! Forty-four! Forty-three! C'mon, mother-fuckers!"

No one in the bar is man enough to tell the besotted giant he's wrong, that 1984 still belongs to the future. Without much fuss, the room simply gives in to the weary group dynamic you saw after both Dubya elections. You know something isn't right, but at some point you just stop resisting the tide.

"Four! Three! Two! One, motherfuckers! Happy Fucking New Year!" An awkward what-the-hell-happy-new-year shrug momentarily unites the bar. Soon after his preemptive celebration, the Viking passes out and everyone settles into a post-midnight funk. Already hammered on the cheap beer and bubbly, half of the crowd is also entering the catatonic period that follows any encounter with Matanuska Thunderfuck, Alaska's legendary smoke from the Matanuska Valley. The twenty-four hours of summer sunlight during the brief but intense growing season there is said to power the weed with the knockout strength of a rutting moose.

Ten minutes later, the bawdy cheers of legit count-downs from fifteen other bars echo down South Franklin Street and through the Red Dog's swinging doors. The miners sit unfazed. To them, 1984 is already ten minutes old, so what's the big deal?

Returning from the bar and dropping two new Rain-dogs on the table, Randy looks at his watch and slams half his can in one gulp: "We gotta get the fuck out of this town."

Drugs changed my life in the seventh grade. Not because I started taking them, but because everyone else did. In the 1970s, Juneau, Alaska, ran on drugs. Amphetamine-fueled fishermen maximizing time on the water. Stoned state employees coping with dark winters and cubicle summers. Coked-up capitol workers more connected to the well-being of South American coca farmers than constituents back home. Even before our national acquiescence to antidepressants, everyone apart from my parents seemed to be on something.

During my first year there, Floyd Dryden Junior High earned brief notoriety for being mentioned on Paul Harvey news for having one of the highest percentages of students in the United States who, according to a recent study, admitted to using marijuana, cocaine, or "hard drugs." If anyone else was taken aback by this revelation, the students of Floyd Dryden were not. The only thing that surprised us was the study's qualifying language. "One of the highest?" Was it possible there existed a preteen community more steeped in narcotics than our own?

I don't recall having been sampled, but the study foreshadowed a life destined for the moral fringes. At the time I was part of the less than 20 percent of Juneau twelve-to-fourteen-year-olds who apparently were *not* spending large chunks of the school day toking up in the woods outside school and memorizing the lyrics to Thin Lizzy's "Jailbreak."*

But the vices that convulsed Alaska in the 1970s and '80s affected more than just the medicated progeny of Floyd Dryden Junior High. (Then nicknamed the Wolverines, Floyd Dryden has since been renamed the "less aggressive" Eagles, and if you want any more succinct indication of how Alaska has been softened up by Lower Forty-eighters you won't find it.) Drugs were only the start. Having embraced one narcotic of the day, young, isolated, unguarded Alaska would prove no match for a pair of even more corruptive influences that went by the genteel names Hospitality and Resource Development: tourism and oil.

Along with me, mega-cruise-ship tourism in Southeast Alaska grew up in the 1970s. To facilitate the early compliance of locals in those salad days, major cruise lines cannily treated Juneauites like VIPs, allowing them to walk right onboard the ships that began tying up at the state ferry terminal. Locals could get a drink in one of the garish bars and gawk at the magnificent vessels that were bringing daily infusions of dollars from Down South.

It wasn't long before ambitious bureaucrats in the state's Department of Tourism saw in the cash cows floating in the sleepy harbor a new gold mine—Juneau's

---

* Years later a former editor in chief of *Rolling Stone* would treat me to a dissection of the sublime logic of the primary lyric from this stoner masterwork: " 'Tonight there's gonna be a jailbreak, somewhere in this town.' A jailbreak? Somewhere in town? Like maybe at the fucking *jail*?"

original A.J. mine having been tapped out in 1944. Despite the fact that the former territorial capital was largely unknown to the outside world, they envisioned it now as the centerpiece of a national marketing campaign. And offered incentives to get it rolling. I worked the push firsthand, sort of, spending a few months as a part-time lackey in the Department of Tourism, stuffing brochures and six-color, spot-varnished posters of hanging glaciers and breaching orcas into cardboard tubes for mailing around the world. If you were one of the many grade-school kids doing state reports who wrote to Alaska in the fall of 1981, I was very likely the guy who sent you all the cool stuff.

Then one day, as if by magic, the most enchanted force in global tourism took note of our efforts. *The Love Boat* announced it would be sailing to Juneau to film a special episode. Fabulous publicity. Town atwitter. Forget that out-of-town rubes and virgin wilderness generally get along like orange juice and toothpaste. This was gonna be huge for tourism.

And it was. Along with half the town, my sisters bivouacked with their empty autograph books (who ever came to Juneau?) at the Mendenhall Glacier and collected signatures. Captain Stubing, Doc, Julie, Isaac. All the giants.

At least one reader on www.jumptheshark.com has since recognized "the Alaska trip" as the episode that once and for all buried the venerable "Fuck Barge." But in truth it was *The Love Boat* that got the best of us. All it took to turn the last unspoiled wilderness in America into a check-it-off tourist destination was a national audience that raised a cultural touchstone from the weekly spectacle of Scatman Crothers, Charo, Reggie Jackson, and Florence Henderson making whoopee on an imaginary cruise ship. Throw in a few "prices slashed" Princess cruise promotions up the Inside Passage and a national marketing campaign jobbed out to some PR firm in New York and you've got the makings of an old-fashioned stampede. This one with gold cards instead of gold pans.

By the summer following *The Love Boat*'s appearance, one or two ships docking in town had become old news. It took three, then four, then five in port to attract the attention of jaded locals. One day, without announcement, the friendly ships you could walk aboard were gone, replaced by larger, oil-belching crypts that anchored offshore and disgorged their charges onto land by covered tender. Soon, more tourists sailed into Gastineau Channel each summer day than actually lived downtown. The floating cities arrived, poured cash into the South Franklin Street wampum shops by day and backlog sewage into the pristine waters by night, then stole away under cover of darkness.

Downtown Juneau vanished. Like Old Singapore and Times Square, the rough-edged city was dismantled by a crowd embarrassed by its history yet eager to profit from it. A wide pedestrian walkway was installed. The line of Indian bars along South Franklin Street was replaced by gift shop, gift shop, gift shop, gift shop, trafficking in Made-in-China T-shirts, mukluks, and cute little stuffed porcupines and otters.

Residents became extras in a tourist show. A busload of cotton tops (as the oldsters were called) once stopped for fifteen minutes to take pictures of me throwing sticks into a pond for my dog to fetch. It was my first experience with the big-time travel industry. Only I hadn't gone anywhere. Big-time travel had come to me.

Juneau's hardscrabble personality was swept out to sea by a relentless tide of packaged tourism. Locals fled downtown in summer. Tourists were helicoptered to the top of the once-hazardous Mendenhall Glacier. The final blow: the original Red Dog Saloon, with its narrow lay-out, sawdust floor, and snowshoes crisscrossed above the bar became such a hit with tourists that they closed it down and opened a big, Disneyfied version down the block. Like most locals, Randy and I sniffed around the new place a few times before swearing it off for good. Not that we had warm memories of the guy, but a Red Dog where our New Year's Eve Viking would be out of place was a Red Dog we wanted no part of.

Despite three decades of steady commodification, the media continues to push the myth of Juneau as an edge-of-the-world destination for hearty adventure seek-ers of the Jack London variety. A 2006 travel story in the *Wall Street Journal* reassuringly labeled the capital of one of the wealthiest states in the Union as "Off the Beaten Track." I resisted the urge to drop the editors a note letting them know that during what the Juneau Convention & Visitors Bureau press kit defines as the official five-month tourist season from May to Septem-ber, Juneau now receives around a million visitors. That's roughly sixty-five hundred tourists a day, 90 per-cent of whom travel to Off the Beaten Track Juneau on luxury cruise ships and whose presence turns down-town into a pedestrian mall of trinkets, tram rides, and local microbrew for nearly half the year.

I can't claim innocence. Stuffing posters in mailing tubes and hamming it up for shutterbugs was only the beginning of my complicity. Sooner than I would have thought, I was giving away "locals only" hiking secrets to readers of *The Atlantic*. Selling out hidden paddling opportunities to *National Geographic Adventure*. Revealing authentic, hole-in-the-wall fishermen's bars for *Maxim* and *Esquire* drinkers. Praising the glories of various natural wonders in the pages of Alaska Airlines' in-flight magazine. With Zero fighters and Betty bombers, the Japanese had managed to take only the Alaskan islands of Attu and Kiska during World War II—the travel industry's swift conquest of the state proved once again the inability of the sword to match the power of the pen.

Most of my travel at the time was limited to boat trips around Southeast Alaska. This made Randy, whom we called MacGyver for his uncanny ability to improvise a fast solution to almost any problem, an invaluable sidekick.

On one fishing trip, drifting perilously in a fourteen-foot dinghy with an engine that wouldn't start, Randy and I paddled to a nearby island where I watched him disassemble our eight-horsepower Johnson outboard with his bare hands and only his pocketknife for a tool as a cold night closed in. With less fanfare than you'd use to make toast in the morning, Randy soon had the engine spread in dozens of horrifying pieces across the rocky beach. The shear pin that protects the drive shaft and holds the flywheel in place—thus allowing it to spin and propel us back to civilization—had caught on something and shattered into sickening little bits. As soon as Randy shoved the handful of black shrapnel in my face, I imagined the fat dude in greasy overalls eyeing the pieces across the counter at Alaska Ship Chandlers marine supply.

"They make that little fucker in Taiwan. Part ships through Hong Kong. Six weeks minimum to get here."

I took the news hard, dropping down on a log and massaging my temples. Randy immediately ran through his impressive catalog of frontier obscenities, yanked out the thin metal handle of our water jug, grabbed a rock, banged out a stubby replacement pin, slid it in place, put the whole motor back together, and crossed his fingers. The engine roared to life on the first pull and didn't stop till we got to the harbor at Auke Bay.

The whole operation had taken about six hours, but we slept in our beds that night. I've watched Filipino mechanics patch car tires with Super Glue and banana leaves and seen two-story houses in Brazil built entirely of scrap metal. But disassembling an outboard motor, crafting a replacement part, then reassembling the motor, entirely by hand, remains the most amazing feat of resourcefulness I've ever witnessed. If Randy was a rare bird in Alaska then, he's an endangered species now.

After tourism replaced real Alaska with "Alaskana," petroleum firebombed the whole package in 1982. With statehood established in 1959, Alaska had settled into a decade of relative oblivion. Then oil was discovered in Prudhoe Bay in 1968. The crusty territorial guys saw what was coming. Senator John Butrovich, born in a mining camp in Fairbanks in 1910, rattled his fist at the legislature in 1969 about the treachery of Big Oil.

"The majors are going to own the whole damn state," he warned. "The majors will own you. They have no souls—robber barons don't change."

Little more than a decade later, 1982, with Alaska

dripping in crude, the first Permanent Fund Dividend checks were issued by the state government to all Alaskans—$1,000 given away to each of the state's 550,043 lucky residents, every penny based on investments made with oil revenues. A pittance for corporate oil even then, but a $6,000 payout for families with four kids, like mine, was big money. Some call the Permanent Fund Dividends pseudosocialism, but the truth is less complex: they're a bribe. Alaska's once-liberal voters haven't sent a non-Republican to Washington since the day that first check was issued.

Alaska today isn't so much a GOP stronghold as it is an oil fiefdom. Having bought the state in 1982, the oil biz to this day continues its annual payoffs to Alaskans. By 2007, the annual PFD check issued to residents was up to almost $1,600. Never mind that the prevailing local mythology remains one of self-sufficiency and rugged individualism, the importance of independence myths is inversely proportional to the degree to which any society has surrendered its sovereignty. Oil now makes 80 percent of the state's income and 100 percent of its important decisions.

As luck would have it, 1982 was not only the year Big Oil purchased the state's soul, it was also the year I arrived at the Alaska House of Representatives, first as a lowly page, then assistant sergeant at arms. An eighteen-year-old who barely dragged himself through high school sitting at the head of the House chambers consulting Mason's Manual of Legislative Procedure and raking in thirty-six thousand dollars a year? For those who haven't seen it firsthand, that's what an oil boom looks like.

Among our forty reps that year, there still roamed a

few leftover coots from the fishing towns and radical loonies from the bush who kept bottles of Old Crow stashed in their desks in the House chambers. The guys I liked most were the Libertarians from Fairbanks, Dick Randolph and Ken Fanning. Randolph drove the page staff crazy by clipping his nails on the House floor, and Fanning, to borrow the description of local admirer and reporter Joe LaRocca, "suffered from the opposite of charisma." But both could rail like drunken Baptists against the Anchorage lawyers running the show and entertain the visitors gallery by pointing out the lies behind the topics of day. Alaskans don't vote for Libertarians much anymore, either.

Dismissed as lefty weirdos by the mainstream, the naysayers, and for that matter the handful of remaining Republican and Democratic independent spirits, didn't seem so much like politicians to me as they did Alaskans. And in the year when Alaska lost its innocence for good, it was easy to tell the difference. Politicians in the capitol did cocaine. Alaskans in the capitol did cocaine. But it was the politicians who made you pay for it, one way or the other.

Having withstood the seduction of illegal narcotics through my formative years—the offerings of slobbery joints from high school guys in sodden wool jackets might not count as seduction, but, still, an element of temptation was at work—I decided one evening for no apparent reason to ingest endless lines of cocaine. My initiation came in the living room of a young legislative aide at a party crowded with pages, aides, lawyers, lobbyists, and at least one government figure well known for publicly stumping for legislation facilitating the ease of resource development.

A guy named J. P. Carrow brought me to the party. J.P. was from Fairbanks, a year older than me. He'd come to Juneau to work in the State Senate. As a favor to an obscure friend of an obscure friend, my father agreed to let him board in my older brother's vacant room through the winter session. As I was in the process of temporarily dropping out of high school, and he'd recently struggled through the end of his senior year, J.P. and I became fast friends.

Smart, clean cut, good-looking—if I saw J.P. for the first time today I'd think of him as a frat boy, though at the time I was unfamiliar with the term. Behind the side part and aftershave, J.P. betrayed signs of a secret life. A couple weeks after his arrival, I was awakened in the middle of the night by a series of urgent taps. Mom spoke through my bedroom door.

"Get up and check on J.P. He's in the hall bathroom."

Four in the morning and the faucet running full blast. No sense knocking. I shoved open the door and found J.P. in the tub, one leg draped over the edge, deader drunk than a Subic sailor on shore leave. Not an unusual condition in our house given my older brother's résumé, except that floating on top of the bathwater was a golden carpet of potato-curry vomit. It must have been there a while, because a little breakaway republic of chicken and carrots had pooled around the faucet and clogged the safety drain. Chowdery bathwater was gushing over the gunwales. A half inch already covered the tile floor.

J.P. was back in top form the night of the party with the well-known government figure, which took place in one of the brightly painted, quasi-Victorian houses that dot the side of Mount Juneau and make postcards of downtown such a hit with tourists. Tom Petty might have been on the stereo, and somebody'd been host enough to put a plate of smoked salmon on the dining room table, but what I remember most is how much coke we snorted and how little effect it had on me. I sucked down someone's expensive Peruvian flake all night long, more than I've ever done in a single sitting since. And nothing. On the way home I told J.P. the experience only confirmed my lifelong policy of abstinence. Drugs apparently made you so stupid that you spent tons of money on shit that didn't even work.

First-timer immunity is, of course, a common enough if inscrutable phenomenon. I had better fortune the following year when I landed my own job with the Alaska House of Representatives. My coke cherry broken, I didn't see any point in turning down the neighborly lines on offer from the young legislative aide from the interior who knew a lot about music and spent much of his time in the fifth-floor supply closet. Then came offers from the staff in the legislators' lounge. Handouts from stringers in the media room. Bumps from the secretary in the junior representative's antechamber. Spoonfuls at the party where . . .

Turned out, this stuff was pretty damn fun. New friends. Barrel of laughs. Coke made me smart. I didn't turn into a crackhead and I did plenty more than jam rolled-up twenties into my nose during my time working among the state's dealmakers. But the inescapable vice in the capitol was a big enough part of life there to forever color my political views. And temporarily make my personal life a little more interesting.

The coke I did that year was always purchased by someone else. All I had to do, when not graciously accepting freebies, was chip in $50 or $75 here and there. Most people didn't even accept it. Then came the day that Randy called to tell me he was coming back into town after fishing all summer out of Pelican. The occasion called for something special.

The friendliest dealer I knew was a recent import from Los Angeles named Rob, a beefy, jheri-curled black guy who wore dark glasses indoors and talked out of whichever side of his mouth the Camel nonfilter wasn't dangling from. He always greeted me with a "solid" handshake and added several baritone vowels to my name: "Chuuuuuk. What up, brutha?" Maybe thirty years old. If you remember the old ballplayer Mitchell Paige, you're 90 percent there.

As one of Juneau's handful of African Americans, Rob was affectionately known as "Rabdul," a brotherly rendering of his name in the grand tradition of it-isn't-racist-it's-funny racism. Rabdul didn't seem to mind. He played along, even called himself Rabdul, though whether this was out of good humor or self-preservation in snow-white Alaska I don't care now to speculate.

Rabdul had always been amiable and generous with me, but it goes without saying that by necessity all drug dealers cultivate a mean streak. Or, rather, it should go without saying. I didn't grasp the concept until the night of my one and only independent coke purchase, a shifty, loitering affair that went down in front of Pizzazz pizza parlor in the Nugget Mall. (A substandard mall very much like the substandard mall in most small towns, only way shittier.) Pizzazz was just down from the make-your-own T-shirt shop, the place that rigged out Juneauites with such classy silk screens as "Makin' Bacon" (pigs fucking) and "Haulin' Ass" (bed of a Chevy half-ton filled with oiled, teenage-girl buttocks). The "Fuck Iran" baseball shirt they sold me once got me kicked out of a high school basketball game.

Oblivious to my intense paranoia, Rabdul accepted my $120—going Alaska rate for a gram in those days— and artfully passed me a small bulge of powder concealed inside a paper triangle made out of a *Playboy* centerfold, another standard of the day. By God's benevolent mercy, no bystanders moved in for a citizen's arrest. Winston Churchill once said nothing in life is so exhilarating as to be shot at without result. Completing a public drug transaction without being arrested must run a close third, after that and finding out your girlfriend's not pregnant after all.

On a clear summer evening, no city in the country surpasses Juneau for scenic glory. Pinkish hue glowing on snow-capped mountains. Spruce-covered hillsides in a thousand shades of green. Running lights from fishing boats reflecting off flat calm water. Northern lights if you're lucky. I don't want to say a coked-up haze makes it all even more magnificent—how depressing would that be?—but I know that night Randy and I never felt so lucky to be alive, Alaskan, and holding.

We met at the harbor at around eleven, just as the sun was melting into an orangey horizon, and drove my beater Ford Torino to all our favorite spots. We checked out eagle trees; cut long straight lines on a vanity mirror held low between the car seats; threw rocks into the ocean at Sandy Beach; pinched one nostril and hoovered acres of spotless powder; scoped out the scene at Skater's Cabin; used scrupulous fingertips to rub anesthetizing snow dust across our gums; poked sticks into the embers of a beach fire while orcas leaped offshore; savored the bitter flavor of coke snot draining down our throats; and had our boners massively harshed when we unfolded Miss July to find all our happy flake gone, me having licked the page clean two minutes earlier. Given that the best time to do cocaine is after massive amounts of it have already been done, Randy and I were instantly united behind a single purpose. More blow.

Rabdul lived in a shit brown, single-wide trailer in a swampy development a few miles from downtown called Lemon Creek, a name careful readers will recall being shared by the maximum-security prison from chapter 1. I dimly remember some brief discussion about the wisdom of making an unannounced house call on a drug dealer at three thirty in the morning. But Rabdul had always been cool with me, and I knew he kept odd hours, so I figured he'd be OK with it. When we pulled up to the trailer, Randy stayed in the car, proving that at least one of us wasn't completely out of his mind.

I tapped on the front door. When no one answered, I moved down the length of the trailer, casual as the cable guy looking for a good place to bring in the wire. Stopping where it looked like the bedroom might be, I rapped a little more firmly on the aluminum planking of the trailer and whispered into the night.

"Rabdul? It's Chuck. Um, you up? I'm out here with Randy. We really need some more shit. Another gram'd be cool. We've only got sixty-five dollars on us, but I can get you the rest tomorrow."

A light clicked on across the street.

It's possible my voice carried slightly farther than I'd intended. Randy later compared it to the screeching of ravens at the city dump. What was I doing outside a coke dealer's trailer trying to swing a deal on blow at three thirty in the morning? It's difficult now to say. Easiest to fall back on the usual excuses of youthful indiscretion, note my limited experience with black guys from L.A. who wore dark glasses indoors, and attest to the sinister grip that drugs can have on even the most late-blooming experimenter.

My last seconds of utter naïveté on this earth were shattered by a vinyl trailer door swinging open with such violence that it seemed to have been ripped backward off its hinges. Rabdul appeared on the front porch—really just some unfinished two-by-four stairs—wearing nothing but a pair of tighty whiteys. His bare feet were planted shoulder width. Resting on his hip at a forty-five-degree angle was a deer rifle with a scope mounted atop its long, cold, black barrel. This was the first time I'd ever seen Rabdul without dark glasses and a cigarette, and at first all I could think was how paunchy he looked with no shirt. I'd later record this among my earliest encounters with what British author John Fowles called "the mystery of other human lives," solid indication of how frighteningly out of touch I was with situational reality at age nineteen.

Randy later said Rabdul fired a warning shot as he stepped outside, but I never heard one. What I do recall is the absolute terror that wrenched my bowels as Rabdul raised the scope to his eye and dipped the rifle barrel directly below my belt. Not at all the reception I'd had in mind. Rabdul's anger shot like a flamethrower as

I backpedaled to the car. The world hadn't yet heard of Samuel L. Jackson, but I was getting a preview.

"Asshole! Get the fuck away from my house! Get the fuck away from my family!" (Rabdul had a family?) "Never come the fuck back here again! Never call me the fuck again! Never talk to me the fuck again! Never even think the fuck about me ag— Did you not fucking hear me? Get the fuck away from my house before I kill you!"

I sprinted the last ten yards and fired up the Torino, but my hands were shaking so badly I had to pull over as soon as we got around the corner. For a long time we sat in silence, watching the sun come up low on the horizon. Across the front seat, Randy stared glassy-eyed through the dirty windshield, not moving a muscle. It seemed like a good time to get the fuck out of town.

3

. . .

Canned Hams, Kendo Beatdowns, and the Penis Olympics: The Education of an Accidental Ambassador in Japan

Japan was my first job out of college and I arrived eager to be taken by its alien embrace—the neon flash of Roppongi, the noble rise of Mount Fuji, the ancient contradictions that produced both Pearl Harbor and anal-retentive flower arrangement. I was ready to become a human bridge to the puzzling culture that was, by all accounts in the 1980s, poised to consume my own. I imagined Tokyo. Strobe lights. Amphetamine-charged nightclubs. Girls with severe bangs and colorful clothes who would giggle when I spoke to them and never say no.

Instead, I wound up in Gifu. The legend that the remote mountain prefecture on the island of Honshu was named for a postwar acronym—"GI Fuck You!"—turned out to be apocryphal. But Gifu was and remains cultural shorthand among Japanese for appalling rusticity. If the Peace Corps operated in Japan, Gifu is where they'd ship volunteers.

In the years since I lived there, I'd often wondered if my memories of the isolation, privation, and general backwardness of the Japanese countryside might not be slightly distorted. Exaggerated, perhaps. Then, in spring 2006, a travel story appeared in the *Atlantic* describing a trip beginning in Okayama, another bucolic venue where I lived for a year after escaping Gifu. The article began by laying down an immutable "Three Laws of Tourism in Japan." Law No. 3 read: "Do Not Go Into Rural Japan: Compared with U.S. cities, Japanese cities bend over backward to help foreigners. The countryside is another matter. It is as free of English speakers as, say, the Ozarks are of Japanese speakers." My own comparisons had more often been with the Appalachians, but the Ozarks reference was a not-so-subtle tip that little had changed over the years. And, with apologies to anyone who lives in those parts of Missouri, Arkansas, or Oklahoma, any time an author compares a place to the Ozarks, particularly in a Brahmin magazine from the eastern seaboard, the intent is not ever complimentary.

I arrived at Giri High School, in a village near the famed samurai battlefield of Sekigahara, under the auspices of Mombushō, the Japanese Ministry of Education, Science, and Culture, which was at the time attempting to engineer a nationwide social movement called "internationalization." Today we know this as "globalization," and people dress up as beleaguered pine trees, outraged salmon, and 1960s hippies to protest the world collective, urging citizens not to eat Quarter Pounders with Cheese and throwing Molotov cocktails through Starbucks windows. In the 1980s, however, few could conceive of burger- and coffee-based empires controlling vast populations with processed animal fat,

mocha lattes, and watered-down jazz CD collections. At
the time, chumming up to your foreign neighbors seemed,
like *The Love Boat*, a largely benign concept, and so programs like JET (Japan Exchange and Teaching Program)
thrived.

The Japanese government conceived JET officially
to forward the cause of English proficiency. Its greater
purpose, however, was to "internationalize" the Japanese population. This despite the fact that since the day
Commodore Perry pulled into Edo in 1853, the Japanese
have practically rioted for anything Western you put
in front of them—silk top hats, cars, the Beatles, Coca-
Cola, rapacious capitalism, amphibious assaults, the
Philippines, rigged financial markets, stagnant bureaucracy, and scandal-inclined politicians. The JET program has been called, by one of its original advisers,
"perhaps the greatest and certainly the biggest education program in humankind's history." While that might
be a bit of overstatement—I seem to recall Spanish inquisitors and a millennium or two of sundry Christian
zealots making the world safe for the New Testament—
it reflects the hubris of those running one of the
strangest shows ever to hit an Asian classroom. Which,
if you've never spent any time in one, are by and large
as dull as an Indian dessert platter.

Although a cultural-exchange program administered
by a faceless Japanese bureaucracy may not sound
glamorous, the JET program was big news in Japan.
There was even a book about it called *Importing Diversity* published in 2000 by an anthropology professor
named David L. McConnell. As you might expect from a
book written by a College of Wooster anthropology prof
about a Japanese government initiative, the narrative is

about as riveting as a bank statement. Even so, no one connected with this insane attempt at cultural engineering could fail to recognize themselves in McConnell's deadly accurate reporting. Just looking at the spine of his book on my shelf gets me misty about those heady days of manufactured change in Japan.

On August 1, 1987, the debut JET class of 848 recent college grads from the United States, Britain, Australia, and New Zealand arrived in Tokyo. "They were greeted with an extraordinary degree of media hype and with red-carpet treatment," McConnell wrote. "These 'foreign ambassadors,' as they were called, were wined and dined at a five-star Tokyo hotel during the weeklong orientation. Their arrival was covered by all the major newspapers and television networks in Japan."

McConnell went on to describe the ponderous procession of official introductions and the gourmet dinner reception, with its river of beer and kimono-clad hostesses provided for the comfort of the JETs. Endless speechifying by heavyweight government officials stressed the select nature of the remarkable foreigners brought to Japan to spearhead the country's historic effort to internationalize.

I'd been on stages before. I'd held down a few on-air radio jobs. But being one of the original JETs—today the program employs nearly six thousand foreign teachers and costs the Japanese government $400 million a year—put the first taste of true celebrity in my mouth. Once out of Tokyo we JETs were, quite literally, poked and prodded everywhere we went. My most memorable interaction was with a ten-year-old boy in a temple restroom who snatched at my pubic hair as I stood at a urinal, his purple-faced father in the doorway giddily urging him on while I jerked away in horror. What the kid planned to do with this apparent treasure I can't say, but knowing how things sometimes operate in Japan, it wouldn't have been surprising to find my business for sale in a sandwich Baggie on some teeming train station platform. Outside of the cultural mecca of greater Tokyo—where one in four Japanese live, and which that year I would see only in fleeting glimpses on TV—tussling with a parade of country folk who had little or no experience with foreigners (gaijin) came to constitute the most significant part of the job.

The Japan most of us are familiar with today was hardly recognizable in Gifu in the 1980s. I lived for a year in a building with neither phone service nor central heat. This in an area blanketed by snow and ice through much of the winter. As we later discovered in Iraq, it takes a while to put a country back together after it's been utterly flattened by war, and the most ass-backward parts tend to get fixed last.

I referenced the Peace Corps earlier because, coming out of college, I resented profoundly any suggestion of public service under a hawkish administration and was as hostile toward that organization as it was possible for an unemployed twenty-two-year-old to be. Judging from the experiences of friends and family who'd signed up for pseudo–government duty in the world's sweltering shitholes, whatever JFK's highborn intentions had once been, the operation now seemed like nothing more than a way for college kids to suck off the government teat for two years of paid vacation. And, more insidiously, a means for America to sneak English—the first wave of corporate imperialism—into unsuspecting countries, purchase diplomatic favors with human pawns, shoehorn Western capitalism into places like Uzbekistan under the guise of "business development," and give corrupt local pooh-bahs and sahibs across the world a free hand with American taxpayer bacon.

I wanted none of that sanctimonious, preachy bullshit on my shoes. I wanted money. I wanted "work." What I got was a year of isolation in the sticks of Japan and a job in a high school for the kind of Asian students no one ever hears about—the ones who don't study for exams like treadmill hamsters and wouldn't recognize Pythagorean theorem if you poked them in the eye with one of its sharp corners. Turns out, Japan needs to produce janitors and gas station attendants just like everyone else. They have places like Giri High where kids can follow those dreams.

At a time when the United States and Japan seemed ready to go to war over tariffs on oranges and automatic transmissions, the fragility of the alliance between recent Western college graduates and the oppressively strict Japanese education system was so palpable that even dry-bones academics like Professor McConnell could work dramatic foreshadowing into their tinderlike theses. As he noted, by the end of August, once JETs like me had settled into local schools and surprisingly primitive towns, the happy high established in Tokyo quickly dissipated.

Culture clashes were inevitable. And complex. I can still recall walking down a narrow country road with a Japanese American JET from Southern California named Steve Murata while he screamed "Motherfucking Japs! Nip motherfuckers!" at passing cars that dared honk at us to move farther into the shoulder.

The real problem, however, was the job itself. Teaching English to the Japanese is like making panda babies— an extremely delicate procedure requiring repeated attempts and resulting in constant disappointment. Test results are rarely positive. The process demands of the instructor an almost godlike capacity for patience; of the student, a Hindu cleric's metaphysical ability to withstand spiritual punishment; and of both, a talent for remaining unaffected by the misery of others.

One of my first assignments took me to a classroom in a neighboring town to perform a planned-to-the-comma meet and greet with thirty or so junior high students. After the inevitable fifteen minutes it took everyone to settle down upon discovering that a lumbering gaijin could be trained to drink tea from a cup and observe basic Japanese etiquette, I made the rounds following a script that required me to repeat the English name each student had been assigned for the class, before moving on to basic pleasantries.

"Hello. My name is John."

"Hello, John. My name is Chuck. Nice to meet you."

"Nice to meet you, too, Chuck. How are you today?"

And so forth. After three or four of these Nobel-level exchanges, digging wells in Gabon was starting to look pretty good. But I soldiered on until I reached an intensely shy boy with an exquisite bowl haircut and wide, watery eyes—the kind of kid they cast as "Simple, Goodhearted Bumpkin" in Hollywood because his innocent, countrified countenance conveys (1) utter human decency, and (2) the immediate understanding that by the end of the second reel, he will have been unjustly ripped to shreds by a racist psychopath or assortment of spinning blades randomly lowered from the ceiling.

Needless to say, the King's English wasn't this boy's strong suit. Straining through near-paralyzing nerves, he gazed at me and, summoning all his strength, cleared his throat and gargled:

"Herro, my name is Rrrllllrrrrr."

I was supposed to stick with the script, which required me to repeat his words back to him. Christ alone knew what that was supposed to accomplish, but we JETs were "team teachers," and I wanted to be a good team player. This despite the fact that any mention of "teams" in the workplace instantly makes the words "two weeks' notice" appear in flashing red letters in my mind.

"I'm sorry, I didn't understand you," I said. "Could you please repeat your name?"

"Please repeat" was a phrase I knew the class had studied and to my relief I saw in his shining eyes that this kid had done his homework, an almost unheard-of feat in Gifu.

"Herro, my name is Rrrlllllrrrrr," he dutifully repeated.

I'm sure the whole British fagging system is a nightmare, but in terms of academic cruelty, calling out a Japanese kid's crappy English in front of a roomful of his classmates is the most effective method of inflicting psychological damage I've ever come across.

I stroked my chin. Making sense of this kid's name was clearly impossible. Improvisation was the only way out.

"Well, it's nice to meet you and . . ."

"No, no, no! You must use the script! You must repeat his name!"

This was the class's English teacher barking orders from the back of the room like Yamashita at the siege of

Singapore. Tanaka-sensei was a short, stocky, and bald sixty-year-old who'd enigmatically introduced himself as an "old-fashioned mountaineer" and welcomed me to his burb the night before by taking me out boozing until four in the morning. He'd spent most of the time regaling me with karaoke renditions of his beloved Kingston Trio ("Where Have All the Flowers Gone," etc.) and forcing me to drink in the typical Gifu fashion, which meant pouring more beer or sake or whiskey or whatever into your companion's glass *while he's in the act of actually drinking it*. In addition to being incorrigible alcoholics, the Japanese absolutely adore peer pressure.

"You must follow the script and repeat his name to him before continuing!" Tanaka-sensei bellowed at me. "That way he knows that you understand his English!"

"OK," I said. "But could you tell me what his name is?"

"Ask him!" Tanaka commanded, pointing a yardstick. "Only he may tell you!"

Twelve hours earlier, Tanaka had been exploring the melodic nuances of "Tom Dooley." Now he was Toshiro Mifune. The kids were beginning to laugh at Rrrlllllrrrrr. I bowed and apologized profusely, confusing the poor kid further.

"I'm *really* sorry (*bow*). I still don't quite understand you (*bow*). Could you please (*bow*) repeat that?"

The kid was game; I'll give him that. I listened like a safecracker as he repeated his line.

"Herro, my name is Rrrlllllrrrrr."

Rrrlllllrrrrr repeated his name three or four more times. Laughter rippled through the room with each miserable attempt. I made pleading gestures all around, to the kid, the class, the teacher. Finally, Tanaka-sensei forced the boy to do the death march to the front of the room and write his English name on the blackboard:

L-A-R-R-Y

Amid eruptions of laughter, "Larry" schlepped back across the room and sank in his seat like the *Edmund Fitzgerald*. For subtle sadism, it doesn't get much more creative than saddling your least talented Japanese student with a name like Larry.

Given this culture of institutionalized linguistic sabotage, you wouldn't think Japan would be filled with adults willing to pay good money to continue learning pretend-English. Yet it is. "Native speakers" without credentials can still arrive there and carve out a decent living, but in the heyday of ESL teaching in Japan, eager expats could make a baron's wage by hiring themselves out to Japanese adults who wanted a little bit of English conversation and a lot of foreign friend—a personal mascot that came with no small cachet in "internationalizing" Japan. One day, a British expat in Tokyo might claim to be getting $100 an hour to swallow bad boxed lunches, babble rudimentary English, and bat her eyes at businessmen. Then a guy from Yokohama would brag about $150 an hour, plus all the drinks he could throw down inside a pricey hostess bar, to translate dirty jokes and get blitzed with gangs of carousing accountants. Japanese salarymen become notoriously grabby with both their male and female conversation monkeys, but this minor drawback was accepted as simply one of the occupational hazards of doing undocumented business in a rich and ancient culture.

A few months after I arrived in Gifu, I was contacted

by a middle-aged woman who explained to me her position as an officer in the local chapter of the Soroptimists club, some sort of "follow your dreams" outfit of do-gooders that claimed to be "Making a Difference for Women." When she asked if I'd be available on Tuesday nights for informal English conversation, ten-thousand-yen bills started doing kabuki dances in my head. With the aged, rural yokels of Gifu, I anticipated none of the legendary indiscretions associated with Japanese businessmen and approached my first freelance conversation assignment with a big gaijin smile and empty pockets—easier for my grateful charges to stuff with bills at the end of the night.

Hanging with the Soroptimists was like chatting up your grandmother's canasta circle for two hours—ball-breakingly tedious and the thermostat high enough to roast a turkey, but compared to digging ditches, not exactly work. There was lots of "Where are you from?" and "How do you like Japan?" and "What kind of girl do you like?" I must have been asked this last question a thousand times in Japan and never once figured out how to answer it. Small titted? Compliant? Breathing? Exactly what information were they after?

Eventually—inevitably—the bored ESL teacher attempts to keep him- or herself entertained by dropping little jokes, witty asides, and rejoinders into the conversation. Anything to keep from falling asleep out of sheer apathy. Yet even this distraction fades quickly since there's no one else around with adequate comprehension skills to appreciate the sparkling, one-sided repartee. After covering the conversational essentials—favorite colors, sports, foods—one of the Soroptimists asked what I did each night following dinner. To which I instantly replied, "Digest." I thought it was pretty clever, but the confused laughs after we had to look up the word in the dictionary took most of the gloss off my little joke. Thus do two hours of informal English education in Japan typically pass.

The end of the evening was signaled by twenty minutes of ceremonial bowing and scraping and good nights and apologies and thank-yous and iron-willed old-lady battles for the title of Most Appreciative of Your Hospitality. Finally, the head Soroptimist pulled me aside with a gentle whisper. This was the moment I'd been waiting for, my meeting with Mr. Fukuzawa Yukichi—he being the even-more-bored-looking-than-me dude on the ten-thousand-yen note.

"We realize that your contract with the local school district prevents you from accepting outside work," she began, painfully earnest. How she knew the details of my JET contract was a mystery, but if she wanted to keep our business on the DL, it was fine with me. Discretion is the better part of tax-free income, and I was as eager as anyone to be let in on the powerful financial secrets of the East, primed back in the eighties to devour the West.

"To avoid any problem," she went on, "we have decided to pay you with something even more valuable than money."

There are only a few things I consider more valuable than money and I seriously doubted she was equipped to give me any of them. I should have turned and walked away. Instead I cemented an idiot's grin of affability to my face as she presented me with a plate of homemade *manju*—a Japanese dessert that tastes like old rubber balls—and a three-pound canned ham.

Her generosity left me unable to speak. A canned ham? In return for one of the most excruciatingly dull nights of my life? Even if no one else was aware that I was supposed to be spending my Tuesday nights in Japan snorting meth and watching Japanese girls make out in the bathrooms of Tokyo rave clubs, this brought my situation in Gifu into enormously depressing focus.

Chump that I am, it took me five more weeks, five more hams, and five more platters of bean-paste "delicacies" before I could face down the Soroptimists' overbearing politeness and cancel the gig. Five additional weeks, ten hours of the exact same agonizing script. I suppose they stock *Lost in Translation* in the comedy aisle because it sells better there, but for a chilling depiction of the suffocating courtesy that almost destroyed me, no media ever produced about Japan has ever been as accurate as that movie. To some she might represent the paragon of sensual womanhood, but every time I see Scarlett Johansson, I get only chilling visions of my evenings with the Soroptimists.

While I spent a good deal of my time in Japan feeling like the tortured rich man begging for a drop of water from the finger of Lazarus, the JET experience wasn't entirely nonstop trauma. The Soroptimists aside, village locals were almost fanatical about seeing that my basic needs were taken care of. The always cheerful calligraphy teacher Nomo-sensei generously dropped by my puny apartment each morning (NO NEED FOR AN ALARM CLOCK SINCE THE GUYS AT THE FIRE STATION ACROSS THE STREET BEGAN DRILLING AT 4:30 AM) to give me a ride to school. Along the way, he'd casually chat about which female students he wanted to have sex with and speculate as to which positions might best suit the anatomical particulars of each.

Responsible for my well-being at Giri High School, the English department head, Kotake-sensei, fussed over me like a Jewish grandmother, but had the purest heart of any human being who ever had to live through his country getting the shit bombed out of it in WWII and then spend the final working years of his life looking after the snot-nosed progeny of the bastards who'd done it. Years later, Kotake-sensei visited me in Oregon. He marveled at the toll-free interstate we drove to Seattle—road fees in Japan for that trip would've cost him fifty dollars. He treasured the informal atmosphere of shops and restaurants, and the boundless courtesy of people on Puget Sound's ferries upon whom he inflicted his rusty 1940s English. He went home and told his wife that he wanted to spend the rest of their lives in America, then died a few weeks later. It wasn't much, but I'm grateful to have been able to give back to Kotake-sensei something of the decency he'd spent a year showing the most ungrateful and impatient version of me that's ever existed.

In many ways, I had more in common with the students than with the teachers. The school's star Ping-Pong player and I could barely communicate, but we battled after school on an ongoing basis. Despite forcing her into dozens of overtime thrillers, I never managed to beat her. She was a mystery to the Japanese as well as to me, a gawky, five-foot-ten, one-hundred-pound girl with a mouth that could go weeks without opening, limbs like a grasshopper's, hair as limp as boiled noodles, slightly bulging eyes (which I mean in a good way—I've never minded a touch of Grave's disease in my women), and the filthiest backspin serve east of Beijing. I'd eat the oldest chunk of raw fish in an Iowa sushi restaurant for a chance at a rematch with her in that freezing, aluminum-sided box they called a gymnasium.

Then there was Hamada-sensei, a burly, highly respected math teacher with a wife and two kids, who spoke that precise, arcane English unique to foreigners who learn the language entirely from textbooks. Over a bowl of ramen one night, he brought up a picaresque aspect of the teaching culture in Japan that he was sure our JET training hadn't included: the unspoken yet tacitly understood tradition of rural teachers hooking up with their students. For purely noble purposes, mind you.

"Chuck-sensei, you must surely know of Koizumi Keiko, who is a student in your second-period class." Hamada-sensei had an avuncular manner and a commanding baritone, so talking to him was sort of like getting advice from a Japanese James Earl Jones. Except for the ramen broth that dribbled down his chin when he slurped his noodles.

"Koizumi Keiko," I said. "Sure. Sits in the front row by the windows."

Hamada-sensei waved his chopsticks in my direction.

"It must be said that she is among the finest-looking girls in Giri High School."

Slurp, slurp.

"She's very cute," I allowed. "No question about it."

"She is also quite athletic. An achiever in Japanese tennis. A very . . . *healthy* girl."

After you've been in the countryside awhile, you start sensing where these late-night ramen sessions are headed. I shifted on my tiny stool. Hamada-sensei dumped Asahi

Super Dry into my glass while I glugged away and attached my eyes to the sumo match on the TV in the corner.

"I happen to know her father and mother," he continued. "Both of them are quite intelligent people. Her father operates his own company with which he has enjoyed abundant success. It is my belief that Koizumi Keiko will soon make a fine mother. She has very strong hips and her youthful breast is quite impressive."

Slurp, slurp.

Koizumi Keiko was fifteen years old. A sophomore. I reminded Hamada-sensei of this perhaps sensitive bit of information. He waved his chopsticks. Flecks of broth landed on my shirt.

"You should be married and have a family soon. For a young man, you now have a good job and can support children. Many of our school's young teachers are jealous of your position. A wife and children will make you happy. Koizumi Keiko is a strong candidate. If you like, I can speak to her father on your behalf."

I knew Gifu was rural, but not West Virginia rural. Get married, have kids was standard patter in Japan, but the solemnity behind this exchange scared me. I spent the rest of the year keeping my distance from Koizumi Keiko in my second-period class. This was a shame, since she was in fact one of the brighter kids at Giri High School. However, despite a growing affection for at least a few national manias—shoes off in the house, the Chunichi Dragons baseball team, excessive drinking—I wasn't yet ready to adopt an appreciation of youthful breasts sheathed in sailor-girl school uniforms, no matter how impressive they might be. Better to satisfy those impulses on late-night runs to the beer and soiled-panties vending machines outside the train station, Japanese institutions that never fail to excite the novice gaijin.

Not that I didn't regret once or twice refusing Hamada-sensei's offer to pimp for me. For the JETs posted in metropolises, life might have been a nonstop poon fest, but hooking up with *inaka* (country) girls was a different story. This was a lesson I learned at the hands of my new best friend, Torizaki-sensei. Nudged by school administrators into befriending me due to our similar ages, Torizaki-sensei was a good-looking young science teacher idolized by the female students, resented by the boys. Every school has one of these just-out-of-ed-school cool types—with-it authority figures who smirk at the system and are destined to win Teacher of the Year awards by dint of popularity rather than skill. I'd never been a fan of these types, but Torizaki-sensei at least had an amiable impertinence that distinguished him from the rest of the pinched-mouth faculty.

Blessed with a "samurai name and samurai spirit," as he loved to tell his students, Torizaki had been a college kendo champion. Once, after I'd inadvertently embarrassed him in front of several students by beating him in a free-throw-shooting contest, he gave me a malicious kendo beatdown to prove it.

"I want to show Japanese culture," he told me by way of introducing me to his "specialty sport." Everyone in Japan has a "specialty sport."

The basketballs safely stowed away, Torizaki led me and an audience of students to the school's large dojo for a demonstration of this ancient fighting art. For those unfamiliar with the bamboo swordplay of kendo, it should be noted that there is perhaps no more graceful way of simulating the evisceration of an opponent's intestines or the lopping off of another's head. My inaugural lesson ended after barely sixty seconds with me cowering on the floor, refusing to get back up until Torizaki promised to strike me no more. Taking advantage of a helpless neophyte was a punishable breach of form for a master like Torizaki, but if he felt any shame about whaling an amateur into submission he did his penance in private.

After the initial kendo humiliation, I actually spent a couple years hopping around various dojos swinging the bamboo sword, but the emphasis on compulsory shouting made me feel ridiculous. In all martial arts there's a heavily ritualized obedience to the dueling principles of humility and domination of a weaker individual. Obsequiousness followed by showy poses, menacing stances, and howls of intimidation have always felt phony to me. Like slurping ramen, I never got the hang of the time-honored shrieking required of the man about to swat someone with a bamboo stick.

This is why I think Bruce Lee became the only genuinely mainstream Asian martial arts star in the West. His kitty-cat squealing and falsetto yelping always conveyed to me an understanding of just how laughable all that in-your-face showboating is. I'm not sure what sound the koala makes in anger, but if I ever get back into kendo, that's the one I'm going to adopt as my battle cry.

I might have held a grudge against Torizaki, but not only was he my only friend in town, he kept talking about getting us laid. Torizaki had a reputation of being a "Japanese playboy"—the Japanese have a habit of pointing out the "Japanese" version of just about everything Western—but after a few unsatisfying trips to hostess bars and canceled double dates drawn from his alleged stable of concubines, I began to sense a more tepid reality. Despite his matinee looks, Torizaki was getting about as much action as I was.

Like many young teachers in Japan, Torizaki lived in an all-male dormitory for public-school teachers. These cramped quarters would be his required home until such time as he was married, a day he hoped would come soon. In the meantime, Torizaki and forty other young men in the dorm operated much like Japanese frat boys—dedicating their off-hours to Asahi Super Dry consumption, pixelated porn of girls in junior high school sailor uniforms, and sporadic episodes of macho competition. The most colorful of these was the Penis Olympics, a deranged festival of cocksmanship I had the honor of witnessing about halfway through my year in Gifu.

In a series of events, the Penis Olympics measured qualities in each contestant such as girth, ejaculatory distance, and, most disturbingly, flexibility. To the surprise of all, the games were dominated by an unassuming little fellow named Kodo—five foot two, 110 pounds, all shoulder blades and rib cage—an agreeable primary-school teacher whose mountain-village upbringing was said to supply the mojo behind his legendary *chimbo*. (Same as me, you just learned your first dirty word in Japanese.) Kodo's nickname was "The Firehose" and his favorite English phrase was "white milk," which meant sperm, a word he wasn't able to pronounce. I didn't bother explaining to him the redundancy of "white milk."

Watching the Penis Olympics didn't make me feel much like the "foreign ambassador" the JET orientation had prepared me to be. Worse, the pressure on me to participate was fierce. A lupine excitement gripped the room at the possibility of seeing a Caucasian penis in the engorged flesh, but the assumption that I was packing a gigantic wad, flattering to be sure, was also intimidating. A white guy back home isn't generally the subject of racial stereotyping insofar as cock size goes, and I can't say it felt all that bad to be objectified in this way. Gossip that I was hung like a California roll—discreetly passed among the locals—couldn't hurt my standing in the community. So long as the actual size remained a secret. Not that I haul into battle inadequate equipment, but next to Kodo-san's stunning endowment, I wasn't entirely comfortable with shouldering the priapic burden of my entire race.

As a side note on the subject of sexual attitudes in Japan, the going presumption is that while black, white, and other foreign penises might on average be larger, the Japanese penis is revered as the most satisfyingly firm unit on the planet. This is the type of cultural data you just won't find in books by anthropologists like David L. McConnell. Also, the Japanese say *"iku iku"* when they reach orgasm, which means, "I'm going, I'm going," as opposed to, "I'm coming, I'm coming." In other words, the expression of a departure rather than an arrival, a fascinating point of discussion among gaijin students of high culture in Japan ever since John Blackthorne and his "heavenly spear" washed up on the shores of Izu.

The final event of the Penis Olympics was designed to measure penile strength, the winner to be determined by the number of bath towels that could be hung from the end of his fully erect member before it bent downward beneath the agonizing weight of terry cloth. A protractor would be employed to measure angles in the event of disputes, but mostly the participants withdrew voluntarily when their hardened organs dropped to an intolerably painful degree, usually after two towels had been carefully hung over the old bald hermit. Effortlessly supporting four towels, the Firehose and his porn-ready appendage won the competition going away. By the looks of things, he could have added a soaked washcloth or two had anyone presented a serious threat.

After experiences like this, it didn't surprise me at all when that Japanese kid came over here a decade or so later and started winning hot-dog-eating contests. Face 'em in a foxhole or behind a plate of pork offal, it doesn't matter. Getting into a test of endurance with a Japanese warrior simply doesn't pay.

Though he'd represented himself well in the games, I was the one who ended up pimping for Torizaki-sensei in a well-intentioned cross-cultural foray that briefly thrust me into the management side of the Asian sex-tourism trade. During a school break, Torizaki and I flew to Guam—the "Japanese Hawaii"—for a weeklong vacation. I was going to visit my brother and his family. Torizaki, so he said, was interested in snorkeling and beachcombing. His back-to-nature tune changed, however, after we boarded the plane in Nagoya. As his participation in the Penis Olympics suggested, Torizaki was a man burdened neither by a searching moral philosophy nor sexual inhibitions. He turned to me shortly after we reached cruising altitude.

"I want sex with Korean girl."

When he said "Korean" it sounded exactly like "Whorean."

"Do you have a particular one in mind?" I thought maybe he'd become infatuated with one of the pubescent singing/dancing sensations that dominate Japanese television.

"In Guam are place where Japanese man can sex with Whorean," he explained. "Before I marry, I want experience Whorean sex."

Torizaki and I had hung out enough by now that we spoke a unique pidgin English/Japanese that took into account the known holes in each other's language abilities. I understood perfectly what he wanted. And my brother—if you told him to pack in ten minutes for an expedition to the Khyber Pass, he'd be ready in five— needed no arm-twisting. Which is how, a few days later, after scouting locations, Mike and I found ourselves drinking lukewarm Heinekens out of the minifridge in the business office of a Korean whorehouse on Guam, chatting up idle members of the staff while waiting for one of Gifu Prefecture's most popular molders of young minds to follow his dream in the back room.

The visit did not begin auspiciously. The three of us, too sober by half for this sort of thing, were greeted at the door by a trio of fortyish slatterns dressed in loose kimonos. Jackson Pollock could have done a better job putting on their makeup. The old tarts spoke to us in peppy, singsong voices normally reserved for animals and small children—it turns out the Koreans are even more awkward with foreigners than the rural Japanese. Torizaki's eyes danced in terror, but my brother grabbed his arm, pushed us inside, and shouted for a round of drinks. You want to go out drinking and alley-catting in a strange town, do it with a navy man.

It was four thirty in the afternoon, we were the only ones in the place, and through the darkness, all we could see were swirls of dust billows illuminated by hard streaks of sunlight slashing through the cracks in the door. The Koreans settled fleshy arms around our shoulders, rested their floppy midsections against our ribs, traced their fingers along the crease where leg joins torso, and demanded we buy them rum and Cokes. You didn't just feel their hot, stale breath in your ear, you tasted it all over the side of your face.

Torizaki began mumbling ancient samurai oaths, and I was about to suggest discreetly taking our leave when, as our eyes finally adjusted to the light, a door opened and an untrammeled vision of lotus-petaled Korean womanhood floated virginally into the room. Eighteen years old, nineteen tops, with wide black eyes and what the old navy guys called a marriage-ending smile. Not a girl who wasted time with ten-dollar ladies drinks. With a silent, purposeful tilt of the head, she took the goggle-eyed Torizaki by the arm and led him away with a snap of red silk, her bullet-straight black hair cutting the air behind her like the wake of a forty-horse outboard.

Down the back, brushing the tops of the shoulders, ponytailed, braided, or bobbed—per capita, no place outshines Asia in the category of laser-straight hair, and the continent obsesses about maintaining its competitive edge. Japanese women have been known to commit suicide over unmanageable cowlicks.

"You hair beautiful" is the last thing we heard Torizaki say before he disappeared into a darkened room.

With that, Mike and I separated ourselves from the ladies out front and managed to convince the old Korean mama-san to crack us a couple lukewarm ones while we waited in the office. We watched her going through the previous night's receipts and chitchatting with the girls just arriving for the evening, as the muted cries of Japanese manhood floated over the wide gaps between the plywood walls and the ceiling. A few minutes later came a crescendo of nails being hammered— or possibly just balled fists being pounded—into the headboard of a wooden bed frame. Rarely do you find Japanese males so completely released of this mortal coil. It had taken the better part of a year, but at last I was doing something constructive in my role as foreign ambassador.

4

. . .

Lost Among Expats: The Shiftless, Debauched, Tedious, and Necessary Existence of Americans Abroad

Not counting letters home—which friends later told me read more like suicide notes—I didn't commit a single word to paper during the two years I lived in Japan. Nevertheless, it was the Land of the Rising Yen and Falling Dollar that turned me into a travel writer. The gradual accumulation of experience helped, but my career development was more sudden and based largely on the advice of a slightly graying expatriate named Robert Glasser (not to be confused with the aforementioned Shanghai Bob) with whom I spent a year in yet another obscure Japanese settlement, a featureless speck of planned suburb in Okayama Prefecture called Kojima.

Prone to peppering cocktail-hour conversation with original Wildean nuggets such as "Experience has taught me that I should have fewer experiences," and "Never let a woman see you in your socks and underwear—she'll never respect you again," Glasser was a figure who it was difficult to believe existed outside the pages of a Victorian novel. A disposition toward formal appearance, or at least the lost art of manners, made him an outsider within Asia's foreigner community—most expats, as David Sedaris has noted, tend to show up in foreign countries dressed like they've come to mow the lawn.

Glasser's venerable style did, however, endear him to the socially rigid Japanese, despite the fact that in all his years there he'd managed to master only one phrase in their language. And not a piece of classic haiku, but a line from Christopher Marlowe's 1604 *The Tragical History of Doctor Faustus*. He'd had a line of it translated even before arriving in Japan to use on romance-starved local women: "Thou art fairer than the evening air, clad in the beauty of a thousand stars." In bars, on trains, over candlelit dinners, in noisy sushi shops, it didn't matter—Glasser's antique eloquence never failed to capture hearts.

I never used the line myself but, then, neither do I wear evening jackets nor smoke pipes in the drawing room. There can be only one Glasser, in this century at least. Among those who know him, opinion remains divided as to who would play him in the movie, Jeremy Irons or Ian McKellan; though Glasser himself wouldn't hesitate to cast the *Lawrence of Arabia*–era Peter O'Toole.

Becoming a writer, Glasser told me, is one of the easiest things in the world. Like divorcing a wife in Islam or going home from Oz, all one had to do was utter the magic words.

"The only requirement is simply *saying* that you're a writer and then believing it," he said. "All writers struggle, very few manage to get published, and almost none are actually any good. It's the 'believing' part that's the trick."

It wasn't so much that Glasser understood the vagaries of the publishing racket as that he understood the lie behind every large enterprise. As a young man compelled to serve at the whim of the U.S. government in 1968, he'd long ago become acquainted with institutionalized deception in its many guises.

"One day you're a theater arts major bounding across a stage at U.C. Berkeley, meeting girls named 'Puppy,' and auditioning for shampoo commercials," he explained to me one evening over a Yahweh, a cocktail he'd invented with ice-cold hundred-proof vodka and a drop of green Chartreuse floating on top. "A month later you're enduring appalling treatment at a boot camp in Fort Lewis, Washington. A few weeks after that you're a foot soldier on night patrol outside the wire at Quang Tri. Believe me when I tell you no man was ever less qualified to carry a rifle."

Despite my fondness for Glasser, as well as my appreciation for his deeply justified cynicism, his strategy for attaining a literary career seemed absurd. Besides, I wasn't interested in becoming a writer. At the time my only mission in life was to see that all 128 million citizens of Japan were armed for the twenty-first century with a remedial fluency in conversational English.

After Gifu, I'd promised myself no more ESL teaching, but, like Michael Jordan watching the Houston Rockets cruise to two NBA titles while he rotted away in minor-league baseball, I believed I had some unfinished business to take care of in the Eastern Conference. I arrived in Kojima eager to put my year of Asia experience to good use. Having a clearer idea about how the future unfolds for itinerant ESL instructors, Glasser's mission was to change my mind. He started with the Rope Challenge.

The Rope Challenge was born in the dark hours of a summer morning in an extremely ordinary Japanese garden, a humble square block crammed amid the acres of asphalt and concrete that made Kojima the unofficial parking lot of southern Japan. Alone in the park that night were Glasser and the previously mentioned charming bastard and Old Asia Hand extraordinaire Shanghai Bob, a man fate had tossed from an idyllic but impoverished posting in Thailand into the more lucrative, commercial armpit of Japan. Powerful entities as individuals, in tandem Glasser and Shanghai Bob created a dynamic not unlike plutonium and fission. Or, at the very least, Dylan and electricity.

Disarmingly simple on the surface, the Rope Challenge worked like this: the pond in the center of Kojima's public garden ran about thirty yards across. On either side stood a wooden platform, about eight feet high, accessed by a set of stairs. Atop each of these platforms was a facsimile of an old, rustic well—the pond and well, as in all Japanese gardens, expressing life and its inevitable renewal. Mounted to each well was a pulley system that connected two lengths of rope, which ran to the platform across the pond at a height of about eight (bottom rope) and fifteen (top rope) feet above the water. Attached to the top rope, an old wooden bucket, usually left suspended midway across the water, could be wheeled to either platform. Presumably, the whole setup served as a comfort to meditating locals not led astray by the surrounding traffic, empty sake bottles, passed-out salarymen, and other detritus of the mid-minor Japanese bedroom community.

Bringing their problem-finding Western natures to this delicate rendering of Japan's spiritual past, and no doubt emboldened by five or six hours of blowing their pay-checks in Kojima's dreary handful of bars, Shanghai Bob and Glasser established the rules of the Rope Challenge by assessing what appeared to be, even in their slurry condition, a reasonably ordinary athletic feat. Balancing between the two ropes—hands on top, feet on bottom—they would see which of them could transport himself fastest across the pond in the step-by-step, hand-over-hand fashion most often associated with black jumpsuits and fatal commando raids.

The crossing looked simple. I'm sure renegade expats stumbling upon it today think the same thing. The prob-lem was the two ropes were actually one rope, strung across the pond in a big loop through hinged gears at ei-ther end. Intended to support merely the small, decora-tive bucket, the design made the rope dangerously prone to swaying, buckling, and flipping once mounted by two-hundred-pound English instructors.

Like *Moby Dick* or a layover at JFK Airport, you didn't fully appreciate the difficulty of completing the Rope Challenge until you were too far in to turn back. In retrospect, the ingredients—unstable rope, pond be-low, besotted gaijin on suicide mission—forecast a pre-dictable enough outcome. The hapless clown attempting the crossing was usually flipped upside down about halfway across and shot ass over tea kettle into the wa-ter for an agony-of-defeat-style splashdown.

By the time I arrived in Kojima, Glasser and Shanghai Bob had already failed the challenge ten or fifteen times between them. It was late and I was seeing double on my maiden voyage—the Rope Challenge having become a Kojima last-stop-of-the-night tradition—and I spilled into the drink ten feet from the starting line. I came up choking on the rank water. Above, the lines across the pond taunted me like a puzzle.

I became obsessed with the Rope Challenge. I pondered its lightning unpredictability during school hours. Ran mental game film while riding trains. Reached back to high school geometry to consider such variables as velocity and weight distribution. Why, for instance, had Shanghai Bob tumbled headfirst into the pond just fifteen feet from the platform, while Glasser's point of impact, only five feet farther down the line, had been at his right hip? My arrival elevated the Rope Challenge from exhibition sport to sanctioned competition. Shanghai Bob and Glasser's primal fires were stoked. A race was on to see which of us would be the first to cross the void.

Living in a foreign country invites the kind of suffering that leads to activities that seem bizarre anywhere else, such as grown men measuring their self-esteem via activities like the Rope Challenge. The threat of complete mental collapse is always an invisible companion abroad, and these sorts of addled endeavors often contain the key to sanity.

When I said "Japan" was my first job out of college, I meant it. I wasn't just teaching at Giri High School. I was enduring an alien place where I had no history, a severely limited present, and negligible future. That sort of thing sounds appealing in the freedom's-just-another-word-for-nothing-left-to-lose kind of way, but it's a monumental trial living in a country where you have no idea what's going on 99 percent of the time. With the Internet, Skype phones, and other technologies that allow the homesick expat to keep minute-by-minute track of everything from Uncle Paul's triple bypass (with photos and video) to back seasons of *Curb Your Enthusiasm*, the invaluable isolation of the expat experience has been diminished. But it's still no picnic to be unknown, illiterate, and surrounded by a race of people who will never understand the massive implications of this week's Cornhuskers v. Sooners game or your feverish need to get the results as soon as possible.

Living in the shadows of crumbled Western empires, expats are social misfits who nevertheless bear the responsibility of being a nation's first line of ambassadors overseas. It's a tricky job made harder by the fact that relatively few are willing to do it. I still find it amazing that only 20 percent of Americans own passports, that only a fraction of those will spend any significant time overseas, and how little the other 80 percent appreciate how the majority of the world operates.

But that's the rank and file for you. They're entitled to be as ignorant as they like. Travel writers, on the other hand, have an obligation to know something more about the places they volunteer to describe. Regrettably, few of them take this obligation seriously enough to actually endure the difficulty of extended periods overseas.

As I'm writing this, a travel book called *Fried Eggs*

with Chopsticks has just been published. It's difficult to believe that a book bearing such a title—describing one writer's trip to China—could have been imagined by someone with even rudimentary insight into Asia. The triumph of globalization pretty much a given, it's no longer relevant to be amused by those funny little wooden sticks the Asians use at dinnertime. If you aren't finished considering them a point of conversation after your second or third trip to the Chinese restaurant back home, much less after a trip across one of the world's great civilizations, you might think twice before taking on the job of interpreting the country for the masses.

Cross-cultural pollution was already old hat back in 1989 when Pico Iyer published the highly respected *Video Night in Kathmandu*. That was two decades ago. It's no longer news—as legions of writers continue to breathlessly report—that kids in Belarus wear T-shirts bearing Beyoncé's likeness, that yuppies in Hong Kong make a fetish of designer balsamic vinegar, that Argentine theaters stage Brad Pitt Appreciation nights. And that half the population of the world doesn't use forks. Not even for fried eggs.

Even so, shopworn observations like these are trotted out every year and perpetuated by publishers who wish us to believe in a paradigm of travel established more than a century ago. Their bidding is done by an army of doltish travel writers whose inability to seize upon anything beyond the obvious and trite is based on either a profound inexperience abroad or by the kind of tittering acceptance that turns everything foreign, no matter how mundane or evil, into a "charming," "authentic," or "hilarious" cultural experience. If a school were ever set up to teach travel writing, a year of menial work overseas would be the first required course. If nothing else, living among foreigners shows you that every society produces dreck. Nothing beats the dilettante out of a soul quite like the discovery that you can still be miserable living in an exotic and beautiful place.

No white man should ever wear a sarong, not even in private. No one familiar with Western fashion needs to be told this. And by introducing him in a silken wrap of fiery orange and fluorescent saffron, I don't want to give the impression that Shanghai Bob actually pulled off the look. Nevertheless, on occasion, leaning against the rail of his apartment terrace, gin rickey in hand, Japanese sun at just the right late-afternoon angle, his lower half encased in a colorful sheet of fabric acquired in some steamy Malay marketplace, Shanghai Bob came as close to appearing born to the sarong as it's possible for a native of Indiana to be.

You don't set out to become an Old Asia Hand, and you don't earn the title simply by making stops in the villages, towns, and sprawling shit holes of Thailand, China, Indonesia, and Japan and hitting almost every other Asian nation along the way. You get it by learning how to parlay your White Man status for gain, when to play the respectful sycophant with regional chieftains and when to bullyrag the locals when they push you too far, as they inevitably will. Honing the ability to drink a Mongolian sheepherder under the table also helps. At six two with dirty-blond hair, blue eyes, the eternal look of a man in his midthirties, and that Midwestern affability somehow interpreted as trustworthy by every ethnic group in the world (no general in history was more underestimated than Kansas-bred Eisenhower), Shanghai Bob strides through Asia as an alien force of nature.

For one year in Kojima, Japan, I lived two doors down from Shanghai Bob. Glasser's apartment was between ours. I battled alongside them both on an ESL warship known as Mt. Hood Community College (endearingly misspelled by our 180 inept students as "Mt. Hoot," "Mt. Hod," or "Mt. Food"), a satellite campus of an American school that folded in Japan after three torturous years. Shanghai Bob and Glasser had arrived at the brand-new school a few weeks ahead of me, sniffed each other out, and decided over copious amounts of brandy that, like San Francisco and the San Andreas Fault, they could piece together a tenuous coexistence. Because I spoke passable Japanese and he did not, Shanghai Bob hated me right away.

Knowing the language vastly improves an incorrigible rake's chances with the local talent, and Shanghai Bob immediately assumed that my youth and semifluency gave me a leg up on the slim pickings he'd already scouted out in town. He needn't have worried. In addition to heartland likability and rugged Scotch-Irish looks, Shanghai Bob had a glorious international-bachelor résumé under his belt that left him adept at establishing an electric rapport with women, verbal skills or no. Once he got his sea legs in Kojima, and my girlfriend, Joyce, arrived from the States, we became pals.

We bonded first over our mutual dissatisfaction with the incompetent American teachers and insufferable gaijin who surrounded us in Kojima. Excepting the few genuinely noble souls who mistakenly wander into every profession, ESL teaching attracts reliably large numbers of dullards, laggards, nitwits, dipshits, dimwits, losers, castoffs, drifters, the verifiably insane, and, most of all, the previously unemployed. Of all these, Mt. Hoot had its share.

Mt. Food's band of expat misfits battled all year. Faculty-room alliances and grudges quickly developed. I fell in with a small group—Shanghai Bob and myself— that raged at the inadequacy of pretty much everyone on staff at one point or another. Glasser was the only one who kept his head during the various school-year dramas, refusing to be pulled into any of several clandestine plots and advising us that the school's infuriatingly sedentary director—nicknamed the Armadillo for his armored, corporate demeanor—was the best type of boss of all because he ignored us.

"There's no point in complaining so much that you ruin a situation as easy as this one," said Glasser, reflecting a wizened apathy I didn't yet appreciate.

To quote John Fowles again, "Like all young men I saw myself as a catalyst, as a solver of situations," and I never managed to settle into school life. Many of us abandoned ship at the close of the final semester, and the school folded two years later amid unconfirmed speculation that our Japanese investors were actually Yakuza mafia looking for a novel money-laundering front. Not the most enjoyable year, certainly no postcard views of golden temples and cherry blossoms, but at least an experience that leaves you with better things to talk about than the goddamn chopsticks.

After the isolation of Gifu, Mt. Hod was a dose of reality. I'd grown so accustomed to blaming Japan for all my troubles, it hadn't occurred to me that the foreigners there could actually be worse than the locals. And that I might be one of them. I suspect now that the Japanese in Kojima hated all of us, and with good reason. We were a self-centered, high-horse, crybaby lot who came in expecting the sweet deal American teachers get back home and never once thought about adjusting our expectations.

And, yes, poor unappreciated teachers, I did say sweet deal. American public school teachers have the world's best PR operation going. Whining every chance they get about how demanding their jobs are, how many "extra hours" they put in, how little they make, how much of their own money they have to spend just to do their jobs, how noble they are working this job that nobody ever asked them to do—welcome to the fucking world.

That's something else you figure out living overseas. You think you've got it tough? You don't got it tough. American teachers would crumble if they ever had to work the real hours of a cabbie, doctor, bartender, fisherman, truck driver, small-business owner, hotel clerk, mechanic, architect, janitor, musician, surveyor, accountant, or the million other jobs that don't observe weekends, much less every city, county, state, and federal holiday on the docket, almost three months' paid vacation a year, and pension programs funded out of the public trough. How is it we all go through school painfully aware that half our teachers are lazy or incompetent or pathological control freaks, then turn around and let them convince us what a bunch of saints they are as soon as we become taxpayers?

Like most institutionalized instruction, teaching English in a foreign country is "easy" because by and large the requirements and expectations are so low, but it's also "hard" because it's nearly impossible to remain interested in the task. It's like trying to stay intellectually engaged for an entire afternoon with someone else's six-year-old. Then going home to a dingy apartment and wondering what the hell you're doing wasting your life in a country where no one will ever really know you. Then popping a beer at four even though you promised yourself that today you were going to wait until four thirty.

Glasser and Shanghai Bob were good to have around because they'd usually start drinking by three thirty, which took a little of the sting out of my descent into a primary form of recreation that traced its roots to a distillery somewhere outside London.

From Glasser, Shanghai Bob and I learned that, like sex, every generation believes it has discovered the martini. And that the old proverb about martinis being like a woman's breast—one is not enough, three is too many—makes sense only after multiple attempts to disprove it. We didn't swill martinis in Japan like the Bombay company was going out of business because we believed that doing so made us debonair—I knew I wasn't, Glasser knew he was, Shanghai Bob knew he didn't need to be. We drank them because they kept the dismal reality of Mt. Foot at bay for a few sacred hours each evening.

One of the best meals I ever had was spent facedown on the bathroom floor of our favorite Indian restaurant, an oasis called the Mughal in Okayama City, a thirty-minute train ride from Kojima. As was tradition on Friday nights, the three of us staggered postmartinis into the Mughal, made a showy consultation of the wine list, and ordered approximately half the items on the menu. Glasser and Shanghai Bob then proceeded to linger over their meals, and make short work of mine, plus two bottles of wine, before knocking gently on the door of the bathroom where I'd been passed out since just before the arrival of the samosas. As I'd taken care to lock the door behind me, no one in the restaurant had been able to get into the restroom for the hour or so it took Glasser and Shanghai Bob to eat, and the staff was beyond the point of agitation.

"Carlos." I heard Glasser's muffled call through the door like an invitation to an exclusive party. "The night's been a smashing success, but it's time to go home."

During our less explosive drinking sessions, Shanghai Bob and I pulled out of Robert most of the essentials of the Glasser Story, including bits about his time in Vietnam. On several occasions, Glasser had hinted that his knowledge of classic poetry had saved his life there, and we were anxious for the details. Some years later I asked Glasser to recount it and encouraged him to commit the rest of his experiences to paper. I told him he'd make a mint selling it, and I'd make a tidy profit as his agent. Here in its entirety is his response to my letter:

Carlos,

As for the Vietnam story, it goes roughly like this. My third day in country at Quang Tri Combat Base, about ten miles south of the DMZ, I was called into a large tent with twenty or so other replacements and told that since a company in the battalion I was to be sent to as a clerk had been more or less wiped out in an ambush, I would be posted there as infantry. And yes, since I had no infantry training and little indication that I might be a natural for that sort of thing, it was pretty much a death or dismemberment sentence.

I came out of the tent and noticed a second lieutenant staring at my helmet, on which I'd written "*Dulce Et Decorum Est Pro Patria Mori*, Wilfred Owen, 1918." Owen was a WWI British poet; the title is from Horace ("It is good and sweet to die for your country"); and the poem (read it, if you haven't) is probably the most savage anti-war statement ever penned.

Lieutenant: That Latin, son? (He was about twenty-five and I was twenty-three but all enlisted men are called "son" by officers exercising combat noblesse oblige.)

Me: Yessir. Horace, sir.

Lieutenant: What's it mean?

Me: It's good and sweet to die for your country, sir.

Lieutenant (*deeply moved*): We need more men like you.

Me: Yessir. Thank you, sir.

Lieutenant: Can you type?

Me: Yessir. Ohhhhhh yessir! My MOS is clerk typist, sir.

Lieutenant: We're looking for someone at Headquarter's company. Come with me.

Me: Yessir, thank you, sir.

And so I escaped certain death to spend the rest of my tour typing for a revolving cast of lunatic officers. True story, but it does sound a little too neat, doesn't it? Too patly ironic, too hooray for the college kid who fooled the lifer lieutenant.

Still, while I vouch for it, I confess I no longer really know what happened and what didn't happen to me in Vietnam. The mind, unbidden, rewrites things, creates new images, makes new connections, draws new morals. War stories are mostly frauds, and mostly unintentionally so. Half my nights in Vietnam I was stoned and what I saw and what I dreamed and what I hallucinated are so intermingled that forty years later I'm damned if I can untangle it all. And some things I remember which seemed completely normal at the time—rolling out of my cot twice a night to hide in an underground crypt during mortar attacks—have startled me years later. Did they happen? Yes, I think so. But I see them as in a dream and as happening to someone else entirely.

And anger, Carlos. Anger distorts reality as much as drugs. And I was Angry most of the time I was in the army and for two years after I got out. You know Fussell's *Wartime*? A very good book, but not, like his *The Great War and Modern Memory*, a great book. I think he never got over his anger—at the Army, at the U.S., at himself for his real and imagined failures, and for the things he was made to do.

So, there'll be no Vietnam memoir for me. But if you're curious, buy me a drink sometime and I'll paste a few pieces together for you. Robert

P.S. The second lieutenant (and this I do recall) was more or less nuts. He used to tie up foot-long centipedes with rubber bands, chop them in bits, pour lighter fluid on them, and set them on fire. On his desktop.

Like starving men on a lifeboat eyeing the weaker members of the party, the expat comes unattached from his social moorings faster than he'd care to imagine. Burning centipedes on desktops is only the start of it.

I found this out the hard way on an obscure island in Indonesia called Bintan where, some years after our Japan adventures, Shanghai Bob had landed a job at a posh Singaporean-owned resort training the local staff on the finer points of catering to wealthy Chinese tourists. I'd brought along gifts from the outside world, a bottle of Veuve Clicquot and a Dwight Yoakam CD. Decent champagne and country music are tough to come by in Indonesia, and Shanghai Bob was particularly touched by the gesture, especially since the CD was signed. I'd recently spent four hours interviewing Yoakam in his suite at the Four Seasons in Austin—he was there filming a movie and still strikes me as the brightest and loneliest celebrity I've ever encountered—and I knew Bob was a fan.

I'd arrived in Indonesia during the upheaval of the late '90s, when killings in East Timor, scattered student demonstrations, the ousting of President Suharto, rumors of another coup in Jakarta, and random Muslim, Hindu, and/or Christian beatings and burnings in the rural provinces threatened to spread chaos across the rest of the country. In Bintan, tensions between the criminally underpaid local labor force, the criminally overpaid expat administrative corps, and the just plain criminal owners of the island's money-churning resorts had recently led to loud public protests and rock throwing. A good number of the expat community had been sufficiently spooked by the "Kill Whitey" graffiti to quit their jobs, pull up stakes, and move on before the bloodshed arrived.

After debriefing me on the general unrest over martinis inside his apartment, Shanghai Bob led me on a two-mile bicycle ride down a dirt jungle path to a small outdoor café that he told me served the best roast chicken in Southeast Asia. No small claim. It was pitch dark; the place was lit by a single anemic string of Christmas lights. Palm fronds sagged against the crippling humidity. Thousands of equatorial insects buzzed around our heads. Three tough-looking boys were listening to tinny Indonesian pop music and leaning on the outdoor bamboo bar, a moldy relic likely taken from some long-gone expat's bungalow.

A resentful-looking character cut like an ex–Thai boxing champ—crazy, opaque eyes, bulging shoulder muscles—sauntered across the dirt courtyard and served us two beers about ten minutes after we ordered them.

"How about a change of music?" Bob suggested to the guy after he'd set the beers down. I had no idea what Shanghai Bob was getting at until, to my horror, I saw him reach into the side pocket of his khaki trousers and produce the autographed Dwight Yoakam CD I'd given him an hour earlier. For a moment, our waiter/fighter looked mildly interested.

"Wat dis?" he said, turning over the CD case in his hand like a grenade.

"Music," Shanghai Bob offered with enthusiasm. "Real music. Put it on."

Waiter/fighter looked at the slouching dude on the cover with the big cowboy hat pulled over his face. He pretended to read some of the song titles, then instantly lost interest and dropped the CD on the table so hard that the jewel box cracked a little.

"No moozik," he said defiantly, tipping his head toward the boys at the bar huddled around a banged-up portable Sanyo CD player. "Only radio."

"That's cool, no problem," I piped up, sensing an acute need for amity. But Shanghai Bob was craning his neck around, and I knew his famous standards-of-customer-service lecture was clawing its way up his throat.

"Look, we're the only ones here," Shanghai Bob told waiter/fighter, the clear implication being that this gave us dominion over the CD player. "Let's hear some decent fucking music for a change. My friend here brought this CD all the way from the States. Special occasion. Play it."

So now it was my request. Waiter/fighter curled his lip and once again nodded toward the bar, though this time without taking his eyes off Shanghai Bob. "Dey listen Indonesia moozik," he said.

"Horse shit!" Shanghai Bob replied. "Those kids are here every night, and they don't spend a goddamn thing. I'm in this place three nights a week eating your overcooked chicken, and I pay actual money." He jingled some of it in his pocket to drive the point home.

The boys at the bar now began looking over their shoulders at us. Waiter/fighter's eyes narrowed. It's showdowns like these that end with machetes unsheathed, flashes of steel in the moonlight, and someone's head rolling across the dirt with its eyes shocked wide open, mouth formed into a black *O* of horror for all eternity. This was how they handled problems just up the coast in Aceh—I knew because I'd seen the footage on CNN International in my hotel room earlier in the day.

Waiter/fighter assumed a red-zone stance in front of Shanghai Bob. I couldn't just abandon my boy here, but I needed to discreetly let this smoldering weapon of Indonesian pride know that if violence was inevitable, he and the guys at the bar might want to consider taking out their aggression on Shanghai Bob first, then see how they felt before committing to any more ass kicking. When waiter/fighter shifted his gaze to me, I seized the opportunity to flash him a complicated shrug, a multi-layered gesture meant to somehow defuse the situation without causing loss of face to anyone. They end up being the butt of a lot of pussy jokes, but it's not easy being Switzerland.

"It'd be one thing if their fucking music here wasn't so bad," Shanghai Bob muttered, further attempting to enlist me on his side. He turned back to waiter/fighter. "C'mon, man, one song."

Waiter/fighter picked up the CD with his right hand and drummed it between the thumb and forefinger of his left. I looked up at him like a kitten in a store window. And then, in one of those undocumented small miracles that save countless tourist lives each year, he reconsidered.

"OK," he said, forcing the barest pretense of a smile. "For you. One song."

You could have inflated the *Hindenburg* with the breath I let out. Of course, I'd forgotten whom I was sitting next to.

"Two songs," Shanghai Bob fired back as the guy walked away. "Tracks two and six."

On the back of that Dwight Yoakam CD, it says that "A Thousand Miles from Nowhere" clocks in at four minutes, twenty-seven seconds, and "Ain't That Lonely Yet" goes just three minutes, seventeen seconds. But listen to a forlorn hillbilly wailing out his despair on back-to-back tracks in a black jungle night while four sets of Muslim eyes and three centuries' worth of racial hostility bore into the back of your skull, and you'll swear that seven minutes and forty-four seconds runs closer to three or four hours. It's nights like these that make you wonder how Shanghai Bob got through his tour of Peace Corps duty alive. One thing I will say for him, though—and maybe those guys on Bintan say it, too, when they're telling the story about the crazy *farangs* ready to die for the sake of some shitty music—Shanghai Bob did leave a helluva nice tip.

For several months during the middle of the school year, Glasser, Shanghai Bob, and I forgot about the Rope Challenge. Or, at least, let it sit dormant. Winter is bitter in Japan, and the prospect of an icy bath seemed less hilarious in January than it had in September.

Then one spring morning as I lay in bed in that half-asleep state, the secret of the Rope Challenge revealed itself to me. It was all about the bucket. The little decorative prop that had been sitting in front of us the whole time appeared in my head and began speaking to me.

"How is it that none of you have seen such a simple solution to such a simple riddle?" the bucket asked me.

Then it proceeded to explain how to beat the challenge. I bolted upright in bed.

"I've solved the Rope Challenge," I said, popping my eyes open and speaking to the wall.

I waited all day to make the announcement in the conservatory, the tiny spare room in Glasser's apartment where we convened every evening for after-school drinks.

"Tonight," I said. "The Rope Challenge. I know how to do it." Glasser looked intrigued. Shanghai Bob was incredulous.

"Bullshit," Shanghai Bob said. "It's been tried every way. It can't be done."

"That's what they said about the four-minute mile," Glasser harrumphed into his martini glass.

"He's got about as much chance running a four-minute mile as he does making it across that pond," Shanghai Bob said.

"I've got ten thousand yen says you're wrong." My expression was granite. Shanghai Bob had no choice but to accept the bet. Glasser came to his aid by ponying up half the amount.

My strategy was based on the realization that the mistake we'd been making had been to adjust the amount of pressure with the hands on the top rope and the balls of the feet on the bottom to accommodate the unpredictable sway of the ropes. The bucket gave the secret away. If as the central visual element of the Rope Challenge the bucket was a mere decoration, wasn't it possible that other parts of the apparatus were decorative, as well? That one of the ropes—in this case, the bottom one—was never meant to support any weight at all? That it existed simply to look good and maybe, like spots on a moth, to baffle potential predators? By ignoring the bottom rope, by allowing my feet to merely glide on top of it while supporting my entire weight with my hands on the overhead rope, I could simply cross the pond as though I were working my way down a set of monkey bars on a school playground.

As we had dozens of times before, the three of us loaded up with beer and stumbled into the Japanese garden shortly after midnight. I stood on the platform at the eastern end of the pond, Glasser and Shanghai Bob on either side of me. Bob brandished a Suntory malt; Glasser puffed on an English cigarette.

"You'll never make it," Shanghai Bob said.

"Good luck," Glasser said, patting me on the shoulder like a brigadier at the Somme.

I extended a bomber pilot's thumbs-up, reached a few feet in front of me for the rope, and swung out over the water. From there it was just as I'd envisioned. Allowing my feet to skim the bottom rope, I used only my arms to carry me halfway across the pond in less than thirty seconds, easily record time. Glasser and Shanghai Bob's cheers faded as I slipped around the dangling bucket and dug deep to concentrate on the final assault. A sliver of doubt raced through my mind as the muscles in my forearm tightened on the uphill climb to the opposite platform, but I'd endured worse during all those Presidential Physical Fitness Awards I'd narrowly missed in junior high. You want to kill a kid's self-esteem, throw some fucking compulsory pull-ups at him and deny him a medal, three years running.

My confidence growing, I knocked out the second half of the crossing almost as quickly as the first. I hit the platform on the other side with a triumphant stamping of feet, spread my arms like Jesus on the cross, then wheeled around to accept my conqueror's salute. But the platform on the other side was empty. Glasser and Shanghai Bob had vanished.

The garden was suddenly small and silent. A devastating loneliness swept over me like an eclipse. I stared out at the bucket, still swinging on the rope above the middle of the pond. "I'm sorry," I said to the bucket, but it gave me nothing in return.

There's a seduction to the expat life, the promise of a world filled with Rope Challenges, close calls with Indonesian rebels, midnight conversations about Vietnam with men who've been there, and a miraculous sense of lone-wolf independence that somehow exists alongside a uniquely intense bond among comrades. The insider's knowledge of a strange place elevates the man abroad above the hoi polloi of his home country, and particularly above the tourist, whose appearance in his adopted country always comes as an unwelcome shock. The romantic attachment to place, even a difficult place, is almost impossible to break.

All expat life is limbo. Lurking behind every discussion, the Return Home, whether it's one or two or ten years away, provides the fundamental tension to every moment you live abroad. Then, one day, you commit to going back to the States, and you either succeed there or you don't. And if you don't, you leave once again, to roll the dice on some other place that requires of you only a passport and the gambler's faith in long odds.

The Rope Challenge, like so many other elements of the overseas experience, kept the real world at bay. Once it was conquered, the spell was broken. As for Glasser and Shanghai Bob, in spite of their own sporadic efforts to repatriate, they were in Asia to stay—they live there to this day—and I knew I'd always envy them for it. But I also knew I'd see them again, that life for all of us after the Rope Challenge was beaten had begun to feel weird, and that the thing to do when the going gets weird, in the words of Hunter S. Thompson, is to turn pro.

PART II
Middle →

5

. . .

Why Latin America Isn't the World's Number One Tourist Destination and Probably Never Will Be

No place needs a good PR agency more than Latin America. For a region with so much going in its favor—food, scenery, the most hospitable locals on earth—it has a worse reputation than the Florida Division of Elections.

On the surface, stumping for Latin America might seem unnecessary. Cancún, Rio, and chalupa didn't become household words in this country because Americans don't love them. With about 19 million visitors a year, Mexico is the top foreign destination for American travelers.

In the murky world of travel, however, statistics rarely tell the complete story. Of the 41.3 million Hispanics living in the United States, more than half are of Mexican heritage. These people don't just inflict loudmouth hacks like Carlos Mencia on the public and make politicians nervous during election years, they screw up travel stats on a year-round basis. Mexican Americans and just plain old Mexicans living in America travel back and forth across the border more often than Major League scouts. Because they frequently speak the language and have family or otherwise feel comfortable traveling in a place most Americans associate with agonizing diarrhea, Mexican Americans don't necessarily conform to the definition of "tourist" as broadly implied in statistical abstracts. Eliminate traveling Mexicans, businessmen who make the country the United States' second-largest trading partner, condo owners, and frat boys permanently squatting at Señor Frog's, and American tourism looks less impressive.

Falling predominantly within U.S. time zones, most of the rest of Latin America still qualifies as "undiscovered," at least in the relative view of the travel industry. After Mexico, no Latin American country even cracks the top ten list of foreign destinations for traveling Americans. With fewer than a million visits a year, massive Switzerland sees more yanqui faces than the legendary nature preserves of Costa Rica. Despite being home to Angel Falls, the Gran Sabana wilderness, and parts of the Andes, Amazon River, and Caribbean coastline, fewer than half a million international visitors venture into the majestic Venezuelan countryside, leaving it, like most of South America, with some of the most neglected natural beauty in the world. This is in large part due to the fact that, fear being the leitmotif of all good propaganda, about 75 percent of Americans are convinced that any trip south of Texas will involve some combination of bribery, kidnapping, armed revolt, the most toxic GI diseases this side of the Congo, knives pulled in macho bar duels, and a probable colonoscopy at the border.

Conversations like the one I had with Glasser several

years ago sum up the prevailing attitude many Americans have about our brethren to the south. Glasser had shown up on the West Coast vacationing with a "lady friend" whom he was keenly interested in showing a good time. He literally snorted when I suggested a drive down Mexico's magnificent Pacific Coast.

"I'm not sure you understand." Glasser addressed me like a Cambridge don explaining mathematics to a particularly stupid eight-year-old. "I'd like to go someplace where we can actually leave the hotel."

I told him I'd been to Mexico and points south dozens of times and always found the paranoia of Americans to be unfounded.

"Will they let me bring my handgun across the border?" he asked.

Venezuela's landscape surprised me, but the country that sealed my impression of Latin America was Panama. Though I had no interest in laying over for five hours in Houston to get there, I'd grudgingly accepted an assignment from the once L.A.-based, now defunct *Escape* magazine because, like all freelance writers, I live in constant fear that every job will be my last and would probably compile an oral history of jock itch if somebody paid me to do it. The three-hundred-word opus I once wrote for a weekly newspaper in Oregon previewing a Chippendale's-like ladies-only cruise may not have been my journalistic high point, but I'm not ashamed of my decision to write it or the fifty bucks I got to do so. (Soothing factoid for struggling writers: Kurt Vonnegut began his career writing PR copy for General Electric in Schenectady, New York.)

I traveled to Panama with such low expectations—
visions of a ghetto Miami, marines blasting Guns N'
Roses at Manuel Noriega outside the Vatican embassy—
that anything short of a junta-backed drug war would
have looked good. From the moment I paddled my
dugout canoe around Panama's palm-covered San Blas
Islands, however, I knew my preconceptions of the
country were as off the mark as the five-hundred-dollar
bet I laid down on the Raiders to cover against Tampa
Bay in Super Bowl XXXVII.

Panama was a paradise of forests, rivers, islands, and
wildlife. Better still, apart from a handful of adventuresome Swedes, wealthy yachties cruising the Panama
Canal, and a mild-mannered group of bird-watchers, no
one was there. I encountered the birders on the outdoor
deck of a bar where we watched massive ships glide like
blimps through the astounding canal and debated the
finer points of white-bellied antbird vs. green-rumped
parrotlet. Not exactly Mary Ann vs. Ginger or even
Cooler Ranch vs. Spicy Nacho, but enough of an argument to burn a good two or three minutes of small talk
with strangers.

"Where are all the Americans?" I asked one of the
Panamanian guides. I was staring at a toucan in a
nearby tree, aware for the first time that the animal existed beyond the borders of a cereal box.

He shrugged. "They're afraid to come here." It was
the same response I'd get at El Avila National Park in
Caracas, in the Andes in Colombia, at Chapada Diaman-
tina National Park in Brazil, amid Mayan ruins in
Guatemala, along the Honduran coast, at the bottom of
Copper Canyon, Mexico, and just about everywhere

else in Latin America that doesn't pump premixed margarita slushies from plastic jugs.

Since the youth of America are almost the only real tourists going to Mexico—though mainly to the party deck at Cabo Wabo—you can't go blaming them for the mistrustful American attitudes toward Latin America. That means responsibility must be pinned on the next best scapegoat: Nicholas Trist.

Sent by President James Polk in 1848 to negotiate the end of the Mexican-American War, Trist arrived in the town of Guadalupe Hidalgo, just north of Mexico City, ready and able by all accounts to carry out his sacred duty. Notwithstanding the recent overwhelming American military victory, however, Trist failed to execute one of his most basic instructions from the Polk White House by somehow managing not to obtain an American naval outlet on the Gulf of California. Trist fouled the job so completely that he accepted, according to one historian, "such terms as Mexico might have imposed if she had won the war." This goes to show you that the tequila they served in Mexico back in the day was every bit as lethal as it is now.

But the Mexicans didn't leave the table smelling like a rose-scented margarita, either. This was the deal in which the United States picked up Arizona, New Mexico, parts of Colorado, Nevada, and Utah, and intellectual property rights on all future Los Lobos albums. Not to mention a little state called California, the entirety of which belonged to Mexico at the time and in which, just two weeks *before* the Treaty of Guadalupe Hidalgo was signed in February 1848, a man named James Marshall discovered a lump of gold at Sutter's Mill. Word of the

California gold strike wouldn't reach the public until March, too late by days for Mexico to make any claims to it. This piece of manifest-destiny-style Providence— or yanqui duplicity, depending on your perspective— altered the fate of North and South America, and cemented in the American psyche the idea that God put all the good parts of the continent above the Rio Grande and that anyone named Gomez, Lopez, or Chavez now had considerable justification for hating our guts.

As it loves to do when given the chance to incite nationalist paranoia, the media has ever since reinforced the idea of a corrupt, third-rate, and dangerous Latin America awash in anarchy, diseased water, and molten-blooded hotties who'll gladly do a striptease one minute and throw a frying pan across the dining room at you the next. I've seen the myth created firsthand. While I was features editor there, *Maxim* magazine hired a writer I'll call Peter Henderson to do a story about Coca Sek, a soft drink being manufactured and peddled by a group of Nasa Indians of Colombia. The hook was that Coca Sek was made from coca leaves— the base ingredient in cocaine—and contained trace elements of coca.

Never mind that the Nasa were using the coca as a way of preserving their indigenous heritage, that Coca Sek bore no resemblance to narcotic cocaine, and that shotgunning four consecutive bottles, as I did in a hotel room in Cali, produced approximately the same effect as downing three Snapples with a Red Bull kicker. The combination of a coke-laced beverage, the world's kidnapping capital, and a *Scarface*-obsessed American public was too intoxicating for the world's largest men's magazine to pass up. Henderson was dispatched to

Colombia. I tagged along as the magazine's official envoy and photographer.

The *Maxim* staff rallied round to say good-bye in case no one ever saw us again. There was a widespread belief that "death wish" described the mental state of anyone who agreed to a trip to Colombia. Everyone figured the company brass secretly hoped Henderson and I would be kidnapped, thrown in jail, or, if things went really well, mowed down in a back-alley shootout with tin-pot drug lords. That's why you send wide-eyed gringos to Colombia with an expense account. Either that or to trawl for mail-order brides in the destitute countryside, which is the story *GQ* sent a writer to Colombia to cover only a few months before the *Maxim* expedition.

Colombia has been a goblin in America's imagination ever since Teddy Roosevelt stole the country's most prized possession, the Isthmus of Panama, in 1903. The story Henderson and I returned from Colombia with echoed the timeless expectations of a trip-wire nation steeped in danger and immorality. While allowing that one had to "take the kidnapping hype with a grain of salt," most of the piece focused on "some of the world's most dangerous countryside," "a land of guerrillas and cocaine lords," "a territory flush with indiscriminate right-wing paramilitaries," "machine-gun-infested FARC land," and "one of the highest murder rates on the planet." It caused a small, angry sensation in Colombia when it came out there.

Meanwhile, *GQ* pandered to another substratum of salacious typecasting by asking its readers to consider the possibility that the subject of its story, a thirty-eight-year-old American with a history of dating strippers who'd traveled to Colombia to exploit Third World poverty by purchasing the affection of an exclusively "model-quality" eighteen-to-twenty-two-year-old girl, wasn't a loser. And people call *Maxim* a magazine for degenerates.

The problem with our story, at least, was that while none of the details were demonstrably false (in fact all were demonstrably true), they were disingenuously skewed for dramatic effect. While middle-class Americans trembling through the territory of narco-terrorist blood feuds might make for compelling copy, the larger truth was that the four days Henderson and I spent traveling through Colombia were some of the most enjoyable either of us had experienced anywhere. This from two guys with seventy or eighty passport stamps between them.

Second only to the Himalayas for mountain drama, the turbulent beauty of the Andes provided a backdrop of overwhelming grandeur. Cafés with courteous staffs served meals alive with flavor—Americans don't realize how bland factory farms, agribusiness, and synthetic ingredients have made the food we eat. We chugged beer with friendly strangers, had lunch in an immaculate shopping mall where we met an easygoing Colombian who gave us a lift across town in his Beamer, and walked fearlessly through the nighttime streets of Cali— "home of the infamous Cali cartel," we reminded readers, even though we saw no blow there. But who buys magazines to read that? Our readers had seen *Maria Full of Grace*, they knew about the latex bullets of cocaine you shit out when you come back from South America. We had expectations to meet.

Once accepted by the public at large, media-created myths such as Latino lawlessness are tough to change. The principle works on more than travel. Consider the absurd revisionism regularly reprised in the music press that's turned Blondie's "Rapture" into the song that introduced white America to rap music. As anyone born before 1970 knows, this is an unmitigated lie manufactured by a myopic New York press so obsessed with its own assumed position at the center of the universe that every five years or so it proclaims another middling New York rock band (Lou Reed, Blondie, the Strokes, Yeah, Yeah, Yeahs) as the bellwether of world hipsterhood. "Rapture" was released in 1981, long after the Sugarhill Gang put out "Rapper's Delight" in 1979, a song whose lyrics I clearly recall memorizing on the floor of Tom Kollin's bedroom in the second-whitest state in the union. (Congratulations, Utah!) By 1981, I was on to "Apache" and revolted by "Rapture"—with Debbie Harry's "pioneering" Fab Five Freddie breakdown—even as a teenager able to recognize shoddy mimicry when I heard it. This might seem like a small-potatoes argument, but the people who care about these things measure their impact in millions of dollars and immortalizing nominations to the Rock and Roll Hall of Fame.

The same self-fulfilling solipsism applies to the parrot-like sports media's baseless proposition that Cal Ripken Jr. and the tainted Mark McGwire/Sammy Sosa home-run chase of 1998 "saved baseball" after the strike season of 1994 presumably raped a nation of its innocence. As though the century-and-a-half-old institution embraced by half of the planet hadn't endured scandal and trouble with the help before. Precisely 27.6 percent of the cynicism I carry around to this day is the direct result of the 1981 baseball strike, which destroyed my "dream summer" vacation that was to have included stops at Wrigley Field (prelights) and Yankee and Dodger stadiums. Somehow the national pastime bounced back from that.

None of this, however, should imply that Latin America hasn't earned at least part of its fearsome reputation. It's possible to defend the region as a whole while acknowledging, for example, that among its most persistent myths, the crooked-cop shakedown endures as a legitimate symbol, perhaps just below don't-drink-the-water, on the traveler's anxiety scale. There's no denying the word-of-mouth power of tourists who return from Mexico spewing tales of bravado, corruption, and near brushes with the inside of a Tijuana jail. Let the rhetorical flames die down, though, and you find the best way to cope with Latin American cops is to understand their side of the bargain.

On a road trip for *Escape* magazine down the entire 1,057-mile length of the Baja peninsula from the border to Los Cabos, I was pulled over at a police checkpoint outside a dusty heap of stone dwellings called Loreto. In the car with me was John May, my laid-back Texan travel companion who'd been christened Juan Mayo for the trip, partly because his superior Spanish was expected to carry us through the rural parts of our journey. The cop asked to see our tourist cards, and when we informed him that neither of us had one, he frowned, shook his head, and stroked his mustache, all time-honored methods of making Whitey squirm while a police officer who earns a few dollars a day sizes up the likely holdings of the rolling ATM before him. I'd seen something in a guidebook about tourist cards, but I hadn't taken the warning seriously, my typical attitude toward bureaucracy being to ignore it and hope it goes away.

While four or five of his comrades smoked and fiddled with assorted Vietnam-era weaponry nearby, the officer asked Juan Mayo and me to step out of the car. We followed him across the road into a dark little concrete hut reminiscent of the bunkers and pillboxes the Germans left all over Europe in the 1940s. He motioned toward a pair of creaky wooden stools next to a desk with a battered Formica top, then took a seat across from us. Inside there were no lights, no electricity, just a pervasive smell like the bottom of a canteen.

"Traveling without a tourist card is a serious offense," he told us. "You will have to leave Mexico immediately. The fine will be several hundred dollars. And we must seize your rental car."

After letting the bad news sink in, he riffed some more about our regrettable lack of proper documentation, then discreetly slid a sheet of ragged notebook paper across the desk. In faint pencil, six words were scratched across the top of the yellowed page: "You help my, I help you." John and I studied the paper like leaves in a teacup.

"We have no desire to leave Mexico, and we need our car to get to Cabo," John said. As he spoke, he slid a pair of hundred-peso notes across the desk in more or less the same fashion the notebook paper had come to us. Without looking down, the cop returned our warm smiles. Minutes later, we were back on the road heading south.

Americans love being outraged by graft in any form, and while this sort of experience might raise a few hackles, it's merely indicative of a more honest and efficient system of police tax than the one we have in the States. Though less transparent, the fines we pay at home for speeding and illegal parking are levied for the exact same purpose: to put food on a cop's table. The only difference is that in the United States the money travels through a more complex apparatus—clerks, assistants, public defenders, judges, and all manner of circuit and county parasites get their cut—which is why it's more expensive to break the law in El Paso than it is in Juarez. But a chunk of any check cashed for a violation in the States ultimately winds up right where Juan Mayo's pesos did in Loreto—inside some policeman's front pocket. In Mexico, they just eliminate the middleman.

For all the anxiety many Americans have about getting along in a foreign country, there's another group who act as though leaving U.S. soil gives them license to behave like the First Marine Division in Fallujah. Often, visitors who run afoul of Latin justice seem to deserve it.

A few years ago, I found myself inside the bathroom of legendary frat-guy hangout Hussong's in Ensenada taking a leak next to a swaying, sun-torched gringo named Clint who'd left his shirt behind somewhere earlier in the day.

"Pretty fucking wild place, huh?!" Clint was shouting and giving me the forty-five-degree urinal glance, enough angle for me to see the redness in his eyes and sheets of saliva flying onto the tile wall as he spoke.

"Pretty fucking wild." I nodded in that condescending way you get around hair-trigger drunks whose good sides turn over faster than the night crew at Denny's.

"This is my first time back to Hussong's in twenty years! We used to drive down here from Long Beach State! Last time I was here I got thrown out with a gun pointed at my head!"

"Why'd you get thrown out?"

"I poured beer down some chick's blouse!"

"Nice."

"Hey, man, your manhood never leaves you, you know?"

With exaggerated effort, Clint coaxed his hog back into his pants, zipped up, and stumbled away. A couple hours later, I saw him on a busy street with a group of paunchy tourists shouting propositions at passing "*mamacitas.*" I don't know if Clint spent the night in an Ensenada jail, but I wouldn't have held it against any cop who hauled him in.

Something about Latin America encourages a lax approach to strictly legal behavior, though much of the thrill has simply to do with escaping the overcautious zeitgeist of an America in which half the population now behaves like insurance adjusters. This is, of course, one of the pleasures of leaving the United States. Forget about immigrants taking over, when did half of this country turn into nagging mothers? When the beer companies start running ads lecturing the public about responsible behavior, you sense a civilization in decline.

Latin America shares little of the stifling obsession with ticky-tack regulations that's turned regular America into the most pussyfooted nation on earth, after Japan. In the coffee region of Panama, I rode on top the cab of a truck—eighteen workers stacked in the bed like Red Army recruits being shipped to the front—clutching the driver's four-year-old son as we lumbered up a rutted mountain road. In Brazil, my body was lifted off the ground, the-Who-in-Cincinnati-style, by a throbbing Carnival crowd. I was carried the fifty most thrilling yards of my life and deposited in the middle of a road just in time to have my foot run over by a car actually trying to force its way through the throbbing madness. And in Mexico, I met Ernesto.

Twelve miles off the coast of Ensenada lies Isla Todos Santos, the legendary surfer's Eden where in 1998 a madman named Taylor Knox rode a thirty-five-foot wave—fifty-two feet, according to one Baja newspaper—to capture the K2 Big Wave Challenge. I didn't intend to mount such a wave, but returning up the Baja Peninsula with Juan Mayo, it occurred to me that the readers of *Escape* might feel cheated if I didn't at least see one.

Getting to the island meant stopping in Ensenada and hanging around the marina until we found a *panga* to take us there. *Pangas* are fifteen-to-thirty-foot open skiffs with high-horsepower outboards attached. The *pangeros* who drive them are jacks-of-all-trades who do whatever it takes to make a living. Sometimes they dive for lobsters, sometimes they commercial fish, sometimes they hire themselves out to visiting surfers and divers and guys like me who aren't quite sure what they're looking for until they find it. The best *pangeros* get snatched up by fishermen at daybreak. By the time Juan Mayo and I arrived at the docks, all but one were gone for the day.

"She is very fast," Ernesto said, bragging about the 125-horsepower Evinrude attached by two rusty bolts to the back of his *panga*, the *Slayamahi II*.

John and I handed over a fistful of pesos and hopped in. Ernesto yanked the engine to life, manfully revved the throttle, flashed a wicked two-teeth-missing smile at the black exhaust filling the air, popped open a can of Tecate, sparked up a doobie, and offered us a hit. All before we'd cleared the marina. If there were any "No Wake in the Harbor" signs, we were moving too fast to see them.

Out in open water, the six-foot Pacific swells might have kept a lesser man from demonstrating the electrifying capacity of the engine. But *Slayamahi II* was soon ripping along at sixty miles per hour, bucking whitecaps, tilting sideways like a Busch Gardens vomit-launcher, and slamming our asses into the bench seats until all four cheeks were bruised. Twice, I was nearly thrown from the boat. After the third time, John swung around to face me with a look of mangled terror and ecstasy.

"We were totally airborne on that last one!" he roared, not realizing that his death hold on the gunwales was producing a set of blisters that would prevent him from gripping anything but a frosty beer for the next two weeks. I shrieked at Ernesto.

"Are these boats supposed to fly *completely* out of the water?"

"Not supposed to, not *not* supposed to. Sometime happens!"

We rammed the chop dead-on, and once more the boat floated into the air for a weightless, pregnant second. Ernesto's oily baseball cap flew off, revealing a bald skull filled with dents, scars, and erratic patches of hair. While I was recoiling from this unexpected sight, all twenty feet of the hull smacked into a swell, rocking us hard starboard. The boat took on about forty gallons of water before Ernesto righted us with a crazy swerve, dumping most of the water back over the port side. The guy had talent; no one could take that away from him. I wheeled my head around to see land slipping into a distant horizon. Ernesto opened another Tecate.

"Does any of this make you wonder what happened to *Slayamahi I?*" John screamed over the din of the motor as Ernesto sped us farther out to sea.

In fact, I hadn't considered the good ship *Slayamahi's* predecessor until John brought it up. Until then, most of my thoughts had been about staying alive, being thankful I was working for the nontraditional *Escape*, and writing off the possibility of reselling my story anywhere else. Death rides in the open sea with shit-faced daredevils at the helm don't line up with the vision most newspapers and magazines expect out of travel writers returning from Mexico.*

Latin America's liberal approach to individual rights and laissez-faire stance regarding personal safety and corporate responsibility can be exhilarating, but it also works against the region's aspirations as a mass travel destination. Americans have grown accustomed to stifling government regulation and control. Any suspen-

---

* It's worth noting that the Ernesto of my memory emerges as a much more sympathetic character than the one he played in real life. For all the cocktail-party mileage I've gotten out of that story, I prefer in the quiet hours of the night to imagine Clint from Hussong's wandering around Ensenada looking for a little chub, and a chance encounter with Ernesto leading to a tragic boating accident involving the untimely demise of them both.

sion of these by business or large public institutions leads to sort of a neurotic leeriness. Leeriness leads to mistrust and fear. Even so, dicey as it can be in places, the fact that approximately 500 million men, women, and children live, eat, work, and go to school, church, and the market in Latin America suggests a stable and mature culture where it's actually pretty easy to get through a day without being killed, maimed, robbed, or disfigured by a runaway *panga*.

A little caution does keep us on our toes abroad, of course, and probably saves lives. Or at least prevents injury and illness. Common sense and a well-honed surrender instinct also come in handy, as I discovered at the check-out desk of the worst hotel in which I ever spent a night.

Following the advice of a pair of Carnival drunks in Salvador, I'd endured refrigerator-sized potholes, a broken fan belt, and vulture-baiting temperatures on an eight-hour drive through a landscape of cactus and dust to a Brazilian backwater called Paulo Afonso. The gritty outpost, I'd been promised, was the launch point for a fascinating cruise down a mighty Amazon rival called Rio São Francisco. The river existed—muddy and emphatically non-Amazonian—but the boat trip didn't. Paulo Afonso was little more than a series of confounding traffic circles, closed restaurants, and asphalt soccer fields.

Hellish drives and wasted days chasing down bad tips, however, are part of the travel writer's lot. In reasonably good humor, I scarfed a bag of stale potato chips and checked into the regally named Hotel Monarch, a freshly painted two-story job that looked like the town's only decent place to stay.

At one in the morning, I stirred in half sleep with a foggy realization that I'd been intermittently scratching at my left leg for the past hour. In the darkness, I clawed at it some more and tried to get back to sleep, but eventually wondered if something beyond just filthy sheets was irritating my legs. I rolled across the mattress, flicked on a light, threw back the blanket, and gagged the way you do when you take a blind swig from a cup expecting water and instead get a mouthful of milk or warm beer.

An army of ants so dense that it formed a garment of solid black was crawling through the canyons between my toes, investigating each stem of hair around my ankles, and engulfing my calves on an industrious march northward. Across the room, a reconnaissance in force was patrolling every cranny of my open pack. It was a green bag and my clothes were the usual hodgepodge of colors, but, like my legs, the bag and its contents had become a black organ of pulsing legs, thoraxes, gasters, heads, and antennae.

My ensuing convulsion of kicking, swatting, and swearing must have triggered little ant pheromones because the alarming though as yet nonhostile swarm began biting me with remarkable ferocity. I cursed in anger and pain, but efforts to wipe the ants off of my legs merely relocated more intrepid units to my hands and arms. Where I come from ants are pretty easy to deal with, but on the horn of South America, it takes more than girlish screams and a heavy shoe to repel them.

Picking up my bag along the way, I charged into the shower and said a hasty prayer ("Please, God, make it work") to the rusty handle. My first stroke of luck of the day—the ants couldn't cling against the torrent. The hot water even lasted a couple of minutes. I spent the next hour in and out of the cold shower rinsing clothes and soaping myself as dry as the surrounding *sertão*. Every time I thought the enemy had been vanquished, I'd towel off and crawl back into bed, only to be attacked anew. In a moment of inspiration, I popped open a can of Coke and poured a large puddle in a far corner of the floor, imagining this would divert the horde. Instead, an entirely new stream of six-legged soldiers issued forth from a crack in the baseboard to lap up the sweet icon of American commercial dominion.

That I finished the night in that room is a testament to how bad rural Brazilian roads are and how closed the Monarch's reception desk was after midnight. In alternating rounds, I showered, stood sentry, dozed fitfully, and battled an insect brigade as relentless as the Chinese at Chosin. At six in the morning, I fled.

Just coming on duty, the front-desk clerk received my complaints with an emotion that somehow conveyed both apathy and hostility. I'd spent the night working up a convincing speech justifying my refusal to pay the bill and had imagined delivering it to one of the welcoming female Carnival types I'd run across all over Salvador. I hadn't anticipated a sullen brute behind the counter who looked exactly like the kind of guy they send back for second and third rounds of training at company customer-relations workshops. Rather than fight the good fight, I sized up the scowling clerk, bowed my head, forked over the thirty dollars, and trudged out the door into the already bright Brazilian sunshine.

Life isn't perfect below the border; I'd known that going in. But sometimes you just have to have faith that you've brought enough nerve to deal with the unexpected, enough cash to make more friends than enemies, and enough perspective to judge a place for what it is rather than for what you've heard it's supposed to be.

6

. . .

Am I the Only One Who Can't
Stand the Caribbean?

In the entire galaxy of travel, the greatest mystery to me is the Caribbean. Not the sea itself, which is aqua blue, clear, warm as bathwater, and nothing to complain about. It's the islands above it and the people who travel there that baffle me.

Specifically, I find myself wondering why anyone—much less the 35 million people who go to the Caribbean each year—would blow presumably limited vacation days and budgets on a place where the definition of "paradise" is fluid enough to include sullen service, neglected hotels, and restaurants where waiting forty-five minutes for a small mango juice is considered an immense honor. The whole place needs a fresh coat of paint, a platoon of chefs who understand how to prepare seafood, and a ban on thirty-year-old white women having their hair cornrowed by fourteen-year-old black girls. This is just part of what makes the Caribbean the evil twin of Latin America—a wretched hole with an artificial culture that everyone has somehow been fooled into believing is a magnificent place to flush away their disposable income.

Give me five minutes and ten blank pages and I'll roll out a list of beefs that will at last expose the Caribbean as the world's largest tourist trap: mangrove swamps billed as exotic sightseeing opportunities, watered-down rum punch on sputtering catamaran cruises, "Hey, mon!" accents brought home by every third visiting frat boy, the tourist ant chain that daily crawls up Dunn's River Falls at Ocho Rios in Jamaica, reggae music that doesn't sound anything like Bob Marley.

Cathartic and childishly easy as it would be to give these observations the public airing they deserve, I realize these are easy targets with applicable counterparts in tourist destinations around the world. I could spend all weekend listing minor irritants of the region—conch and other low-tide gelatins as culinary mainstays, aggressive "guides" who badger tourists for work and payment at every corner, nothing-special duty-free shopping that turns ports like St. Thomas into sweaty outlet malls—but what would be the point?

Filling a chapter with a laundry list of complaints— hotel dinner buffets set out at noon to wilt in the tropical heat, Asian-made baskets pushed on bewildered visitors at the straw market in Nassau—wouldn't convince anyone, as I've tried to do in the past, that the world should declare a travel moratorium on the Caribbean and give it the next decade off. Kind of the way no one went near Croatia after the war there or how you leave your hungover friends alone for a few days to get their game face back after a big night out. Everyone sees the birthday girl the night she turns twenty-one—no one sees her for the week after. Likewise, the Caribbean needs some alone time to put itself back together. It shouldn't be that hard for 35 million people to find somewhere else to go for a while.

Building a convincing case out of such an extreme position might appear to demand a lot of thoughtful analysis. But if rabble-rousers like Mussolini, Rush Limbaugh, and Dr. Laura can construct entire careers out of crackpot observational zealotry, I don't see why I shouldn't give it a shot. Demagogues make a lot more money than travel writers.

Before presenting the brief on the pestilence of the Caribbean, it might be useful—if only in the interest of context and full disclosure—to list a few other beloved places I'm supposed to like, but don't. These include but are not limited to:

Graceland: Or any Elvis kitsch. If the guy wasn't overmarketed before, he is now. When exactly did Presley make the transition from American icon to White Trash icon? I blame the trustees in charge of marketing Graceland.

Most of Las Vegas: We went to the moon in 1969. Big fountains, replica pyramids, and endless rows of twenty-dollar craps tables aren't that impressive. Nor is a city where you can't walk to the building next door without burning six hundred calories.

Colorado: Give me a year in a proctologist's waiting room, or even Utah, over a Midwestern state posing as a Western one, the soul-crushing blandness of

Denver, and McCondos covering every other decent hillside.

Austin: Apologies to "Big Dick" Friedman, but if it wasn't surrounded by Texas, it'd be called Sacramento.

New Zealand: Nice people, nice mountains, but unless you live in Australia, save yourself the time and trouble and visit British Columbia instead.

Baltimore's waterfront: Or any once-relevant city's $65 million downtown renovation project.

B&Bs: Whenever I see "B&B" on a Web site or brochure, I imagine sharing a bathroom with strangers, awkward chats with the owners, and "savoring" breakfast with a talkative couple from North Carolina.

Florida: Excluding Amelia Island and certain parts of the Gulf Coast and the Keys.

Yankee Stadium: When the new Yankee Stadium finally opens, the sports media will go on a yearlong caterwauling binge bidding farewell to the House That Ruth Built. Don't believe a word. The stadium's mid-1970s makeover destroyed whatever traces of authenticity were left in this claustrophobic rat hole. New Yorkers deserve a place to watch baseball that's at least as good as what they have in cities like Milwaukee and Arlington.

Minor League Baseball parks: While I'm on the subject, it's always annoyed me that as a baseball fan I'm obliged to revel in the purity of the remarkably dull product you get in these temples of the mundane.

St. Tropez, France: Amazing how shit service and one lousy dinner can put you off a city for good. And, really, how many $23 million yachts do you need to look at to feel crappy about your life of chronic underachievement?

Distillery and brewery tours: Hey, they make booze in giant vats! Who knew?

Natchez, Mississippi: Impressive mansions, but any slave-state locale that runs glory-days "heritage tours" should take me off their mailing list.

Eric Clapton: OK, not an actual place, but I've been needing to unburden myself of this for years. I suppose it's not Eric Clapton's fault that he's the most overrated guitarist in history, but the fact is twelve-bar blues is the absolute most basic and boring musical form ever invented. Wonder why every bar in America can put on an impromptu "Monday Night Blues Jam" and have half the failed musicians in town show up and put together a set that actually sounds pretty good? Ten-year-olds can play blues scales. If you want to make a god of a white British blues guitarist from the 1960s and '70s, take Peter Haycock from Climax Blues Band. Start with the perfect guitar solos in "Running Out of Time" from

1975's seminal *Stamp Album*, then move on to 1976's *Gold Plated*. On the topic of unpopular rock guitar opinions, the guitar solo in "My Sharona" is one of the greatest in rock history, right up there with "Free Bird" and "Stairway," and you don't even know the name of the guy who played it, which is Berton Averre. This observation says more about the nature of rudimentary rock guitar competency than it does about Jimmy Page, Allen Collins, Gary Rossington, or the Knack.

So that no one comes away with the impression that I'm a joyless crank except when listening to my complete collection of Climax Blues Band recordings, here are some places I like but am pretty sure I'm not supposed to:

Utah

Queens

Orange County

Interstates

El Paso/Juarez

Caracas

Singapore

Manila

Volgograd

Hotel beds in dumpy cities, flicking channels till four in the morning.

That Wilson Phillips song that goes, "Hold on for one more day."

To help me better understand why I like presumably lame things like "Hold on for one more day" yet hate presumably awesome things like the Caribbean, I decided it would be helpful to speak with a person who actually likes the place. I concede enormous holes in my knowledge of the Caribbean, and it's possible I've simply had a run of bad luck down there, somehow managed to miss the best parts. In a remote, rational corner of my brain, I know the entire Caribbean can't be reduced to those annoying Red Stripe "Hooray, beer" ads and the dead reef at Buck Island off of St. Croix used to lure "eco-tourists" on fish-free snorkeling excursions. I decided to call David Swanson.

Already I've gone out of my way to complain about travel writers, and I'm going to do a little more before I'm through. David Swanson, however, isn't the type of travel writer I complain about. He's a solid reporter and good writer who's more interested in presenting facts about a place than details about himself. Like all people of maddening contradictions and redoubtable hypocrisy, I apply a double standard when it comes to narcissism and self-indulgence in my own writing.

David and I have one of those convenient relationships that was established on the phone and Internet and remains entirely outside the physical realm. Based solely on the sound of his voice, I've constructed a picture of David—about five ten, well dressed, fifteen or twenty pounds overweight, brown hair over the ears, and a beard that's always neatly trimmed, though not irritatingly so. David and I have spent enough time discussing business that we're comfortable talking about superficial personal stuff, but I'm not sure if it's fair to say we're friends.

Most relevant to my immediate purposes, David has a ton of experience where I do not. He's made a career of the Caribbean. Written entire guidebooks covering the region. Been a contributing editor to the *Rum and Reggae* series of travel books. Works for magazines like *Caribbean Travel & Life*. By his own accounting, he's been to every island in the Caribbean that has a hotel room, and then some. Most astonishing, after all that schlepping through what I consider a miasmic hellscape, he claims to retain positive feelings for the region.

Although I hadn't had much contact with David in the past year or two, I observed the absolute minimum of perfunctory telephone niceties before launching into the nuts and bolts of the issue. My appeal went like this:

"David, in the past I haven't been entirely honest with you about my feelings toward the Caribbean. This is because I know that the Carib has pretty much been your bread and butter, and I don't see the point in unnecessarily criticizing another person's work. That would be rude. In many situations I'd rather lie than be troublesome. For example, I'm not a fan of antidepressants, and I worry that our nation's doctors, as willing dupes of the pharmaceutical industry, have tricked a dangerously large percentage of Americans into a nefarious addiction that's secretly intended to keep them dependent on the government-supported corporate drug lords for the rest of their lives. Nevertheless, in the company of my good friend Dr. Bahr, I do the best I can to stick to conversation topics like New Mexican folk art, how cute his baby daughter is, and how much I'd love someday to visit his villa off the coast of Sicily. Same thing, sort of, that's kept me from revealing to you how intensely I dislike the Caribbean, how much pretrip stress I endure every time someone wants to send me there and I say 'yes' because, like you, I understand that as a freelance writer to decline work is to invite death. Whereas accepting work in the Caribbean is more like inviting an extremely uncomfortable illness, such as the flu or a persistent bronchial infection. The point is that I'm now engaged in a sort of legal discovery, a serious attempt to examine and understand my feelings of contempt for the Caribbean. In doing so, I'd like to confront the possibility that I might actually be wrong—it's happened, have we ever discussed Super Bowl XXXVII?— that the Caribbean might not be as intolerable as I've built it up to be. Would you agree to engaging me in a discussion, consider it a friendly debate, in which you take the pro-Caribbean point of view and try to persuade me and an imaginary jury that I'm wrong, that the Caribbean is indeed a fabulous destination that deserves my sincere reconsideration?"

David agreed to accept my challenge, with one proviso. "Just don't make me look like a shill for the Caribbean Tourism Organization," he asked. I assured him I would not. I had no idea how easy a promise it would be to keep.

I'd called David on the kind of rainy, chilly Pacific Northwest day that's supposed to make people pine for sandy beaches, tropical breezes, and cheap rum made by companies they never heard of. I came out swinging with my well-rehearsed rant about the surly locals I've run into on every Caribbean island I've visited. I told David I didn't want to sound insensitive—and, yes, I know that whenever someone begins a sentence with "No offense, but," someone is about to get offended—but the white races pretty much populated the Caribbean by forcing Africans there in slave ships, and that although slavery has been abolished for well over a century, the economic die was more or less permanently cast. This means that the people who live on the islands today seem to be stuck there doing pretty much the same thing their ancestors did. Namely, serving a bunch of (comparatively) rich white people and not getting a whole lot in return. It's not that I blame the locals for not liking me. I'd feel exactly the same way and probably behave even worse if our roles were reversed. It's just that I don't see the fun in traveling to a place where I'm treated with open disdain.

Toss out blunt commentary like this and you typically get back a stern lecture about racial stereotyping and the implication that in a former life you were most likely a shift supervisor at Buchenwald. David merely chuckled politely, ignored my more inflammatory rhetoric, and told me he sympathized.

"It varies by island, but there is some truth in what you're saying," he said. "There's a certain burnout factor, even in hotels where I stay, when I realize that I will be the one doing the work in every relationship."

Exactly, I said. So why would anyone want to travel to a place where even the clerk at the hotel makes them scratch and claw for a shred of humanity?

"Well, you have to adapt and that's true of any destination," David responded. "It's not fair for you to assume, for example, that what goes in Seattle necessarily goes in Paris. You wouldn't wear the same clothes to a coffee shop in Paris as you would in Seattle, and you shouldn't expect to."

Paris seemed like a long way to go to defend the honor of the Caribbean. And it annoyed me that like everyone else David reduced the whole of the glorious Pacific Northwest to "Seattle" and once again assumed that I lived there, even though I never have. I chalked up a point for my side and moved on to my next complaint: the Caribbean's ubiquitous freelance "guides" who work the islands with the mean-spirited tenacity of NFL cornerbacks. You can't walk forty yards from a dock or runway without being accosted by an army of belligerents, each one insisting that you're incapable of so much as buying a T-shirt at the palm-roofed gift shack down the street without their assistance. David laughed again and told me he knew what I meant.

"My first experience in the Caribbean was in Jamaica about twenty years ago," he began in a gentle tone that I assumed presaged a story with a surprise ending. "We stayed in Montego Bay. The first morning we left the hotel, and this guy on the street came up and asked us if we wanted a guide. We said no. Long story short, we ended up spending the next eight hours with this guy, walking in the rain, buying him lunch, meeting his uncles, taking them all out for beers.

"One thing I tell everyone, don't ever admit it's your first time in Jamaica. If someone asks if it's your first time on the island, just say no. They're more likely to leave you alone, because they assume you know the scams. If you say yes, you get a different line of patter."

This was interesting information and sound advice, but I didn't feel like it refuted my charge. Two-oh. We'd been on the phone five minutes, and already David was playing from behind.

I took a chance on a knockout blow with an argument

that's always tricky, because while it's emotionally im-possible to disagree with, it can be blown out of the water with a fairly simple accusation that the person making it is an arrogant snob. To wit: All the best beaches in the Ca-ribbean have been ruined by tourists. And by "tourists" I mean beaten-down worker drones from the Northeast corridor of the United States who flee the winter snow-storms of their homeland to "recharge their batteries" on some presumably lustrous beach, only to find that getting drunk and high and staring at hotties in thongs for five days in places more beautiful than the one they live in doesn't reinvigorate them at all, it only makes them even more profoundly resentful of the job/life/spouse they'll soon be returning to. David replied by telling me the story of Tortola.

Five or six years ago, he said, people on the island of Tortola in the British Virgin Islands looked across the ten miles of water that separates them from more pros-perous St. Thomas. Taking stock of the obvious in-equity, they came to the conclusion that the citizens of St. Thomas were able to buy large-screen TVs and new cars because that island attracted more cruise ships. The cruise ships dispensed more tourists who pumped more money into St. Thomas businesses, which in turn employed more St. Thomas residents.

Seizing upon this most fundamental premise of the trickle-down Caribbean economy, Tortola came up with the idea of expanding its own cruise-ship facilities. They went to work and quickly increased their port's maxi-mum docking capacity from one or two medium-sized cruise ships a day to three large ones. Their efforts were successful. Cruise-ship tourist arrivals in sleepy Tortola leaped from 203,000 in 2001 to 467,000 in 2004. The twenty-one-square-mile island didn't get any bigger, but in three years its number of annual visitors more than doubled.

"Tourists spend their nights on the ship, but they need help once they're in town," David said. "As a result you've suddenly got a lot more taxi drivers in Tortola. And just like in St. Thomas, the taxi drivers pretty much run the main towns. They form strong political groups. Their votes count and they vote for whatever puts more people in their taxis."

I asked David what this meant in practical terms.

"Ten years ago, Cane Garden Bay on Tortola had one of the most beautiful beaches in the Caribbean," he said. "Now, locals are cashing in with wall-to-wall beach chairs rented for five dollars a day to cruise-ship passengers. I went there and literally couldn't see the sand anymore. I asked locals about the development and felt like I was talking to the Mafia. I was told to butt out. 'Well,' I thought, 'there goes another one.'"

I'm not challenging anyone's desire to own a gigantic TV or make their life easier by renting a beach chair to a guy from Philly. If Tortola wants to jam up its beaches this way, fine. I've never been to Tortola and couldn't care less how they run their show. It's just that I'd come into this discussion not understanding how a Mafia-run beach with no visible sand and five hundred guys in matching black socks manages to attract almost half a million tourists a year, and I wasn't getting any closer to figuring it out.

By now I was feeling sorry for David. I'd known all along I was drawing him into an unfair fight, but at this point I liked the Caribbean even less than I had before calling him. This wasn't what either of us wanted. The only noble thing to do before letting him off the phone was lob him a softball that would allow him to save a little face and not piss off the Caribbean Tourism Organization too badly. I trotted out my old line about the entire Caribbean needing a fresh coat of paint and ten years without tourists, figuring he'd seize the opportunity to tell me about some of the pristine new condo developments and golf courses and all-inclusive resorts opening across the islands. Instead, he began talking about an oil refinery and a cemetery.

"Curaçao is an island I like," he said. "It's written off by most people because it's not lush and green and filled with resorts. In the middle of Curaçao is a big oil refinery that belches soot all day. Right next to the oil refinery is the oldest Jewish cemetery in the New World. It's called Beth Haim cemetery. It was established in 1659. This place is like hell on earth. It sends chills up my spine. Because of all the soot, the gravestones are eroding so badly you can't even read a lot of the names."

David put a bow on this enchanting package by saying something that I immediately made him repeat. I did so because I knew as soon as I quoted him, it would sound like something I made up in order to pound home a baseless rhetorical point. The expert I'd called to explain the lure of the Caribbean actually said of an oil refinery, a cemetery, and a collection of decaying headstones: "It's one of the coolest places I've been in the Caribbean."

If it didn't change my mind about the Caribbean, our conversation did remind me why I rely on writers like David Swanson for travel information. Not because they confirm things I already know—it didn't surprise me that the best thing about the Caribbean is a culturally significant oil refinery—but because they're not interested in changing my mind. They like what they like, they give me the basics, and they don't get uppity if I disagree.

Figuring any more discussion about the Caribbean was pointless, I began asking David how the family was doing and about his recent trip to Dubai. We chatted awhile along these lines, but he kept circling back to the Caribbean. I began to sense that I'd overestimated his willingness to concede the argument. After misdirecting me with a few innocuous anecdotes from Middle Eastern hotels, he swooped in for the kill.

"If we break down your opinions point by point, maybe we can isolate the source of your hostility toward the Caribbean," he suggested. I've never been to counseling, but this is how I imagine they start you off. For the first time in our discussion, I was on the defensive. "You like sunshine and warm weather and sparkling water and you will admit that not every Caribbean beach is a shithole, right?"

I allowed that most of this was probably true.

"You may have run into jaded tourist-industry touts in Jamaica or Trinidad or wherever, but you've encountered those types all the way from Bangkok to Belgium, and you wouldn't condemn an entire nation of people based on the actions of a money-grubbing few, would you?"

I told him that I'd never met a Belgian I didn't like—most underrated country in Europe, by the way—but that his point was valid. Gaining confidence, David went on dissecting my knee-jerk assessments and comically limited point of view for another minute or two before hitting on what he considered to be the essence of my objections.

"Most of the tourist complaining I hear about the Caribbean is about the visible poverty there, and I don't have a lot of sympathy for that," he sniffed. "Most of the issues you bring up ultimately have to do with economics—it takes five minutes of research online to figure out how low the per capita income is for most of these islands. If you're going to travel in a place where poverty exists, you're going to have to take it as it comes. There's something appealing about the soft crumbling of old Havana. It feels like history is happening right in front of you. If you can't appreciate that, fine. But hating a place just because it's poor is wrong."

If I'd let him go on five seconds longer he'd have me nominated in a Republican primary somewhere, but I appreciated his sentiment. It took thirty minutes of talking, but David had finally helped me put a finger on the real reason I've disliked the Caribbean for all these years. Only it isn't because I hate poor people.

One of my first trips to the Caribbean was to Casa de Campo, a sprawling resort on the southeastern tip of the Dominican Republic that "boasts" (God, these self-fellating travel-industry euphemisms) three golf courses, nine restaurants, sixteen pools, 350 rooms, and 150 villas. Along with most other reputable guides, *Fodor's* will tell you that Casa de Campo is the Dominican Republic's "swankiest and most famous resort." It's the kind of rarefied retreat where megawattage celebrities like Michael Jackson might sneak off to get married—which the then King of Pop had done just recently with Lisa Marie

Presley. Within hours of my arrival at Casa de Campo, our guided tour of the grounds stopped for a reverential moment in front of the luxurious *casita* in which the future not-guilty child enthusiast and the Queen of Deadpan had done one of pop history's most puzzling deeds.

I was working at the time for *American Way,* the inflight magazine of American Airlines. The reason for my trip was to help publicize the fact that the airline was inaugurating direct service from Miami to the resort itself. This meant Casa de Campo's discriminating guests no longer had to fly into the impoverished Dominican capital of Santo Domingo, then endure a two-hour drive through the countryside to the resort. They could board a plane in Florida and step off a few hours later surrounded by orchids and lackeys. To highlight this historic moment, the first commercial jet to land on the resort's newly modified runway was greeted by a brass band, dancing sexpots, and white-shirted waiters who marched onto the tarmac bearing trays of champagne and hors d'oeuvres for disembarking passengers.

The whole boondoggle was a classic media junket. In addition to me, a number of airline PR people, and my girlfriend, Joyce, whom I'd somehow managed to get on the guest list, a gaggle of travel writers had been invited along for the trip. There was a far-too-serious staffer from a major daily newspaper in the South, a pair of pudgy homemakers from California who'd become travel-writing pros by accepting whatever free trips came their way in exchange for effusive reviews no matter how lousy the accommodations, two or three amusing-in-that-jaded-sort-of-way magazine freelancers, and one or two other shadowy scribes whose affiliations and motives I can't recall.

For most of a week, all of us were herded around by a rambunctious PR flack from Atlanta who kept us on a bustling schedule—7:00 AM breakfast, 7:45 AM meeting with pool manager, 8:00 AM reception with assistant vice-minister of tourism, 9:30 AM viewing of tribal pottery artisans at work. That sort of torture. The PR flack resembled a sun-wrinkled version of the character actress Annette O'Toole, famous for her role as Nick Nolte's stressed-out girlfriend in *48 Hours* and, later, more than twenty appearances on *Nash Bridges.**

Beyond her looks, the PR flack's distinguishing habit was of proudly reminding her hostage entourage every thirty minutes that her Latin lover of the moment was an extraordinarily passionate jazz flutist renowned throughout the Dominican Republic. Her skill at working this information into virtually any conversation was so impressive that it served as an ongoing point of discussion and ridicule among the entire group. One of the highlights of the trip came on the final night when the evening activity turned out to be a concert by none other than the jazz flutist himself—an inside booking if ever there was one—a man whose nonironic, sensual relationship with his instrument was later channeled with more subdued attention to form by Will Ferrell as Ron Burgundy in *Anchorman*.

Casa de Campo is so big and its guests generally so rich and lazy that everyone gets around the grounds via personal golf carts. Even if you aren't rich and lazy, this is actually pretty cool, except that Joyce and I kept getting issued carts that broke down, requiring us to call

---

* Bet-winning *Nash Bridges* trivia: the show's pilot was written by Hunter S. Thompson.

guest services at least once a day to come pick us up from some isolated corner of the property. Annette O'Toole lost a little patience with me each time she heard about this, rolling her eyes as though I was trying to make the resort look bad by stranding myself on rocky shores, miles away from the dessert station at the Mango Tango pool. My standing was further eroded by Joyce's freeloading insistence on ordering lobster at every meal, including breakfast.

Mostly, though, Casa de Campo turned out to be almost as spectacular as we were constantly being reminded it was. We were plied with free booze and all the local cigars we could cough through. Although the staff was Carib desultory—seriously, forty-five minutes for a fucking mango juice?—there wasn't much beyond the derelict golf carts and jazz flute to complain about.

The memorable part of the trip came on the day Joyce and I rented a car and drove across the island. We were headed to another resort I was researching for a story on overseas honeymoon destinations I'd talked about with an editor at the now-defunct *Mademoiselle*. Sometimes, the only way to get back at a place for making you have coffee at eight in the morning with the assistant vice-minister of tourism is to sell a two-hundred-word blurb touting one of their competitors.

The moment we exited the guarded gate at Casa de Campo, we had the sensation of entering a new world, like the moment when *The Wizard of Oz* shifts from black and white to color. Part of this had to do with liberating ourselves from Annette O'Toole's itinerary, but most of it had to do with finally seeing an actual living, breathing piece of the Dominican Republic. The national highway and rugged countryside stood in epic contrast to the fussily manicured resort. Yellow, green, and blue shacks with peeling paint and corrugated tin roofs lined the highway. Scraggly goats wandered through barren fields nosing around for clumps of dry grass. Groups of young men loitered at virtually every corner staring at the wealth and prestige zipping past them with the windows rolled up against the suffocating heat. We felt for the first time that we were visiting a foreign country. It wasn't necessarily a pretty scene, but it was real.

I don't mean "real" here in the self-important tour-guide sense of some mythical place that presumably represents the "real" Kenya or the "real" Norway, a remnant of authenticated nostalgiana somehow left untrammeled by centuries of tourism. One of my favorite examples of this type of travel-writer disconnect with reality came out of AAA's *Essential London* guidebook, which I reviewed for a magazine some years ago. Like an appalling amount of others in the guidebook genre, it was full of useless advice such as the bit instructing readers on "10 Ways to Be a Local," one of which was "Eat in one of London's few surviving pie 'n' mash shops." If only a few such shops remain, of course, it stands to reason that not many of London's 12 million locals are eating much pie 'n' mash. But never mind, this was the "real" London according to AAA.

If tourism applies artificial respiration to traditions like pie 'n' mash and Dominican folk dancing, I suppose that makes these things no less "authentic" than anything else. Even so, in this case, I use "real" per its traditional Webster's definition, as in "not fake." And fake is what Casa de Campo had become as soon as the scent of bougainvillea and Amaretto-soaked cigarillos faded in our exhaust fumes.

Our dalliance with the "real" DR lasted only a few hours. We stopped and paid a dollar or two for lunch. We chatted with a few people, all of them pleasant. We took some interesting pictures of a donkey painted like a zebra that also happened to be sporting a massive erection. Alas, these were pleasures enjoyed in haste. We had a schedule to keep.

At the resort across the island, which was almost as impressive as Casa de Campo, Joyce and I were scheduled for a dinner that turned out to be both the most romantic and most uncomfortable of our lives. While hundred-dollar wines and four-star dinner plates arrived at our candlelit table in a small island at the center of a man-made pond, a group of Eastern European violinists, cellists, and Baroque oboists floated around in a rowboat serenading us with a selection of classical numbers meant to complement our dinner in paradise. Because I was a visiting writer with loose ties to large-circulation American magazines, the scene had been carefully prepared to show me the unparalleled luxury available at the resort. With the fantastic dishes, respectable service, and floating musicians, Joyce and I should theoretically have spent the meal semidiscreetly feeling each other up under the table before rushing back to our honeymoon suite overlooking the beach and humping like safari animals.

The trouble was, the resort's director of marketing, a congenial Dutch woman in her early thirties, was joining us for dinner. With a superlative forced smile glued to her face all evening, our perky host spent the meal breaking down the fascinating details of the resort's golf course (I have no idea who Pete Dye is, but he must be rich as Croesus because everywhere I go he's designed another golf course), its new family-friendly package deals, top-flight chefs imported from the best culinary schools in France, and other property renovations (always with the property renovations) that totaled in the tens of millions. I'd suffered through these obligatory PR meals before. Even so, my mind was as dull as a butter knife by the end of the soup course. Glassy-eyed across the table, Joyce appeared to be taxidermied.

The meal lasted three and a half hours. Everything Mozart ever scribbled on a napkin was performed. The Dutch woman didn't get up once, not even to go to the bathroom. (Glasser wisdom: Never trust a woman with an iron bladder.) There was, of course, no way to ditch her so that Joyce and I might enjoy the lilting tones of Bach's Concerto No. 3 in G Major while plotting unspeakable acts of sexual exploration over the gratis veal cutlets and vintage Pol Roger. She was just doing her job, which meant making sure the hotel's visiting VIPs saw exactly what they were supposed to see and not much else. By the time dessert arrived, I was so exhausted from manipulating the demands of professional flattery that I couldn't eat. One of the problems with accepting comps at swanky resorts is that you end up paying for them with dinners so boring they leave you wanting to scrape your own face off with a souvenir conch shell.

Among the great joys of travel is catching a break and dropping into a situation you might otherwise never be able to afford. Circumstance puts an unexpected first-class ticket in your hand. A friend of a friend just happens to need someone to look after his Mediterranean estate the very week you were planning a tour of Greek youth hostels. As a gift at the end of a job editing a travel guide, a publisher once presented me with a three-night stay at the famed Danieli Hotel overlooking the Grand Canal in Venice. Joyce and I clung to every second of it.

In the event that luck doesn't favor us, most travelers are willing, on occasion, to pony up egregious sums to feel, even if just for a sweet, fleeting moment, the intoxicating freedom from financial constraints only the very rich can appreciate. Limousine services, for example, pander to the splurge instinct intrinsic in these illusions of momentary affluence. Most of us suffer financially at some point for binges of extravagance, but, on the whole, the mirage is worthwhile.

Not in the Caribbean. Had the director of marketing not joined us at the table, I might have enjoyed the dinner with the classical music more, but I still wouldn't have been completely comfortable. The drive across the island had brought the economic disparity of the Caribbean into ugly focus. It wasn't the poverty that offended me. It was the adjacent luxury behind guarded gates. It wasn't hard to figure out which side of the fence the waiters and busboys would be going home to once dinner was over. The average Dominican earns sixty-three hundred dollars a year; unemployment is at 17 percent; one of every four people lives below the poverty line.

Talking to David Swanson about the Dominican Republic helped me realize after all these years exactly what it is about the Caribbean that I don't like.

Brochures, magazines, and TV ads sell luxury and comfort, but the product ends up being a stark reminder of the world's dreadful injustices. Going to the Caribbean isn't like going to Cameroon or India, because those are places you know are going to be fucked up before you even get there. Disheartening as they are, reminders of America's affluence vis-à-vis much of the rest of the world—kids with distended bellies, open sewers, cardboard shantytowns that stretch for miles—are good for us to face. Americans could stand a few more buckets of cold reality splashed on us. Just not when we're supposed to be in "paradise."

Harsh as it might sound, I don't want to spend a week sunbathing in a place with a cultural foundation so poisonous that even the pirates who made the place famous didn't stay long. Call it white guilt if you like, but I've watched people of every possible ethnic designation lord their wealth and status over the local plebes. No race does it any better or worse than the other.

It's not that I feel the need to turn away from poverty. Manila is one of my favorite cities in the world, and conditions there can be as bleak as anywhere. Same goes for Rio de Janeiro. It's just that pockets of extravagance in the midst of widespread destitution depress me. If you're selling me luxury, give me luxury, not a reminder that my comfort comes at the expense of someone else's poverty. If that's what I want out of a vacation, I'll invite Sally Struthers along.

Following the breakthrough articulation of my Caribbean complaint, David suggested I give the islands one more look. He said he knew the perfect place.

"It's on their license plates and, yes, it's a cliché, but Aruba really is 'One Happy Island,'" he said. "People there are generally friendly and warm. But that's not why I think you'd like it."

David told me that a recurring complaint among Caribbean travelers concerns places that fail to keep the region's essential promise: escape. "I grew up in California and at first I didn't get the Caribbean, either," he said. "Then I moved to Boston and experienced blizzards. I started looking at the brochures and posters in airline office windows with a little more appreciation."

As Caribbean tourism expanded and competition between islands became fierce, he explained, offerings became more elaborate. Golf. Eco-tourism. Native culture. In the beginning, though, the masses didn't go to the Caribbean for the activities or culture. They went there because of the blizzards in Boston.

"The degree to which each island delivers on the Caribbean's original promise varies," David told me. "Aruba has always remained true to the basic message. It doesn't promise you anything more than sun, a beach, and a clean bed. That's it, that's what they give you, and they do a great job with it. I'm always delighted to write a favorable review of Aruba."

After David and I finished talking, I did some research on Aruba. I was surprised to learn that it gets about a million American tourists a year. That makes it the fifth- or sixth-most visited island in the Caribbean, depending on whether or not you still hold the *Revolución* against Cuba.

In books and online, Aruba looks pretty basic. Crowds of tourists, cruise ships, car traffic, fast-food chains, casinos, shopping. Not exactly the classic image that springs to mind when someone says "Caribbean." Which is why I sent David an e-mail a few days later telling him that if I do go back to the Caribbean, Aruba is going to be my first stop. Just as soon as someone buys me a ticket.

7

. . .

What Lazy Writers, Lonely Planet, and
Your Favorite Travel Magazine
Don't Want You to Know

In the spring of 2000, a former employer called me with an intriguing proposition. Former employer was a publisher negotiating for the contract to launch a magazine for Travelocity.com. Based in Dallas, the pioneering Internet company was anxious to bolster its position as the leader in online travel booking against bloodthirsty competitors such as Expedia and the soon-to-be-announced Orbitz. Looking at the model of critically successful magazines like *Yahoo! Internet Life*, Travelocity.com concluded that putting out a legitimate newsstand magazine—not just a corporate marketing vehicle—would produce a media synergy that would raise its brand to profitability, a plateau no large Internet company had achieved at the time.

Dot-com profiteers of the ill-fated late 1990s catch a lot of hell now, but even if their boom did go bust, without it you'd still be calling sixty-year-old Sylvia at the travel agency downtown and getting the runaround for three days before being told you have to connect four times to get to Istanbul and the only place to stay once you get there is a Holiday Inn. In the 1990s, I didn't have jack shit to invest, in retirement hedge funds or anything else, so I tend be philosophical about the whole stock-collapse thing. God bless the Internet and everyone who took a hard hit so that I could spend my weeknights booking apartments in Macedonia on Craigslist and downloading Daft Punk B-sides instead of wasting time watching *JAG* and *Dharma and Greg*.

Following the independent tradition of Travelocity .com and its mercurial founder Terry Jones, *Travelocity* was to be a travel magazine like no other, a publication that would break the mold of what had become a timid, unreadable genre. In the same way the company believed it had radically altered the travel landscape—which it sort of had—it would radically alter the way the world looked at travel in print. The magazine also needed to beat the rumored launch of Expedia.com's already-in-the-works publication to the newsstand, a bomb expected to drop in a matter of months.

This meant that while finding an editor in chief who burned with a desire to rewrite the travel-publishing template was crucial, it was even more important to find some schmoe willing to put together an entire magazine—from concept to staff hiring to prototype to first issue—in about 120 days. All for about half the salary of his industry counterparts. Most critical, said schmoe had to be willing to relocate to Dallas. These criteria tend to narrow a field considerably. I'm not sure if in fact I had any competition for the job.

I was at a vacation house in Bend, Oregon, getting mildly intoxicated and watching NCAA March Madness with some college friends when the call from Dallas came. Between the skiing, hoops, and drinking buddies, I had no good reason to want to be anywhere else, but the more I listened to my old employer, the more I began to consider a change of scenery. Talking about travel magazines with people who were putting together a new one was exciting, and I started selling myself right there on the phone. One nice thing about being an opinionated son of a bitch, you've always got a few intractable positions handy on those rare occasions when they can actually do you some good.

Practically speaking, I said, people travel for all sorts of reasons, not just vacations. They travel to ink a killer deal with Hewlett-Packard. Attend Aunt Lucy's funeral. Wage war. See their kids' soccer tournament. Move from Dayton to Fresno. Yet this type of travel is never reflected in travel magazines.

"If you look at the stats, a hundred million undupli-cated Americans travel each year," I rambled. "Yet the combined circulation of every travel magazine in exis-tence is about five million. That means ninety-five per-cent of travelers aren't getting what they need from travel magazines. The potential audience is massive."

More significant, whether for fun, work, or whatever reason, more and more travelers were hitting sites like Travelocity.com to book that travel. What could set a *Travelocity* magazine apart, I said, is that it might legiti-mately appeal to all travelers, not just the AMEX Gold Card crowd in junior suites overlooking the south rim of the Grand Canyon that most magazines cater to. As I'd later beat into our staff like a GOP spokesman at a Fox "News" strategy session: "We're going to be the travel magazine for people who don't like travel magazines."

Travelocity.com liked the pitch. Within a month, I had an apartment in Dallas almost equidistant from Dealey Plaza and the affluent Highland Park neighborhood where George Bush was a member of the Highland Park United Methodist Church and Dick Cheney lived on Euclid Avenue.* By mid-August, after the four busiest months of my life, the premiere issue of *Travelocity* magazine rolled off the press.

Dallas Mavericks owner Mark Cuban was recruited to serve as celebrity host of the magazine's inaugural launch party. We rented out a popular bar called Club Clearview for the event. A retro-'70s band played. Tons of good-looking people showed up. Flash bulbs from society-page photographers popped all night. If there was ever a time to be in Dallas, I recall thinking, this was it.

Cuban drove himself to the gig, arrived on time, and without an entourage. Along with jazz guitarist Pat Metheny, he remains the most humble and considerate celebrity I've ever met. Beneath an enormous replica of our first cover, he opened the festivities by delivering an enthusiastic speech about the new world of travel magazines being ushered in that night. To the amazement of our staff, Cubes had actually taken the trouble to read the magazine. He referenced specifics buried deep in jump copy and had kind words for the overall editorial direction. Question: don't NBA owners and tech kazillionaires have better things to do with their time? Answer: apparently not in Dallas.

---

* Two guys not just from the same state but the same fucking *neighborhood* running on the same presidential ticket being as unconstitutional as Jim Crow, and why nobody else sees this shit is beyond me.

That speech was the last unmitigated praise for the magazine anyone in Dallas would ever publicly express. To this day I love Mark Cuban for it and almost always root for the Mavericks (except in games against the Lakers with play-off implications) even though I otherwise enjoy feeding a pathological hatred for all sports teams from Dallas, including high school girls' teams.

Semirelated and completely valid note substantiated by any replay angle you care to find: Texas was handed a gimme touchdown in the second quarter of the Rose Bowl against USC. Vince Young's knee was clearly down on the eleven-yard line. So that 2006 national championship is not legit.

You don't move to Dallas for fun or the kind of money they were paying me. Unless you were born to it, Dallas is impossible to appreciate. The city embodies the worst of L.A. (vanity-plate car culture, general lack of personal integrity, smog, fake tits) without any of the redeeming parts (the beach, nice weather, nine NBA titles, classic Randy Newman theme song).

At this point it's imperative to note a significant distinction between "Dallas" and "Texas." For understandable reasons, non-Texans have a tendency to lump the two together. This is unfair to Texas. In the same way that Anchorage has very little to do with the Alaska of popular imagination* and New York City is considered a foreign country by many residents of its state, Dallas is largely a city of carpetbaggers and ambitious hacks

---

* It's impossible for me to be civil about Anchorage given the fact that those scheming oil whores have been trying to steal the capital from Juneau ever since I was a kid.

who have nothing in common with the state's cow punchers, country outlaws, and salt-of-the-earth types who enunciate all three syllables and pronounce the *h* in words like "vehicle." On those occasions that I got out of Dallas and made it to Texas, I actually had a pretty good time, despite the truly odious politics that prevail there.

What I wanted out of the Travelocity deal was the chance to apply the lessons of my years of travel to correct what I saw as the travel-writing racket's multitude of shortcomings. Apparently I wanted this badly enough to move to Dallas for a second time.

I'd gotten my first daily exposure to these failings in the mid-1990s in Dallas as an editor for *American Way*, the venerable in-flight magazine—well, the first one, anyway—put out by American Airlines. In the publishing industry and by the public at large, in-flight magazines and other "custom publications" aren't considered "real" magazines. This is due to the fact that their primary purpose is neither to entertain nor edify readers but to blatantly represent the interests of the corporate entity that sponsors them. This may be true, but it's only the blatant part of the equation that separates in-flight magazines from the ones you buy on the newsstand. As with Third World cops, the "corruption" of in-flight magazines is simply more transparent than that of their otherworld brethren.

Almost all magazines exist for a single purpose—to move product, or, less artfully, to sell shit. Introduce consumers to new products. Put them in a buying mood. As conditioned purveyors of the sell-sell-sell mentality, magazine editors routinely dismiss story ideas if something new to sell can't be attached to them. This limp editorial practice prevents thousands of good stories each year from seeing print and reinforces the contemporary magazine's standing as a cleverly concealed catalog. It doesn't matter if they're peddling lipstick, financial services, movies, or hotel rooms. *Cosmopolitan* sells L'Oreal and *Entertainment Weekly* sells Warner Bros. the same way *Delta Sky* sells Delta Airlines. *Delta Sky*'s just more open about it.

Perfect example: Spend five minutes with *Sports Illustrated* and you'll find that the cross-pollination of commodities like Gatorade, the NFL, and any number of steroid-chomping jocks makes many editorial and advertising pages virtually interchangeable. I still have the *SI* issue that ran an absolutely ball-sucking, eight-page feature on ESPN—a little photo of Chris Berman tucked in the banner across the top of the cover—followed the next week by an issue in which ESPN purchased a prime-placement, two-page, inside-front-cover ad that included the same photo of Berman that had run on the cover the week before. Not that anyone at either organization would admit to a connection between an eight-page blow job and a pricey ad buy.

Worried that my favorite *SI* example was a little dated and maybe unfair, I opened a recent issue. It was the annual college football preview. Just for fun I began looking for all the Nike logos I could find in the magazine. Without trying very hard, I counted 175 reproductions of the famous swoosh on editorial pages, 32 more on advertising pages. That's 207 swooshes in a magazine just 138 pages long. That's called branding through repetition. It's also called you're-not-gonna-see-too-many-realistic-stories-about-underpaid-workers-in-Indonesian-sweat-shops-or-wife-beating-heroes-in-this-magazine. Demean in-flight magazines all you want. Just don't think the ones you pay for aren't shilling every bit as hard.

One of the most discouraging examples of the power that advertising holds over even the best magazines is Paul Theroux. One might presume Theroux has established a name big enough to allow him to make his own rules, but—and this should come as some small comfort to travel writers hacking away in obscurity—it turns out that even a respected best seller isn't immune to the travel industry's remorseless demand for gloss.

Theroux is indisputably the great American travel writer of the Jet Age. He's also been described—by me, for one, though I'm sure I read it somewhere first—as the most unhappy man who ever packed a suitcase. To longtime fans this is understood as a compliment, not an insult. For the writer, not to mention the reader, misery is a far more interesting state than happiness, and Theroux's ability to tap into the universal frustrations of the road is justifiably legendary. Want a quick take on the squatty, unattractive natives copulating like jackals in some distant hellhole? Theroux's your man.

The travel world's original antihero is also, however, unable to resist the lure of magazine work. From time to time the master still bangs out short pieces for newsstand consumption. For examples, pick up a copy of *Fresh Air Fiend*, a collection of Theroux articles written for publications such as *National Geographic*, *Travel Holiday*, *Condé Nast Traveller*, and the *New York Times*.

Theroux made his name as the sworn enemy of luxury travel, but it's been a long time since his stint as a

Peace Corps volunteer. I still like to think of him walking the old walk, but these days he's less inclined to do so if it means skipping the gratis champagne service in first class. In the introduction to *Fresh Air Fiend*, he advises travelers—and travel writers in particular—to "stay away from vacations, holidays, sightseeing, and the half-truths in official handouts." This before proceeding to mount every corporate perk available to the famous travel writer scribbling away for big-time magazines, of which there are many.

In the service of adventure-hungry *Outside*, Theroux bad-mouths a megaresort on the Philippine island of Palawan as "one of those trophy hotels that is half obscenity, half joke." He exhibits no compunction, however, about staying at the Ritz-Carlton in Hong Kong and having room service boil up his Chinese herbs while on assignment for the *New Yorker*. In an introduction to the paperback edition of his landmark book, *The Great Railway Bazaar*, Theroux rips passengers of the resurrected Orient Express as "wealthy, comfort-seeking people who have selfish, sumptuous fantasies about travel bearing no relation to the real thing." Yet in *Gourmet* magazine, he registers no complaints about reclining in his own private gourmet-dining railcar and traveling through the Rocky Mountains with a world-class chef to answer his every culinary whim. "Bliss" is how he describes the food orgy. Though one can imagine *Travel & Leisure* and its advertisers not liking it much if he did, when devoted kayaker Paul Theroux can boat through South Florida's Charlotte Harbor, call the place "ideal," and barely remark upon the decimation of the state's swamplands and waterways, you know you aren't dealing with the travel scribe of legend. You're dealing with an ordinary man of needs writing for a sales vehicle that doubles as a magazine.

One of the unavoidable truths about travel is that it often isn't fun, but this isn't something hotel companies and airline executives like to see acknowledged in the publications they're funding. In travel magazines, writers who attempt some facsimile of the truth are usually accused by editors of being "too negative," magazine-speak for "That's not an effective sales pitch." This by design leads to boring writing, most notably for its lack of the fearless honesty that made guys like Theroux famous in the first place.

Should we hold it against Theroux if like every other schlub who can't stand flying coach, the man just wants to enjoy a decent meal and a little extra legroom now and then? Of course not. If anyone's earned his shit-eating dues on the road, it's the man who suffered for *The Mosquito Coast* and *The Happy Isles of Oceania*.

It's just that too often, it seems, writers are pressured away from invoking Samuel Johnson's famous words upon visiting the Giant's Causeway in Northern Ireland: "Worth seeing, yes; but not worth going to see."

At *Travelocity* magazine, I assumed that forging a new foundation by breaking writers and editors of their more corrupt practices would make us immediate superstars in the business. Long before I arrived in Dallas, I'd been nurturing a list of bad habits and a ruthless attitude that I'd someday spring on an unsuspecting profession. This was to be my chance.

A big problem with travel writers not named Theroux is that they're all essentially required to share the same opinion about everything. As a result, their copy tends to be defined by how many clever variations they can conceive while riffing on the same themes. How "exquisite" this hotel is. How "romantic" that mountainside vista is. How "convenient" or "perfect" a given destination is for burned-out workers in need of a "quick getaway." Travel writers are a lot like recovering alcoholics. All they can talk about is their own trip, and it always boils down to more or less the same story.

Travel writers are typically enabled by travel editors, themselves recipients of compromising perks— like my junket to Casa de Campo—that they'd like to keep getting more of. Then there's the matter of tightwad publishers who pay nothing in expenses and allow airlines and hotels to "host" writers, thereby tacitly influencing their recommendations. Bribe would be too ugly a word, but it's closer to the truth given that travel magazines also generally pay poorly for copy. Most writers work for about a dollar a word, the same rate they got in the 1980s. Babysitters' fees have quadrupled over the same period. Low wages and stingy expense budgets mean that countless stories are now written by "travel" writers who never leave home. Find a travel story less than a page or two long and chances are high it's nothing more than information pulled off the Internet and disingenuously written up in a way that suggests insight borne of direct experience.

My list of directives for writers and editors addressed the sins that have made most travel writing such a slog. A few highlights:

No Cabbie Quotes

A certain sign you're reading the work of a lazy travel writer is when you see quotes from taxi drivers, hotel clerks, and maître d's. For most writers, the single most degrading part of their job, even worse than the crappy pay, is talking to strangers.

This is why writers often satisfy the obligation to provide quotes and local color by taking the easiest route and chatting up those already in their midst, such as taxi drivers, leading to the reader's false impression that the secrets of any burg can be extracted in a five-minute conversation with an immigrant man who spends his days in the company of those least likely to know anything about the city they're in. Namely, out-of-towners and locals without the resources to drive themselves around.

There's a complex psychology that explains why the average travel writer recoils from journalism's most basic information-gathering technique. First, the palpable awkwardness of a contrived conversation undermines any sense of natural give-and-take banter the interview is supposed to replicate. Second, interviews create a social hierarchy of two, making the interviewer supplicant to the interviewee.

This second point can be tough to cope with, since all writers have massive egos—if they didn't they wouldn't seek jobs encouraging them to broadcast their every mundane observation to the world—and very few are good at hiding this unflattering side of their personalities. For the writer, hanging around a locker room until eleven at night hoping to pry a nugget of wisdom out of Carmelo Anthony is one thing. Pretending to be interested in a sales pitch from the manager of a "hip" and "trendy" new patisserie in Savannah, Georgia, is quite another. The whole time an exchange of ideas about mocha-cinnamon breakfast muffins is taking place, the smiling writer is thinking, "If anything, it is I who should be getting interviewed, I whose wisdom the world should be seeking. I'm the one who's been to the Giant's Causeway and am on speaking terms with Carmelo Fucking Anthony."

The only reason a writer quotes cabdrivers or other service-industry minions is to disguise the fact that he or she didn't want to deal with the hassle of drumming up any authoritative local sources. Think of all the cabdrivers you know. You don't know any. That's because in every major city in the world—London excepted—taxis are driven by impoverished foreigners who don't know Sukhumvit Road from Euclid Avenue, work insane hours, talk to their buddies on the cell phone all day, and fall asleep as soon as the off-duty sign lights up. Cabbies having their fingers on the pulse of a city is the biggest travel myth since "Hey, we can stop and get reliable directions at the gas station!"

Quit Playing with Your Food

- Unless it's directly related to something edible, I flinch anytime I hear something described as "tasty" or "delicious." If you see an old blues guitarist in concert, find another way to describe his "tasty licks."
- I don't want to eat any food that needs to be preceded by the word "edible." Edible bowl. Edible flowers. Edible panties. If something isn't clearly meant for consumption, stop acting like it came out of Mario Batali's private kitchen.

- Travel writers make a wonder of the most ordinary meals. I once encountered this jewel in *Frommer's Santa Fe, Taos & Albuquerque* guidebook: "The place to eat in town is Back Road Pizza on NM 14. . . . Feast on such delicacies as the Hawaiian, with pineapple and Canadian bacon."

Forget that we're not merely eating or even "dining" at a pizza joint located on a state highway, but that we're "feasting" like Tlingits at a potlatch. Forget that the use of "delicacies" should be reserved for the fine or exotic—lizard tongues from an ancient Hohokam recipe, perhaps, or at least a handful of chanterelles flown in from France. Pretty much everyone knows what the inside of a pizza place looks like, and no one has gotten excited about ham and pineapple on a pizza since Duke Kahanamoku won his first longboard championship.

- No more labored food metaphors touting a destination's ethnic diversity. Unless it's made with carrots, celery, and onions, don't make a "stew" or "sauce" out of it.

- Every combination and relevant application of "chocolate" and "sinful" has already been published thousands of times. Worse, any use of these two words in the same sentence makes you look like someone who shops for her mom pants at Target.

- No straight man has ever used the word "scrumptious" in conversation.

- As a photographic image, nothing's as tired as the wide-angle shot of the smiling chef proudly shoving a platter of his specialty mussels/shepherd's pie/pecan-encrusted caramel brownies in front of the lens. Find another way to shoot your food porn or just leave it to *Bon Appétit*.

Death to Clichés

Because I've yet to find an audience willing to endure my complete two-hour lecture on the words, phrases, euphemisms, and clichés that have become the dismal backbone of travel writing, I won't reprint the entire transcription here. Point number one in that address, however, is the mealy, default city descriptive that highlights a destination's "bewitching blend of the ancient and modern," its "intoxicating brew of the time-honored and trendy," or its "enchanting collision of the classic and contemporary." What place on earth cannot be described this way? The captivating-combination-of-old-and-new war horse is the most meaningless notion ever presented to any audience anywhere ever, yet some redaction of it can be found in virtually every travel magazine currently on newsstands. Yes, Lisbon has a history, it has a present, and evidence of each can be found there. Same goes for Colby, Kansas, Stockton, California, and my fucking backyard, so there's no reason to invent a "delightful stew of Old World and disco influences" to promote the most obvious point since the concept of time was first elucidated.

Other words that identify travel stories as subpar:

hip	magical
hot	nestled
happening	liquid sunshine
meander	the wet stuff
luxuriate	the white stuff
cozy	mouthwatering eat
rapturous	tasty treat
exclusive	Big Easy

Big Apple	eye candy
Windy City	pamper
duty-free	wine and dine
savvy traveler	One of Hemingway's favorite . . .
sun-drenched	Not your father's . . .
undiscovered	Tocqueville

If You Want to Preach, Join a Church.
Or Lonely Planet.

I've always believed that just about all of us are one or
two bad decisions away from sleeping on a moldy
bedroll and lining up for lunch at the soup kitchen
downtown. Since cosmically speaking no one is really
any better than anyone else, the corollary follows that no
adult has the right to instruct any other adult in how to
conduct their personal business. I hate people who tell
me what to do even if, *especially if*, it was something I
was already going to do, anyway. This is why few things
get under my skin quite like perk-snarfing writers who
dole out unsolicited advice like cold pancakes at a Ladies
of the Parish breakfast.

Though typically a borderline-dweebish lot in person, travel writers on the page become an insufferably
high-handed bunch. The moment they settle in behind
a keyboard, they succumb to the travel writer's imperative, a verb tense that turns every sentence into a de-
ceptive command. In Paris: "Get up early and take a
morning stroll through the lush gardens at Luxembourg
Palace." In Utah: "Take the short hike at sunset and bask
in the mesmerizing orange and saffron rays at Delicate
Arch." In a restaurant in San Jose: "Order the succulent

grilled shrimp and follow it with a scrumptious dessert of nine-layer banana-rum-apricot cake. Ask for the sinfully good chocolate-poached pears on top!"

Don't miss. Be sure to. Eat this. Buy that. These camouflaged directives—in the retail trade it's called "suggestive selling"—are the magazine equivalent of those irksome Post-it notes little Napoleon coworkers leave scattered around the office "reminding" everyone about project deadlines and how long a Tupperware container of leftover chicken salad can sit in the communal fridge before it gets thrown out.

It's bad enough being told what to do. Worse is being told how to feel about it. The most obnoxious pusher of travel attitudes and politics in our lifetime is Lonely Planet, the Aussie publisher that's made a fortune putting out guides aimed at the kind of traveler who might roll over at the hostel and ask to borrow your toothbrush. I know it's wrong, but I can't help imagining the typical brown-rice-addicted Lonely Planet reader as one whose MySpace page describes them as the author of self-published, mean-hippie-feminist memoirs with titles like *Your Cock Tastes Lousy* and *You Shoulda Been Here Five Years Ago When the Full Moon Parties Didn't Suck So Bad*.

With its well-researched and crisply written guidebooks, including accurate local maps and color photo inserts, Lonely Planet has been propelled to the top of the budget-travel heap in no small part by me. In my home an entire bookshelf sags beneath the weight of dozens of their irrefutably bang-up books. The metric-to-normal conversion chart printed in the back of every *Lonely Planet* guide alone has saved me from countless opportunities to reaffirm my mathematical incompetence.

Rather than questions of accuracy or insufficient detail, it's Lonely Planet's ceaselessly strident PC tone that finally pushed me into the slightly less competent arms of *Time Out* and, in a pinch, *Rough Guides*, when traveling in unknown lands. It was London that broke me. Loaded with the usual pulpit fare, the *Lonely Planet* I hauled there was the last I ever carried. I'd finally had enough of the sanctimonious asides on animal rights in the section on London's world-renowned zoo; snotty cracks belittling the masses who are unable to appreciate the treasures of the British Museum; provincial put-downs of "loud-talking City types with mobile phones"; and the needlessly insulting instruction not to stare at locals on the trains. Gee, really? Thanks for the tip. I returned from London and swore off Lonely Planet forever.

During the four or five years of my self-imposed Lonely Planet ban, I'd occasionally cruise past the colorful guides in bookstores and begin thinking that upcoming trips to Ecuador or Ulan Bator might profit from their collected wisdom. Then I'd remember London—and Malaysia, Amsterdam, Brazil, and others—and stop myself. Inevitably, of course, the day came when I could hold out no longer. Prepping for a trip to Budapest, I picked up a copy of the *Lonely Planet* guide to Eastern Europe, hoping the publisher had seen fit by then to exercise a little less judgment. I'd have been better off waiting for the Born Agains to come around on evolution.

I hadn't leafed through ten pages before I came across a section titled "Responsible Tourism." This condescending copy made full use of the travel writer's imperative to address readers the way one might a classroom of compliant third graders: "Be sure to follow the local code of ethics and common decency and pack up your litter." This from a bunch of Australians who laid the groundwork for the hordes of faux-rasta back-packers and unwashed freeloaders that launched the near-total tourist holocaust of old Siam.

The mention of ethics was a particular crock given that Lonely Planet is the only publisher I know of that seems to actively dislike its readers. Or at least insult and hang its own pseudomorality over them anytime it finds an opportunity. Their Costa Rica books are a model case. Take a look at the lead section on the gorgeous Manuel Antonio National Park taken from the publisher's 1991 first-edition book on that country:

> Fortunately, Manuel Antonio was declared a national park back in 1972, thus preserving it from hotel development and encroachment. Although the park can be busy during dry season weekends, it quietens down midweek, and during rainy season weekdays you can have the place well-nigh to yourself.

Now check out the same section from the 2006 edition of the Costa Rica guide:

> Parque Nacional Manuel Antonio was declared a national park in 1972, preserving it (with minutes to spare) from being bulldozed and razed to make room for a crucial development project—namely an all-inclusive resort and beachside condominiums. . . . Unfortunately, the volume of visitors that descend on Manuel Antonio can sometimes make it feel like you're tromping through a safari park at Six Flags.

The 2006 version then goes on to berate "camera-clicking hordes" and takes proprietary interest in Costa Rica's monkeys by issuing a scolding sidebar titled, "Don't feed the monkeys! Dammit we're serious!" This pissy chestnut begins, "We at Lonely Planet respect the environment" (as though no one else does) and proceeds downhill. The whole section winds up with more bitching about all the damn tourists and ends on this dour note: "With the inevitable influx of cruise shippers that will follow the completion of the marina in Quepos, it's hard to be optimistic about the future of the park." So now blame for the destruction of yet another once-remote wilderness can conveniently be transferred to cruise-ship passengers, leaving Lonely Planet to go its merry way wearing down the path to Honduras or El Salvador.

Brief though they are, these passages leave much to review. The threat of development in Manuel Antonio having been all but vanquished, Lonely Planet nevertheless feels the need to ratchet up the preaching by adding bulldozers and sarcasm to its scary review of a thirty-year-old blueprint to build a hotel in a monkey-filled location they wanted to promote their way. And promote it they did, so well that lots of people came—many more than likely would have to an all-inclusive resort. Then, having made their money off the deal—I don't know how many Costa Rica guidebooks Lonely Planet has sold, but the 2006 book is a seventh edition, so we can assume it's doing pretty well—the publisher turns on the very people it's selling books to by comparing adventure travelers to camera-clicking theme-park dullards. (As though taking pictures of your kids at Disneyland is a crime.)

Lonely Planet wants readers to believe it's still the

cult newsletter "written at a kitchen table and hand-collated, trimmed and stapled" in 1973 by company founders Maureen and Tony Wheeler. It's not. It's a massive business that publishes more than six hundred titles in English and others in Spanish, Italian, French, Japanese, and Korean. It uses ink and paper instead of bulldozers to build visions of idyllic vacations and attract customers, then cries foul when they show up.

There's an old Chinese saying that goes, "One of life's greatest pleasures is to meet a countryman in a strange land." This might have been true during the Tang Dynasty, but it's unlikely that China's ancient wanderers ever suffered the disappointment of trekking miles to the quintessential Thai café, ordering a bowl of the country's most exemplary noodle soup, then looking up to find three tables of scraggly travelers opened to the exact same page in their dog-eared *Lonely Planets*. This actually happened to me in 1997.

At this point, most of the world isn't lonely enough. And that's the real problem with Lonely Planet. Along with all the sermonizing from the hyperenlightened stoners who write it, those guides also have to go and be the most insidiously effective motherfuckers to hit travel since the wheel.

At *Travelocity* magazine, if there was one thing we were willing to borrow from Lonely Planet and other travel-publishing success stories, it was the "effective" part of the equation. Deals and information on flights, rooms, cars, restaurants, and related money soakers are essential parts of the consumer travel magazine, and we meant to hit them hard at *Travelocity*. We intended to augment the basics, however, with a presentation that would, at a glance, distance us from the field.

Given what should by now be the obvious fact that I'm suspicious of almost all travel writing, I was an interesting choice to head the magazine. Other than the fact that I was willing to rush to Texas for substandard compensation, I initially assumed my antipathy was a big part of the reason I'd gotten the job. I quickly learned otherwise.

The first whisper that *Travelocity* magazine was in trouble came in late May, less than two months after my arrival in Dallas. During this period, our impossibly small and talented staff had put together a magazine prototype, gotten early drafts green-lighted by Travelocity.com CEO Terry Jones, and taken what we had out to focus groups in Dallas, Chicago, New York, and L.A.

The focus group reactions were mixed, running a nose in front of lukewarm. I didn't consider this a problem, nor did anyone else. Focus groups are famously fickle and, besides, we were going for a radical reconstruction of the travel-magazine form. Humor. Edge. Honesty. A travel magazine for people who didn't like travel magazines. You anticipate some resistance to change. As it turned out, it wasn't the overall concept but the cover of the magazine that led us into dark waters.

As one might expect, intense but friendly debate over the cover of our bold, new product had been a constant since day one. None of the focus groups was conclusively supportive of any of the options we'd shown them. Any magazine, particularly a new one, needs its cover to "pop" off the newsstand and must convey in the fleeting instant a consumer might glance at it a complete sense of what the magazine is about, who its target audience is, and why that audience should buy it. The job is made tougher by the fact that there are thousands of extremely talented people already out there working hard to crush your magazine by making theirs even better.

After several weeks we agreed the inaugural cover should emphasize the principle upon which Travelocity .com was based: the merging of travel with Internet technology. Taking this cue, our steady-handed associate art director, Chris Philpot, conceived and sketched a gatefold cover, which is the term for that kind of cover that opens up with an extra panel so that a second page of premium, inside-front-cover advertising can be sold against it. Chris's sketch played against the old message-in-a-bottle concept, except in his version, instead of a note, the bottle floating on the sea had a computer mouse inside. When you opened the gatefold, the mouse cord—in those prewireless days—was revealed to be running from the ocean onto a deserted, tropical beach. It was a clever twist on a recognizable archetype, and Chris drew a handsome illustration. A South Seas idyll, a computer hookup. Everyone easily grasped the concept. We began looking at photographers who could bring the idea to life.

Despite the general sense that the magazine was coming together, our advertising department was getting nervous. Publishers, ad directors, and sales-account reps are always nervous because modern corporate culture demands their quarterly sales goals be set high enough to collapse Dale Carnegie's right ventricle. Salespeople are also notoriously skittish about anything high concept or "artsy" since the only colors most of them acknowledge are black and red. As Emily Dickinson once noted, "Publication is not the business of poets."

Our publisher and sales staff didn't understand the mouse-in-a-bottle cover. They didn't trust my instincts. They didn't trust themselves. With considerable enthusiasm, however, they were ready to embrace and place total trust in the aesthetic vision of a stranger, so long as that stranger had taken the trouble to identify himself as a "magazine consultant" on his business card.

Thus we were treated one afternoon, mere weeks from the day we were scheduled to go to press with our masterpiece, to a visit from Simon Spencer, PhD, a self-styled magazine authority from a southern university who called himself the "Magazine Master." Though the bio on his Web site would seem to suggest that the Magazine Master has never actually *worked* at any magazine, he has nonetheless become a go-to "magazine expert" for networks such as ABC, CNN, and PBS. He's also consulted for or spoken at seminars before an impressive number of major American publishing companies. Understandably, the *Travelocity* office buzzed with excitement in the days leading up to the Great One's arrival. This wasn't Helen Gurley Brown or even Tina Brown, but the magazine biz produces few outright celebrities, and a visit from even a B-list one seemed kind of cool.

The Magazine Master turned out to be a stocky, manicured, blond bundle of energy with blazing eyes, a pit-stained pink dress shirt, and lots of opinions. A great number of these opinions involved sex. Not just ordinary sex either but raunchy, hard-core, barely legal sex. He took one look at our prototype cover and shook his head.

"Do you actually want to sell copies of your magazine?" he asked us.

Oh yes, we said, we most certainly wanted to sell magazines. The Magazine Master shook his head sagely, as if this was just the response he'd expect from such an intelligent group of people. Shifting into a gear that indicated he was ready to start earning his outrageous consulting fee, the big brain from the publishing hotbed of southern Appalachia hit us with this piece of finely crafted insight:

"Sex sells." The Magazine Master let the news sink in for a few stage beats before continuing. "Your magazine needs more sex."

While this groundbreaking information percolated in our minds, our advertising director flashed a toothy smile—I'm sure he wasn't literally rubbing his hands together, but that's how I remember the moment—and led the staff into a conference room. Here the Magazine Master dimmed the lights and ran us through a slide show featuring faded line graphs and pie charts interspersed with a series of photos of escalating sexual intensity. Cheerful girls-next-door in bikinis gave way to sleek models in suggestive poses. Next we knew, grainy images clipped from European stag rags hit the screen in front of us, ten feet tall. Topless Teutons faux-fingering themselves. Saucy MILFs anticipating backdoor action. Hot interracial foreplay. All of it with the vaginas and wieners blacked out, so as not to stir offense.

Against this surreal backdrop, the Magazine Master delivered in high-strung tones a lecture explaining the success of lad mags like *Maxim* and *FHM*—in case none of the people in the room who actually worked at a magazine had walked past a newsstand in three years—accompanied by images of beaded sweat on legal-this-week cleavage.

"This magazine moves about four hundred thousand copies a month," the Magazine Master said.

Click. Pubescent nipple bulge.

"When this magazine began running exposed breasts, sales tripled."

Click. Resplendent melons, fully iced.

"This is a very popular Italian magazine."

Click. Massive hair pie.

"There are many magazines for specialty audiences."

Click. Naked black woman pulling pendulous breasts upward within tantalizing reach of her tongue.

"More graphic equals more sales."

Click. Full-spread beaver, *O* face.

Part of me feels lousy trashing the Magazine Master. Aside from everything else, he was actually a pretty nice guy, smart, with an oddball charm. He liked me, told our company brass I was a great choice to lead the magazine, and wrote an article about me and the magazine on his Web site, predicting success.

But he was also a joke. And, worse, a convincing one. At least to our publisher and advertising director. By the time the Magazine Master left Dallas, our gatefold cover with the tech-meets-travel theme was deader than Pets.com stock. "Sex sells" had become the mantra on the other side of the office, the side with all the money.

During its run of just over a year, *Travelocity* magazine was hurt by a number of poor decisions. On a day-to-day basis, no one made more than I. A magazine editor in chief is uniquely positioned to undermine a product that hundreds of people rely upon for their livelihoods and potentially millions read—or don't read. Story selection. Cover lines. Sales calls. Corporate tie-ins. Media interviews. Internal negotiations with company executives. I was presented with a number of chances to stumble and did so often, usually with little elegance. Still, no decision was as portentous for the magazine as the one made on that dark afternoon. From the moment the Magazine Master's musk-scented hook sank into the open mouths around our conference room, *Travelocity* magazine was doomed.

Before proceeding, one point should be made clear. I've got absolutely no moral objection to exploiting blazing-hot young ass to sell whatever you need it to. Sex and sexuality are huge parts of life, and anyone who doesn't want to allow pop culture geared for adults to reflect that is a fascist. Or a moron. Or a eunuch.

What the hustlers who push cleavage and camel toe conveniently neglect to mention, however, is that while sex does indeed sell, so does a lot of other stuff. The *New Yorker, Popular Science, Redbook, Field & Stream, Reader's Digest*, and most other magazines manage to stay in business without relying on poontang to move copies. In the case of *Travelocity*, my opposition was based less on morality than context. Even if the "Come and get it, boys!" approach was somehow deemed appropriate for Internet travel bookers, I knew the Puritan confines of corporate Texas—the Bible study lunches in our office were well attended—wasn't the place to kick off a risky, experimental magazine with a marketing strategy lifted from the febrile imagination of a southern academic with an eye for European smut.

The popular image of the dot-com company often includes a brilliant, shaggy-haired, iconoclastic entrepreneur blithely breaking old establishment rules while allowing employee creativity to run wild in a laid-back atmosphere of strewn pizza boxes, copay day care, and Dinosaur Jr. looped into the company's telephone hold music. Not so, Travelocity.com. The company was born out of American Airlines' old Sabre Travel Network—which was to the travel industry what sites like Travelocity.com are now to the consumer—and remained almost as stiff-necked as the country's largest airline. When I was at *American Way*, we referred to the colossus that is the American Airlines corporate complex as the "Death Star." It's officially called CentrePort, and you can see this cube-stuffed cluster of massive, colorless boxes looming out of the dirt fields as you head out of DFW Airport on Highway 183 toward Dallas. Few sights are as heartbreaking on the return trip from a strip-mall lunch at Chili's with embittered coworkers.

Also worrisome was the almost cultish reverence in which Travelocity.com employees held their CEO, Terry Jones. The WWTD (What Would Terry Do?) fallback assessment of all situations might have been a humorous play on the South's ubiquitous "What Would Jesus Do?" bumper stickers, but it wasn't exactly a joke. People at the company said it all the time and they meant it. When I applied WWTD to our cover dilemma, I couldn't imagine the CEO erring on the side of "more pussy."

When none of my arguments convinced our publishing executives to abandon the hot-chicks strategy, the only options were to resign or get on board and produce the best babe-on-cover magazine possible. I've stormed out of jobs on principle before, and I'm a firm believer that once or twice in life everybody should say, "Fuck you, I quit!" then march out in a blaze of self-destructive glory. This, however, was not one of those occasions.

We spared no cost, hiring Walter Iooss Jr. of *Sports Illustrated* swimsuit-issue fame to shoot our first cover— a blue-eyed blonde in a Neoprene bikini carrying a surfboard down a California beach. Even as sexy-girl covers go, I didn't care for it. For starters, the model looked as much like a surfer as John Madden does. To my astonishment, however, Terry Jones approved it. Sort of. He was a man busy with things like testifying before Congress on behalf of the travel industry and staying two steps ahead of the extremely hard-charging competition, and I could tell he was more interested in coming up with new ways of moving airline tickets than selecting magazine covers.

He also appeared to have other issues on his mind. Leaving his office that day, Terry took me aside and leaned in close. "My brother is a professional photographer," he said. "He does beautiful nature shots. You ought to get him to take pictures for the magazine."

As I left Terry's office, my mind was racing in a hundred directions. Why would the CEO tell me about his brother? Why had our advertising director ambushed editorial by bringing in an eleventh-hour cover consultant? Why hadn't the focus groups been just a tiny bit more receptive? (OK, I did care about those results.) I didn't know the answer to any of those questions, but one thing was clear. Dubya and Cheney didn't even have the Republican nomination yet, but already the mood in Dallas seemed ominous.

Travelocity managed to beat *Expedia Travels* to the newsstand by a few weeks, and though being first to market was a small victory, I'm not sure it brought us any lasting advantage. As far as the public was concerned, both magazines came out at roughly the same time, and media reviews predictably made head-to-head comparison the focus of their coverage.

You might not think media reviews of other media would matter that much, but they do. All people are desperate to be loved by their peers, none more so than those in the media. This is why media "awards" are such long-running and successful business enterprises.

Magazines pay to enter most industry competitions, which are run by organizations that know enough to keep the customer satisfied. Winning an award is a matter of basic economics. Pay to enter enough "competitions" and eventually you'll probably "win." If you didn't win once in a while, you'd stop paying. Same principle applies to the carnie midway.

Reviews for both magazines were generally favorable, though I was amazed at how the media beat "experts" so thoroughly missed the point of each. *Travelocity* and *Expedia Travels* magazines were competitors only by virtue of the fact that they both operated beneath the very large tent of online travel sales. Otherwise, the magazines were going after contrasting audiences. The fact that two similar Internet travel companies had chosen to market their magazines to completely different groups of people should have struck media observers as interesting. Or at least struck them. Of the many stories published, only one, a Liquid Media piece by a guy named Ryan Meech, managed to pick up on this. Whoever Ryan Meech is, I hope he's written a bestseller and become a millionaire by now.

Expedia Travels magazine was put out in New York by Ziff Davis Media, the same company that published *Yahoo! Internet Life. Expedia Travels* hit the newsstands as a highly polished product focusing on top-end destinations. It was geared, in the words of its editor in chief, Gary Walther, "toward an affluent, fairly sophisticated audience." *Expedia Travels* featured lots of brochure-friendly pictures of hermetically sealed hotel suites with no people in them, photos such as might have been provided by the hotels themselves. When we looked at *Expedia Travels*, we concluded that it was a well-designed, solid magazine with an incredibly stupid marketing plan. No matter how nice a magazine you put together, there was no way you were going to dethrone *Condé Nast Traveller* at its own game. I had *Expedia Travels* on suicide watch from day one.

I'm sure the Expedia people were even less impressed with our magazine. Next to their sheen, we were all ragged edges, showy irreverence, and, of course, babes on the cover. There were traditional elements. A well-researched story dealt with animal-related tourism and its impact on wildlife. Pulitzer Prize–winning photojournalists Judy Walgren and Jay Dickman—whose photos had brought female circumcision in Africa and Central American revolution, respectively, to the attention of Americans—were dispatched to Southern California and Croatia's Dalmatian Coast. Both returned with images worthy of gallery framing. I remain happy about our decision to feature Croatia five years before the rest of the travel media decreed it Europe's "hot new destination." If any readers actually took our advice back in the day, they got to a few remarkable spots ahead of the heavy traffic.

As important as beauty travel, however, were our edgier stories: a pale, unattractive Dutchman who'd somehow become an African chief; the high incidence of romantic breakups caused by the stress of travel; and gripes about wasting precious annual vacation days on obligatory trips to in-law family functions. A short bit on a San Francisco boutique that sold stuffed mice dressed as punk rockers and Hamlet made us the target of a never-ending form-letter protest campaign from animal-rights activists around the world. Stories like these satisfied the part of our mission intended to capture the attention of a mythical, young audience then hopefully referred to by dot-commers as "the Internet generation."

Our worst review came in *USA Today* from a critic named Laura Bly, who called the magazine "more sophomoric than sophisticated." It was accepted as gospel at Travelocity.com that Bly had some sort of axe to grind and that her criticism of the company long predated the inception of the magazine. No one at Travelocity.com, I was assured, took her comments seriously.

This turned out not to be true. Terry Jones and many others in the company hated Bly's remark, it festered in their craw, and for the rest of the magazine's life we heard the refrain "too sophomoric" in response to innumerable creative ideas. "Too sophomoric" was no tipping point, but it loomed large at the magazine from that moment on.

Part of this is because it was accurate. To me, Laura Bly's snippy complaints proved we were sailing in the right direction. As a stodgy, humorless *USA Today* columnist, she was as far from the "Internet generation" as we wanted to be. Whether you're selling hip-hop records to fourteen-year-old kids or Armani suits to Mafia dons, the first rule of image marketing is defining precisely who you are *not*. Flower Power, for example, was first about hating the establishment. Everything that followed was a reaction to that, from LSD to Hanoi Jane to fourteen-minute drum solos.

By my reckoning, Bly's review proved we'd passed the what-we-are-not test. We were emphatically not *Condé Nast Traveller*. Or *Expedia Travels*. This was positive news. I concede, however, that it's tough to win an argument with travel-company executives in which your basic contention is that it's a good thing that *USA Today* just took a big dump all over you.

This is especially true when the CEO's underlings start asking with broadening emphasis why the CEO's brother's photography hasn't shown up in the magazine yet. When you begin hearing worrying remarks about the board of directors wanting a magazine that looks more traditional. When the phrase "too negative"— referencing stories about overpriced hotels, cramped coach seats, whatever—begins creeping into discussions with the publisher. And most especially when a group of angry women in San Francisco is planning a sexual-harassment lawsuit that could bring down the magazine you're editing.

Travelocity magazine's second issue—cross-legged brunette in bikini kicking back on a Mexican beach on the cover—was the scourge of the company. Employees removed it from the tables in waiting areas. Cringed when they passed it on newsstands. It was postmillennium in the rest of America, but this was Texas, and I felt like the scorned Hefner of the 1950s. Only without the pipe, smoking jacket, and attendant nymphettes making the pain go away. The outrage peaked in Travelocity.com's San Francisco office, a place you'd imagine might be a little more tolerant than Dallas. Turned out the Bay Area team wore its PC straitjacket like a burka.

It was mid-October when we received word that a group of Travelocity.com employees in San Francisco were contacting a lawyer about filing a sexual-harassment lawsuit against their own company, presumably on the grounds that a provocative image of a woman on the cover of a magazine promoted a sexually hostile workplace environment. That every travel magazine on the planet—from *Islands* to *Travel & Leisure* to *Arthur Frommer's Budget Travel*—often features good-looking women on the cover was beside the point. San Francisco's impractical legal threat was reactionary sexual politics to its core.

I'd see the same thing a few years later when I worked for *Maxim*. Despite the contrary evidence of one hundred thousand years of human reproduction, half the country had somehow come to believe that that magazine had invented human sexuality in the late 1990s. From friends to total strangers, people loved venting as soon as they heard I worked for *Maxim*. I once got into a late-night shouting match with a couple in a West Village bar over my immense responsibility for the eroding intellect of America's youth, as though the nation's

massive public-school system was powerless against a
single magazine. In the end, I had to laugh, pretend to
concede a few points, and leave them to their fantasy of
enlightenment. As I'd already learned at *Travelocity*, people can't get enough of easy targets, and there's no rea-
soning with hysterical militants.

Back in Dallas, emergency meetings were convened
behind slammed doors. Everyone knew the San Francis-
cans were nuts, but no company can afford to ignore
accusations of sexual harassment. Travelocity.com execs
screamed that the magazine was ruining their company's public image. Though it was tempting, I decided
not to assure them that the damage was actually pretty
minimal, since almost nobody was buying the damn
thing yet, anyway.

After some righteous soliloquies about journalistic
integrity and branding through repetition, the magazine
relented. We literally ripped our next cover off the
press—Caribbean hottie in bikini frolicking in surf—and
slapped together a less threatening substitute. Though it
was a loss of face for the publisher vis-à-vis the parent
company, I was secretly as happy as I'd been since
April. Finally, we could put out a magazine that would
reflect both Travelocity.com's technical virtues and a
new publication model for the industry.

With the passing of the cover crisis and lawsuit threat,
the staff established a tenuous rhythm, improved the
magazine on a weekly basis, and even got a few cordial
smiles at the company Christmas party. We embarked
on a new cover strategy—studio concept shots depicting

travel trends—that produced some genuinely impressive results and consensus approval. But we never really recovered the trust of the parent company.

The March 2001 issue was our best. Southern Italy. Last-minute booking tips for NCAA basketball tourney travel. Internet travel scams. To promote its move to Las Vegas, we put the Blue Man Group on the cover. Given our shaky footing and my complete lack of What Would Terry Do insight, I knew sending prominent gay columnist Dan Savage to anchor our Las Vegas package was dicey. I didn't anticipate his offhand remark about Circus, Circus getting company investors in such a snit that I'd have to personally apologize for it. "When I found myself alone in a clown-theme hotel room, which I had to ride to in a clown-theme elevator, I curled up on my clown-theme bedspread and cried," Savage wrote. Soon, however, the goodwill of Vegas casinos became the smallest of my concerns.

In the end, it was a guy named Bob from Oregon, a chubby dude with back hair and stretch marks enjoying a Princess cruise off the coast of Haiti, who sank our ship. Specifically, it was a picture of Bob from Oregon—raising his arms in victory after winning a cruise-ship belly-flop competition—that ended my career at *Travelocity*. We splashed Bob from Oregon in all his flabby, poolside glory across a two-page spread to open our feature on cruise ships. It was a helluva photo, but Bob from Oregon's portly frame was too much for Terry Jones (no distance runner himself) to abide.

Another flurry of hard-faced meetings followed the "Bob" photo. I recall someone saying, "No one wants to see a fat white fuck in a swimsuit in a travel magazine and no one ever should!" Maybe they were right. Either way, it was clear that Travelocity.com had had enough of their experimental foray into publishing. Or at least enough of me.

Travelocity magazine had its minor triumphs. We eventually built a respectable subscriber/newsstand base of somewhere around a quarter of a million (though like most magazine-circulation figures, this was an educated guess), and many readers noticed the difference in our product and wrote nice letters saying so. My preference for hiring nontravel writers brought in sharp voices like Joe Queenan, whose essay on *SkyMall* was one of the funniest travel pieces written that year, and whose inventive piece on homesickness was cited by execs as an example of my unfitness for editor in chief duty. Toward the end of the first conversation I ever had with him, after I'd laid out the blueprint of the revolutionary travel magazine I was recruiting him to write for, Queenan told me that he expected me to get fired.

"Guys like you don't last very long in those jobs," he said with all the empathy of a weatherman announcing the fifth straight day of light drizzle and sixty-five degrees. "But keep in touch if you manage to make it."

The magazine comparison I like to draw now is with the first season of *Seinfeld*. Watching those reruns makes you feel uncomfortable. They're almost depressing. The characters aren't developed. The timing is off. Jerry and Elaine's relationship feels forced. George comes across like a warmed-over Woody Allen. Kramer's haircut isn't right.

Yet even in those clunky early episodes, you can see that the pieces for what might develop into a great show were in place. The foundation was there. That's how I feel now when I flip through old copies of *Travelocity*. Had the powers that be stuck to the original business-plan commitment of three years, *Travelocity* might have become a successful magazine. Not *Seinfeld* successful, but it would have developed into a compelling product. One that might have changed at least part of the travel landscape.

On a sunny evening in mid-April, almost a year to the day after I'd been hired, the president of our publishing company called me at home to fire me. This stung a little—despite his canning me, I liked our publisher, he'd given me a lot of rope, and I knew he wanted a successful magazine as much as I did—but it wasn't much of a surprise. I'd been asked to resign a few weeks earlier, an offer I refused on the principle of not quitting on a tough situation. I'm nothing if not tenacious. And occasionally delusional.

Hanging up the phone, my mind leaped to an article Joel Stein had written before he became a columnist for *Time* magazine. Hired for the launch of *Martha Stewart Living*, Stein recalled a pep talk given to the staff about how theirs was going to be a new kind of publication, an animal utterly different from all magazines that had come before it. As the months wore on, heady start-up promises were betrayed one by one, and Stein was eventually fired (then quickly rehired). In the aftermath, he concluded that whenever someone said they wanted a radical new product, what they actually meant was that they wanted an unconditionally conservative product that looked exactly like everything else on the market, with the notable exception that it made a ton more money. I didn't follow Stein's logic at the time. Now I understood.

Travelocity limped to a doleful finale. The first issue after my departure featured Mickey Mouse on the cover pimping Disney World above the line "Mouse Control." One more thin issue—Hawaii, Spain, New Mexico—was printed. Then came September and planes flying into buildings in New York. All at once, our year of back-room politicking, legal threats, and arguments about fat guys on cruise ships seemed foolish and irrelevant.

The magazine's last issue was dated September/October 2001. Ziff Davis Media shut down *Expedia Travels* in November 2001, citing the post–September 11 downturn in travel and advertising markets, but it was on its way out anyway. Both magazines lasted about a year. Both performed about the same insofar as advertising and readership went. Neither managed to make a lasting imprint on the market. Companies like Travelocity.com and Expedia.com might have changed the way travel is booked, but not really the way it's perceived. Open any travel magazine today, put it next to one published in 2000, and you won't find significant differences.

Terry Jones retired from Travelocity.com in 2002. He's now the chairman of the board of travel search engine Kayak.com, public speaker—eighteen-thousand-dollar keynote fee—and consultant, assuredly a better one than Simon Spencer, who's still the Magazine Master. Though I don't believe he felt the same about me, I liked Terry, appreciated his moxie, and wish we could have convinced him to hang in there with *Travelocity* for another year or two. Not that I blame him for playing the deal the way he did. There were a number of negotiations above my head—between Travelocity.com, the publisher, various corporate partners, advertisers—and in the end he came out looking like the smartest of the lot. Plenty of money was spent launching *Travelocity* magazine, but I don't think he or his company's investors put up a dime of it. And if there's one thing I took away from my time at *Travelocity*, it's that when the CEO asks you to run his brother's photography in the magazine, it's probably wise to get the brother's number, go back to the office, and call the guy. Immediately.

After getting sacked, I spent a couple months in Oregon, weary of the whole racket, wandering around like a weathered Lakota chief looking for an empty piece of desert or lonely mountaintop where I could fold my legs, stare at the sky, and quietly pass into the next world. After a while I realized I still loved travel and that my malaise was merely the cumulative effect of trying to fashion a literary existence in a city where Bush/Cheney bumper stickers were given away at the front counters of bookstores, next to displays of *Left Behind* DVDs and other apocalypse merchandise. The indignity of getting the boot took a couple weeks to fade, but it's easier to count your blessings in some places than it is in others, and I was at least happy to be back in the Pacific time zone, surrounded by mountains and clean air.

Going-away parties are nice reminders that every place is filled with good people. If I've come down hard on Dallas, I should note the excellence of the staffs at Travelocity.com, *Travelocity*, and *American Way* magazines, and the dozens of fine people who befriended me during the combined two years, eight months, twenty-one days, nine hours, fourteen minutes, and fifty-two seconds I lived in the city. It's increasingly rare, but there does remain in Texas, and sometimes even in Dallas, some of the old Lone Star spirit of self-reliance, honor, and generosity. Even so, it's perhaps only outsiders who can completely appreciate the magnificent sense of relief and elation you get watching that fucking town disappear in your rearview mirror. Even if you did get run out of it a little sooner than you'd planned.

PART III

Window →

8

. . .

The Curse of Chinatown:
And Other Updated Wisdom
for the Modern Traveler

Maybe it makes me sound like a hypocrite, but for all the complaining I've done over the years about the travel industry's hidebound ways—at *Travelocity* and elsewhere— I've also developed an appreciation for its astounding intricacy and the overall excellence of many of those who make it work at ground level. And come to understand that a Zen-like acceptance of travel as a highly unpredictable animal is the most effective way of approaching it.

Hit the road enough and you eventually acquire a workmanlike knowledge that goes well beyond knowing what you want at the Panda Express in Terminal C before you even look at the menu. It doesn't take a travel writer to get a basic handle on the industry, which is why it always amazes me that you almost never find anything novel or particularly useful in those "savvy traveler" columns every magazine and newspaper in America trots out two or three times a year to announce for the millionth time that you should drink plenty of water while on a plane and "check the Internet" to find deals on hotels. Wow. I'll bet no mileage-club gold-level account rep crisscrossing the country ever thought to do that before.

In fact, most of our ideas about tourism and the companies that facilitate it are pretty old—Victorian influence on contemporary life is never ending. In the 1800s, rapid economic growth among the working class of Britain coupled with development of the steamship and railroad opened the globe to citizens of the world's foremost imperial power, leading to the almost unheard-of idea of travel for travel's sake. With money and transportation flinging open the doors of the world to the common man, the Victorians established a massive new industry. The template for modern travel was created around British tastes for the beach, wilderness idylls, museums, cities of antiquity, and, critically, the opposite sex. Queen Victoria's plebes didn't exactly roll like spring breakers at Panama Beach, but they were quick to seize upon romantic opportunities that became more available the farther one got from the restrictions of home.

For a century and a half, give or take, all proceeded swimmingly. But technology, which made tourism a mass phenomenon in the first place, has transformed the beast entirely. In 1950, international tourist arrivals around the world totaled 25 million. By the turn of this century, the number was 693 million. On a global scale, tourism accounts for more than $450 billion annually, a volume that, depending on how you count it, rivals oil and petroleum exports as the world's largest industry. Groups like Global Exchange, an international human rights organization, claim the travel/leisure industry is actually the world's largest, accounting for 10.4 percent of the world's

gross domestic product and 4 percent of global employment. Whatever the exact numbers, it's time our expectations about travel were brought up to date.

SMILE WHEN YOU'RE LYING

From the ant brigade of Brazil crawling across my body
to being left broke and homeless on a Thai beach, I've
endured the most stone-hearted indignities travel dishes
out. Even so, I've been averaging a trip a month for the
past decade and will in all likelihood continue to do so.
Just because the reality doesn't often line up with the ad-
vertised fantasy—that the staff will be competent, that
none of the previous fifteen hundred people who've
crashed in your hotel room will have dried deep into the
crack of their ass with the towel you just used to wipe
your face, that the locals actually want you there for reasons that have nothing to do with your money—doesn't
mean you should stop traveling. It simply means that you
need to travel smarter.

After giving up on finding anything new in those
workhorse rundowns of tired tips, I began keeping my
own list of ways of making life easier away from home.
Though constantly in flux, my list (abbreviated below)
always culminates in the single golden rule meant to
equip any twenty-first-century traveler with the proper
attitude to travel like a pro.

Lie

Chances are, you already lie a little bit when you
travel—and, by the way, when you complain that you've
been on hold or waiting in line for thirty minutes, they
know it's only been ten—but chances are also good that

you should be lying a lot more. For the same reason parents lie to children about that farm in the country where Dad took Friskies the pregnant cat so she could enjoy life on her own feral terms, travel companies lie to you—because it makes their lives easier.

You'll never be able to fool the industry to the degree that it hoodwinks you—the airlines' vaunted "on-time" departure records, for example, are finessed in any number of undetectable ways—but you can play their game to your advantage. The easiest involves lying to phone reservation agents with hotels, resorts, and car agencies. The next time you're booking a reservation and the agent asks if you have a corporate rate or discount, immediately answer yes, then provide the name of a Fortune 500 company you "work for." If you actually do work for a company that entitles you to a corporate discount, name a higher-profile corporation and see if that gets you a sweeter deal.

Better still, offer the information before being prompted. After a car or hotel reservation agent quotes a rate, try this: "Geez, that's a little higher than I paid last time. I'm a regional director for Microsoft (or United Airlines or IBM) out here in Phoenix, and I'm pretty sure we have a rate with you guys." That'll get a 10 percent discount on the spot, sometimes more. And don't worry about someone checking up on your bogus employment credentials. Once your rate is logged into a computer, no one down the line has any reason to question it. Every travel transaction is a negotiation, and the easiest place to front is on the phone. How do you think sex chat lines stay in business?

Because they operate on doomsday margins—the price of jet fuel alone tripled between 2004 and 2006—the airlines are the Nazis of the travel industry and take more effort to deceive. Even so, the airport offers innumerable opportunities for dishonesty. You're prone to deep-vein thrombosis and really need that bulkhead seat—I know a writer who carries a phony doctor's note for this ruse. You just pulled a red-eye shift at work and you're the best man at a wedding in Tampa and the minute you get off this plane you have to race to the rehearsal dinner, so if there's any way they can block out an empty row in the back so that you can get some rest, you'd really appreciate it. Female counter agents are suckers for wedding stories, and details about things like rehearsal dinners establish your credibility.

On some flights, there's legitimately little a counter agent can do to accommodate special requests, so the sob-story routine isn't a guaranteed winner. But if you're creative and willing to sacrifice some personal integrity, deals will fall your way more often than not.

Hang Up on Morons

Because your telephone instincts are always right, disengage from half-wits as soon as you get one on the line. Not regarded as a keenly self-motivated group to begin with, telephone reservation agents perform a repetitive and stressful job for little money—hotel and motel reservation clerks average less than twenty thousand dollars a year. They increasingly work from home, where the distractions of kids, dogs, dinner, and Oprah divert attention from the disembodied entity in Nevada looking for a deal on a Reno-to-Boise hop. Reservation agents quit all the time—25 percent annual turnover at call centers is considered good, 100 is the norm in some places.

If the voice on the other end of the line suggests a creature with the problem-solving capacity of a juvenile bonobo and the interpersonal skills of a Calcutta cabbie, cut your losses and hang up. Keep calling back until you're connected with a voice that conjures the competent, smiling woman in the headset they show on TV cheerfully booking first-class flights to Venice. There are more than 300,000 travel reservation operators working in the United States. Don't waste time on the 150,000 lousy ones.

Downsize

The best way to start packing for a trip is by reaching into the drawer next to the bathroom sink and grabbing a handful of trial-size toiletries—mini shampoo, conditioner, toothpaste, aspirin, shaving cream, Band-Aids, sunscreen. If you don't have a drawer like this, start one. Like old ladies who hoard cat food, I'm a habitual collector of handy-sized personal items, tossing random tubes into the basket every time I pass that shelf at the drugstore, lifting them out of hotel bathrooms, plucking them from maid carts left unattended in hotel hallways. Keep enough of these plastic bottles around and you can be out the door for Kabul ten minutes after *National Geographic* calls the house.

Spicy Is Almost Never Spicy

In the United States when they tell you it's spicy, it's not spicy. In the rest of the world when they tell you it's spicy, there's a 20 percent chance it's spicy. In Thailand when they tell you it's spicy, it's going to taste like someone shoving a blowtorch down your throat for the next twenty-five minutes.

Steal an Extra Inch of Legroom

For an average-sized adult, cramming into a coach airline seat is perhaps the most dehumanizing requirement of the travel experience. And once you've been hectored about sharing overhead compartments, been spoken to like a child for twenty minutes,* obediently stowed your carry-on beneath the seat in front of you, and settled in with your luxurious twelve inches of legroom, what does the airline do? It steals up to another inch of that space—legroom you paid for—by jamming the seat-back pouch in front of you with magazines, catalogs, and other promotional pieces that make money for the airline and its publishing partners at your expense. As soon as you buy a ticket, the airlines sell your eyeballs—and legroom—to advertisers. You don't really think the TV programming is there for your enjoyment, do you?

Rolling back this crafty territorial incursion is as easy as throwing out the trash, yet few people think to do it. Since you're under no obligation to accept the airline's clutter, the next time you're on a plane, take everything they've put in the seat-back pocket, and stick

---

* One of the best things about leaving the United States is being addressed like an adult. Once overseas, the haughty demeanor, simpleton instructions, nursery-school tenor, and scripted happy talk that exemplify the American travel industry's idea of "service"—the chirpy banter from flight attendants on Southwest Airlines being the pinnacle of infantilism—are replaced by straightforward, competent voices delivering information in a crisp, capable manner. I love England because it's like a grown-up America, a fact I'm reminded of as soon as I get on a British Airways flight or hop into a London cab and people stop treating me as though I'd just learned to finger paint.

it in the overhead bin. Voilà! You just bought yourself an extra inch of legroom.

Never Eat Airplane Food

There's a reason the "bistro bags," box lunches, and assorted snacks—as well as the meals served on longer flights and in first class—are referred to as "earthquake food" by the flight attendants who serve them. Anything with an unrefrigerated shelf life of up to a year ought not technically be considered "food." The smartest way to prep for a flight is to eat a big meal beforehand and pick up some fruit or deli items on the way to the airport. The same rules apply to international trips. And, yes, it's a long flight, but if you can't go ten hours without eating, you shouldn't be visiting Sri Lanka in the first place.

Resurrect Dead Batteries

If your batteries die while you're in the air, rub them briskly for a minute or two on your pants leg. The static electricity will give them a recharge that'll last as long as an hour or two. This also works in cheap hotels where they never change the batteries in the remote.

Don't Be That Guy

As your mother should have told you, the easiest way to make someone like you is to like them first. With no group of people is this truer than the overworked, underpaid customer-service army that runs the day-to-day operations of this country's travel monolith.

In recent years I've spoken several times off the record

with a flight attendant for a major airline. I've been ac-quainted with this woman for a decade and can attest that she's one of the most pleasant, professional, and decent people I've ever known. Not in any way one of those surly dragons who uses her ill-gotten seniority to grab all the Honolulu routes and make life miserable for everyone crossing the Pacific because she's thirty pounds overweight, her third divorce is hung up in court, and her dye job looks like shit. Some people just aren't cut out to work with the public, and the airlines have an uncanny knack for finding them. Here's what my perfectly agreeable, mentally stable flight attendant friend told me about passengers who try to play tough with airline employees.

"Every encounter at an airline starts with the cus-tomer's attitude," she said. "If a person comes on all de-manding or confrontational, I will do everything in my power to make sure they don't get their way. If someone's a dick, I will get on the radio and word will spread and everyone at this airline will line up behind each other to shut that person down. It's the same wherever you go."

Kiss Ass

The trick to getting what you want out of an airline em-ployee is to get on their good side before they even know there's a problem. This might mean being pre-pared with small gifts inside of carry-ons—boxes of chocolates are good. In Arabia this is called baksheesh, a romantic term to keep in mind if "bribery" offends your fragile sensibilities.

Next time you've drawn the middle seat that nobody on the phone or at the front counter is willing to change for you, subdue the uglier side of your nature and approach the departure-gate agent with an easygoing smile. When she asks how she can help you, explain that a client has given you this box of chocolates, but that, alas, you're allergic to the nuts in it, or whatever. Since you hate to see such generosity go to waste, and because you have a sister who used to work for Continental and know what a demanding and thankless job our nation's counter agents face every day, you're wondering if she'd like to have the chocolates? Of course she would. And maybe after a little more chitchat about your sister, during which you slide in a reference to the lousy seat you've drawn for the flight, she might be inclined to see what she can do about making your life more comfortable.

At this point you're perhaps asking yourself, "Why bother with this charade?" The flight is "completely full"—the lady on the intercom has harped on this every five minutes—so what can the gate agent do about it? As it turns out, plenty.

In addition to those unclaimed great whites up in business and first class, many commercial jets have "special" seats they leave unassigned until the last minute. These are typically saved for handicapped passengers, solo kids, honeymooners, preferred customers, or, assuming none of the aforementioned show up, fellow airline employees. On some Boeing 767s, for example, seats 17A and B and 17H and J are more comfortable coach seats designated as crew rest seats for international flights. On domestic flights, however, these prime seats, like those in the bulkhead and exit rows, remain open until just before takeoff, when, along with some of the unsold business- and first-class seats, they're given to traveling employees and counter-agent favorites. Such as the passenger formerly in 33B who was nice enough to drop off a box of candy and talk to the agent like she was an actual human being, not a prison guard.

Tip Early

When staying in a hotel for more than a day or two, don't wait until the last day to tip the maid. Leave ten bucks on the nightstand the first morning. The maid who cleans the room will do a better job, and she'll make sure she's the one who takes care of you again the next day. She might even be good enough to forgo the daily round that requires her to barge into the room at three thirty in the afternoon when you're on the bed in your underwear watching *SportsCenter*.

If you aren't tipping hotel maids, you need to start. Tipping is a lousy system—business owners should pay their employees a living wage, not force them to beg from paying customers for tips they "depend on to make a living"—but we're stuck with it. As long as we are, it's near criminal not to recognize that hotel maids work much harder than the valets, bellhops, and coffee slingers who get showered with tips every time they lift an eyebrow. Since maids generally exist farther down the socioeconomic ladder, they need the money more, anyway.

Avoid Chinatown

It doesn't matter which one—San Francisco, Vancouver, Toronto, New York, wherever. Every Chinatown in the world distills the worst of the obligatory tourist trap. Most of these brochure institutions are either no longer vital or were fakes in the first place. London's Chinatown, for example, was established way back in 1970—Old Blighty's original dockyard slum of opium dens and red lights was leveled long before that. Unless you belong to a triad or your name is Fast Eddie Chan, Chinatowns offer no surprises. They're loaded with worthless trinkets that look even more worthless once you remove them from the context of reeking fish markets and Chinese calligraphy. There are no public bathrooms; the food's never as good as you think it's going to be; the service blows; the fortune cookies are stale; and since it takes an hour to park, everyone feels compelled to get their money's worth by hanging out well past the point of ennui. Chinatowns have stolen more time from weekend vacations than weather at O'Hare.

Pay Through the Nose—and Like It

If you're going all the way to the Grand Tetons or the Virgin Islands or Rome, pay the upcharge for the nicer room with the panoramic view. You're on vacation—let the travel writers worry about living like an animal on a scratch-and-claw budget. As Robertson Davies wrote, "When one is traveling, one must expect to spend a certain amount of money foolishly." Accept this inevitability with equanimity and you'll enjoy the trip more.

Ignore Jet Lag

Jet lag is a mental game you don't have to lose. The best way to beat it is to pretend it doesn't exist. When you arrive in a new time zone, simply force yourself into a behavior consistent with the local time. Stop being so weak willed. Either that or drop a melatonin pill, the "natural" sleeping pill that actually works without leaving you feeling like a sedated rhino on *Animal Planet*.

The first time I encountered Glasser outside of Japan was at the San Francisco airport. I was in the city for my sister's wedding; he'd come for the sole purpose of introducing me to Gaylord's, the Indian restaurant he'd spent a year waxing rhapsodic about while Shanghai Bob and I picked through the seaweed-wrapped bar snacks at one of Kojima's dismal sake clubs. At SFO, Glasser staggered off the jet bridge like a ghastly shell tumbling out of a boxcar at Auschwitz. He confessed to me a lifelong battle with jet lag that he'd long ago given up hope of winning. Finally, I was in a position to help Glasser off the floor. One melatonin pill and twelve hours later, the man was inhaling tikka masala and saag paneer like it was the last days of the Raj.

Learn Language the Right Way

Language acquisition games and abstract communicative method are bullshit. The second-best way to learn a foreign language is alone in a room doing skull-numbing rote memorization of vocabulary, grammar, key phrases, and colloquialisms. The best way is in bed.

Stop Feeling So Entitled

The numbers thrown around in this chapter—some in the billions—should have been a tip-off to where all of this is heading. For those needing a more detailed accounting of the colossus modern travel has become, here are a few more facts that apply to the United States alone:

Each day in this country, about 1.8 million people travel on thirty thousand flights from approximately 450 commercial airports. That's not even counting general aviation traffic originating from thousands of private airports, 150 of which are in the Dallas area alone. At any given minute during daylight hours, between six thousand and seven thousand aircraft are in the skies over North America. If you get inside the FAA's Air Traffic Control System Command Center (aka "Flow Control") in Herndon, Virginia, and see the real-time computer tracking system that uses a green blip to represent every plane in the air across a map of the United States, you'll see a pulsing mass of solid green with very few open areas.

About 3.2 million hotel rooms are occupied every night in this country. The nation's in-service car rental fleet stands at 1.7 million vehicles. Amtrak carries 25 million passengers a year—68,000 per day. Greyhound hauls 22 million more—60,000 per day. At this very minute, 27,000 North Americans are trying to talk themselves out of a third trip through the buffet line of the cruise ship they're currently fattening up on.

Offensive as it may be to hear, no matter how much you spend on travel, your bottom-line value to the industry is so insignificant that it can't actually be calculated. Feel free to go on and on about how this country was founded upon customer service—it wasn't, by the way, it was founded on tobacco and land speculation—and how the impertinent attitude you received from some overworked assistant manager at an Enterprise car-rental counter is yet another grim indication of the whole country going to hell in a handbasket. You can fly over to Myanmar or Laos or Hong Kong and find whatever bamboo paradise Shanghai Bob is living in right now, knock back thirty or forty beers with him, and have one of the most memorable all-nighters of your life commiserating over the decline of standards and Western civilization. He'll add layers to that discussion you never even dreamed existed. But the fact is there's a reasonable chance that the freight in the belly of the plane you take to see him—invisible to you, commercial goods are the lifeblood of many routes, particularly international ones—will be worth more to the airline than all the passenger fares combined.

When you shout at a reservation agent, "I'm a loyal customer and I'll never stay in this dump again!" or "I'll burn in hell before I spend another dime on this airline," the company thinks, "Good!" They're thrilled to let someone else waste time appeasing a troublemaker. A customer who doesn't conform to the predictive models of consumer behavior is a customer who *costs* the company money.

Cliché that it is, "time is money" is the unofficial motto of every travel company in the world. The time you spend on the phone, waiting in line, hanging out at the gate, en route, standing at the luggage carousel—all of these activities are calculated to the second and penny. Airlines employ teams of engineers to shave seconds off of routes they've been shaving seconds off of for decades. They pay millions to companies like the Preston Group in Australia for software programs that forecast incremental changes that might save them fractions of pennies on "seat mile cost," pennies that translate into millions of dollars a year.

Travel execs care about good customer relations and they do worry about negative word of mouth. But they sleep well enough knowing that disgruntled consumers are a statistically predictable part of the business and that shafted customers get passed around the industry more or less evenly. For every passenger Royal Caribbean loses to Princess, they'll gain one back from Carnival or Holland America. Enterprise, Hertz, Avis, and Budget share the same understanding. So do Northwest, Continental, and JetBlue.

You need proof? In 1986, 47.5 million people flew on American Airlines. Ten years later, the number had grown to 93 million. In 2006, it was up to 130 million. This despite thousands of complaints ranging from mishandled baggage to racial profiling, and stories like a recent *Washington Post* piece (covering the entire industry, not just AA) that ran beneath the headline, "Airlines Rally, but Customer Service Falls." Trust me, if you never fly American again because you got weathered out of Cedar Rapids and some counter agent rebooking her two-hundredth itinerary of the afternoon got a little snippy, they're not going to convene a board meeting because you've decided to take your business to Allegiant Air.

Taking into account its leviathan proportions and considering its essential role in the economy—Boeing is this country's largest single exporter and has been for five decades—the U.S. travel industry is a miracle of efficiency. It's one of the most complex, cooperative, and successful private systems ever constructed. For all the manipulation, the missed connections, bitchy employees, cramped spaces, and thousands of ways it doesn't care about you, the American travel industry's reliability and safety are impossible to beat.

Given their enormity—Denver International Airport covers fifty-three square miles, more than twice the size of Manhattan—modern American airports are operational marvels. At DFW Airport in Dallas, for example, a wildlife control office keeps a freezer filled with birds—barn owls, doves, geese, and so on—collected from troublesome avian populations that refuse to be driven from runway areas. Because birds can damage and potentially bring down a plane if enough of them get sucked into an engine, autopsies are performed on the salvaged birds to determine what they've been eating so that attempts can be made to eradicate their food source. That's called obsessive attention to detail, and an A-plus commitment to safety rarely seen by the public.

Around 658 million passengers took more than 10.5 million domestic flights in this country last year, and pretty much all of them made it there and home. That is probably the most overlooked fact in the entire business, but it's how the real "savvy traveler" views the equation. Achieving the professional's attitude and expertise isn't about lowering expectations. It's about lining them up with reality, then working the angles that are revealed when you pull back the curtain and appreciate what it takes to get the biggest show on earth off the ground in the first place.

9

. . .

Boys Gone Wild: How the Philippines Became the Friendliest Country in the World Despite/Because of the U.S. Military

September 11, 2001, made a decade-old idea of mine fashionable overnight. In 1992, in a ten-by-six, bamboo-veneer room I was renting in the back of an expat bar called Midnight Rambler, not far from the U.S. Naval Base Subic Bay in the Philippines, I sat on a tiny bunk and scribbled down the outline for a book called "A Field Guide to World War II Sites in the Pacific." My idea was to travel to every place where combat had occurred in the Pacific, walk the old battlefields, and document all extant traces of the war, from the fall of Singapore to the assault on Guadalcanal to the signing of the Japanese surrender in Tokyo Bay aboard the USS *Missouri*. The data would be put into a concise travel guide that would give like-minded history geeks the nuts-and-bolts information they needed to locate everything of war-related interest—abandoned tanks in Saipan and the hallowed invasion beaches at Peleliu—a perfect Christmas gift for the man who gets misty in the presence of battleships and black-and-white newsreel footage.

Throughout the nineties, I pitched the proposal to a dozen or so publishers and always got back more or less the same comment: "Interesting idea, too costly to produce." Then came 9/11. Suddenly, patriotism was back in style. "God and country" hadn't been the point of my book, but given recent events and the Greatest Generation spin that accompanies virtually all treatments of World War II, patriotism—not travel or history—revived interest in the project. Two publishers who remembered my proposal called to ask if anyone had ever picked up the rights. I ended up selling the book to Greenline Publications, a small company in San Francisco.

Some might prefer the cafés of Paris or the coast of Spain, but fresh off the *Travelocity* magazine fiasco, the dense foliage of Asia seemed to me a decent place to disappear for a year or so. You say "tomato"; I say "banana ketchup." I shook on the deal and decided to start my research on familiar turf, the Philippines, a country I'd been taking regular trips to for more than a decade.

Arriving in the Philippines for the first time in 1990 was a shock. The tight security at airports that irritates American travelers today had by then long been a way of life in Manila. Only ticketed passengers were allowed inside the airport, a restriction that forced welcome parties to wait in a large fenced pen outside in the tropical heat. Given that entire Filipino villages sometimes empty to herald the return of a beloved cousin, the crush of humanity in front of the arrivals terminal at

Ninoy Aquino International Airport turned the greeting area into a giant rugby scrum.

From the antiseptic tranquility of the airport, I walked past a pair of armed guards into a blinding sun and was confronted by a sea of brown faces, each one mashed against the ten-foot-high chain-link fence. The crowd roared and lunged into the fence as passengers appeared. Taxi drivers stuck their arms through holes in the fence and clawed at my sleeve, offering to take me to whatever I wanted—girls, drinks, drugs, hotels. Above the incomprehensible racket of two thousand people screaming for the attention of two hundred passengers, the humidity descended like a blast furnace, leaving me glazed in a thick sweat. I retreated from this theater of the surreal back into the terminal to figure out my next move.

"Jesus H. Christ," I said to no one in particular. At that moment I heard a voice calling my name. From a hundred yards away I recognized my brother walking toward me and waving.

"I paid a security guard to let me in the terminal," he said, grabbing my bag. "No way you would have found me out there in Thunderdome."

Leaving the chaos in our wake, we drove past the cardboard and sheet-metal shantytown that still surrounds Manila's airport and got on the highway. With his wife and two boys, Mike was stationed at Cubi Point, part of the gargantuan Subic Bay naval base, at the time home to the largest community of Americans (twenty thousand, including dependents) living outside of the United States. Somewhere on the highway, we passed through a time warp. Three hours from the cacophony of Manila, I opened the car door and stepped into 1950s Kansas.

America's large overseas military bases operate as if the last fifty years never happened. More wholesome than Ward and June Cleaver's annual missionary hump, they're an isolated nirvana where all is clean and orderly, flags fly from every building, and children are never late for school. Men go to work during the week and fire up the backyard grill on weekends. Shopping, cooking, and household chores are the domain of wives and domestic help drawn from the local population, young women who often become integral parts of the family structure. Pulling up to Mike's house inside the base, I noticed a sign on the lawn.

"We won this month's 'nicest yard' competition," Mike said, explaining the placard. "Second time this year."

The Philippine town that neighbored this airtight island of Americana was called Olongapo. It was to Subic what Woodstock once was to upstate New York. Each day at the base's main gate, navy, marine, and air force personnel—squids, jarheads, and zoomies, in the argot of the culture—dropped their facades of military sobriety as they left Little America and dove into the shameless intoxication provided by a town that existed to meet a military man's every need and desire.

Following the primal call of metal, hip-hop, and other stripper music blasting from giant sound systems in bars abutting the base, America's finest crossed a small bridge over the "Shit River"—a chunky flow of open sewage that separated the United States from the Philippines in the same disconcerting way that rivers, ditches, and gullies separate prosperous America from down-at-the-heels Mexican border towns. First stop in Olongapo was the row of smiling money changers, where U.S. dollars were traded for "carnival tickets," the military's euphemism for Philippine pesos and an indication of the arrogance of the Americans who patronized the legendary collection of go-go bars, taverns, and whorehouses that awaited along neon-lit Magsaysay Boulevard and Gordon Avenue.

Top Gun, Florida Club, Hard Rock, Solid Gold Disco, Cindy Bar, Body Shop. Unanimously regarded as the most potent arrow in the navy's quiver of reenlistment incentives, Olongapo's bars came fully loaded with available women, San Miguel beer, and Tanduay rum. In the economically depressed P.I. (as military men have always called the Philippine Islands), recruits who struggled with menial jobs back home found that their navy paychecks vaulted them near the top of Olongapo's economic ladder. Like thousands of Ray Liottas in *Goodfellas*, eighteen- and nineteen-year-old kids suddenly had the run of the town, blowing wads of cash on cars, women, alcohol, weed, blow, and whatever else they wanted, then going back to "Mom" (enlistee-speak for the U.S. Navy) for another pile and starting over the next week.

An army may travel on its stomach, but it sets up camp around booze and poontang. Olongapo provided sparkly diversion to the thousands of men permanently stationed in Subic and millions of round hats who over the decades poured off American ships like second graders set free for recess. Olongapo was the U.S. Navy's last great liberty port, a Wild West, free-for-all holdover from the World War II and Vietnam eras that, as one young marine assured me on my first visit there, "made anything in Bangkok look like a Campfire Girls bake sale."

Having seen both red-light strips operating at full bore, as well as Singapore's famed "four floors of whores" and other landmarks of Asian debauchery, I believed I was in a position to judge the respective levels of decadence on offer across the region. I told the marine that though there was much in Bangkok to recommend to a man of libertine interests, I couldn't argue his basic premise that for widespread depravity, Olongapo was impossible to beat. He beamed like a lighthouse at this pronouncement, declared us the kind of guys who could be buddies back home, then wandered off to hoot at a pair of bar girls in micro-miniskirts stepping out of a cab down the street.

I traveled to Subic Bay twice in 1990, first in August, just days after Saddam Hussein invaded Kuwait. By the time I arrived, the American government had already begun its massive military buildup in the Middle East under the umbrella Operation Desert Shield, and President Bush I was putting together what looked like an authentic coalition to stand up to the Iraqi aggression. By the time I returned to Subic in late December, Wolf Blitzer had become a household name, and the imminent invasion of Kuwait by U.S. forces was only weeks away.

Always alive with military commotion, Olongapo that December was electric. Subic Bay had been designated a major staging area for Operation Desert Storm. Seventh Fleet troop ships from the West Coast by way of Pearl Harbor were arriving almost hourly, dropping their anchors in the harbor and disgorging an endless stream of combat-primed soldiers ready for one last liberty before war.

Through the sterility of press conferences and grittier field correspondence, it's possible to get a sense of the American fighting man's dedication to duty. These staged affairs do not, however, convey the gut-churning thrill of watching an army united behind a single purpose assembling for battle before your eyes. During that last week of December, I spoke with dozens of sailors, marines, and flight crew around Subic, and what remains most vivid nearly seventeen years later is the absolute certainty they felt in their mission and their unwavering support, without exception, of the orders issued by their commander in chief.

The run-up to the Gulf War was the last great spasm in the long history of Subic Bay, and it peaked on New Year's Eve 1990 in Olongapo. Following an anxiety-filled month of interminable sea voyages, combat maneuvers, and amphibious landing exercises with names like Operation Quick Thrust, most of the troops heading to the Persian Gulf already had their orders to ship out after the first of the year. Word of what was going on at Subic spread throughout the provinces, and by Christmas every bar girl, dancer, marriage hopeful, and straight-up streetwalker in the country had descended on Olongapo alongside an army of drug dealers, tattoo artists, pimps, and pickpockets to work the exodus.

I was up early on New Year's Eve, but Olongapo hadn't even gone to bed. At eight in the morning, Magsaysay Boulevard looked like Times Square. Every bar was open, every stage jammed with bikini-wrapped girls, every million-dollar sound system on the strip shook the earth with Guns N' Roses, AC/DC, Metallica, and the miraculous sound-alike Filipino cover bands who played even louder renditions of the same. In front of a club called Sierra, I stopped on the street and watched small clouds of dust literally being stirred up by the sonic waves rumbling from the wall of speakers inside.

A lone American didn't have to stay that way long. You couldn't walk ten paces without a girl appearing in a doorway, throwing an arm around you, and trying to drag you inside for a drink. Sailors with two and three dusky hotties clamped around them spilled out of jeepneys, staggered into bars, groped their trophies on sidewalks, and retired to hotel rooms for "short time" recreation before flinging themselves back into the bedlam. Fireworks exploded throughout the day, at times so powerful and sustained that drunken marines assumed a live-fire ordnance test was taking place on a training range across the Shit River.

After wandering around the circus for a couple hours, I ended up in a restaurant where I bumped into a well-spoken navy-enlisted guy I'd met in a bar earlier in the week. Over beers we'd gotten into a friendly debate, and though we disagreed on many issues, I'd come away impressed with his sensitivity and historical insight into the forces and plans at play in the Middle East. In the restaurant he recognized me, left his besotted companions in the company of a gaggle of laughing teenage girls, and brought his plate over to my table. We immediately picked up the geopolitical discussion we'd left off days before.

Minutes later a slightly chubby Filipina shortie with large eyes and a flapper haircut sashayed across the room and asked if she could join us. We made space and she got down to business, placing a warm hand on each of our thighs and offering backroom hummers at a considerable discount. My amiable buddy accepted at once. The cordial apology he extended as he draped his arm around the girl and stood up led to a brief conversation that now strikes me as one of the most absurd in my life.

"You mind?" he said, nodding at the girl.

"No, not at all," I said. "Go right ahead."

"Don't let them take my plate away. I'll be back in a few minutes."

And he was, with a smile on his face, completely at ease with himself, to finish our discussion of troop deployments, Iraq's Revolutionary Guard, and the putative effectiveness of smart bombs. There's a lot to admire in soldiers. There's a lot to deplore. And there's a lot that leaves you shaking your head.

In any review of the Philippines, particularly one written from an American perspective, military operations must provide the backdrop, if only to stick a finger in the dyke of the public's stunning ignorance about the war machine it's been feeding for the last century. History isn't necessarily Americans' trump suit, but that's no reason to stop telling people about the touched-by-an-angel similarities between presidents G. W. Bush and William McKinley, why Japan really bombed Pearl Harbor, and what made a guy named Robert Beightler one of the biggest jackasses in U.S. Army history.

The 7,107 islands of the Philippine archipelago stretch like a curse across one of the most strategically valuable expanses of ocean in the world. From deep-water ports in the Philippines, a military or merchant fleet has direct access to shipping lanes that feed most of East Asia, including China, Taiwan, Vietnam, Thailand, Malaysia, Singapore, Indonesia, and in a pinch, Japan and Korea. This was true a thousand years ago and it's true today. It's the reason why at some point in your lifetime, battles will once again be fought over control of the Philippines.

As the eighty languages and dialects spoken by its people attest, "the Philippines" is one of those products of colonial convenience, not ethnic, religious, or political reality. Scattered in early times with independent merchant fiefdoms established by seafaring Malays, Chinese, Muslims, and other groups, the islands became a political collective only after the Spanish arrived to claim them in the name of King Philip II. Spain's rule began in 1565 and ended in 1898 when the Spanish-American War was settled with a treaty giving the United States—which had recently squashed the Spanish fleet in Manila Bay—dominion over the Philippines, as well as a rapidly swelling head as it thundered into the twentieth century.

Having endured three-hundred-plus years of Catholic muskets, the locals were less than thrilled about another crop of sanctified foreigners putting them to work in cane fields and shipyards, then siphoning the profits back home. Eager for independence, the Filipinos fought the Americans in a vicious, atrocity-filled war that lasted almost three years, involved at its peak seventy thousand U.S. troops in the field, and left as many as two hundred thousand Filipinos dead. Historians now consider the village-burning, civilian-terrorizing, small-unit jungle fighting in the Philippines to be a precursor to the Vietnam War. The P.I. is where words such as "gook" and "quagmire" entered the American lexicon to describe fighting in Southeast Asia.

In the Philippines this period is referred to as the Philippine-American War. In the United States, if it's mentioned at all, it's called the Philippine "insurrection," proving once again that political euphemisms never die, they just get recycled by sleazy campaign advisers. Though now largely forgotten, the "war" or "insurrection" was, much like Iraq, the singular political question that gripped Americans around the turn of the century. The defining issue of the 1900 presidential campaign, the Philippines was America's first foray into European-style colonialism. Debate in Washington over whether the nation should head down this unholy path was bitter and divisive.

In favor of enveloping the Philippines in a snuggly Yankee Doodle embrace were such heavyweights as Teddy Roosevelt and President William McKinley, the latter of whom claimed God had specifically told him to annex the islands. Opposing were prickly moralists such as Andrew Carnegie and Mark Twain, the latter of whom suggested that the new Philippine flag might be "just our usual flag, with the white stripes painted black and the stars replaced by the skull and crossbones." Like social critics such as Jon Stewart today, Twain won the war of words, but the imperialists won the congressional vote. The United States officially declared sovereignty over the Philippines in 1902, and for the next four decades proceeded to run the place like a combination military base/Christian youth camp.

Unhappy with America's creeping influence into

what it considered its rightful sphere of rape and pillage, Japan seized the Philippines from the United States in December 1941. Most Americans know December 7 as the date that will live in infamy, but Pearl Harbor was only one American target attacked by the Japanese that day and was, in fact, something of a sideshow. The Japanese attacked Pearl Harbor to cripple the U.S. fleet anchored there, thus ensuring that its roughly simultaneous invasions of the Philippines, Guam, Malaysia, and, eventually, Singapore wouldn't be seriously threatened. In the Pacific, Southeast Asia, not Hawaii, is where the significant ground action of the early war took place.

Japan controlled the Philippines from 1942 until late 1944. When American forces returned, they came with such a vengeance that they burned the capital city of Manila to the ground. This was done to save the lives of American invaders and to make the kind of statement back-from-the-dead militaries love to deliver to friend and foe alike. In his activity report for the Thirty-seventh Infantry Division, General Robert Beightler, among the chief architects of the indiscriminate artillery attacks that killed one hundred thousand Filipino civilians, tactfully wrote: "I have no apologies to make. . . . So much for Manila. It is a ruined city—unhealthy, depressing, poverty stricken. Let us thank God our cities have been spared such a fate."

After most of the country's assets had been reduced to smoking rubble, the United States kindly gave the Philippines its independence—with conditions. These included the continuing presence of massive American military installations (presumed necessary to thwart budding Russian ambitions in the region) and political sway that would ensure guys like Ferdinand Marcos could remain in power long enough to empty the country's bank accounts before retiring to a Hawaiian estate. In the postwar period, the United States poured vast capital into reconstructing its former enemy Japan into a first-rate economic titan. Meanwhile, the P.I. struggled to rebuild itself.

After all of this war and destruction and betrayal, you'd think the people of the Philippines would hate us. By "us," I don't just mean Americans, but Muslims, Spaniards, Chinese, Japanese, and any other group that has arrived through the years to extract what resources they could from the islands while exploiting its inhabitants. And yet the Filipinos don't hate us. After centuries of foreign oppression and injustice, Filipinos remain the most optimistic, friendly, and generous people on the planet. In a world of takers, they inexplicably remain givers. Which is why, despite the abundant poverty, natural disasters, and man-made catastrophes, whenever I'm asked what my favorite travel destination is—travel writers get this question all the time—I always say the Philippines.

Though you wouldn't have gotten hundred-to-one odds on the proposition at the time, within two years of the Gulf War, the virile arsenal of democracy at Subic Bay and the riotous business center of Olongapo had become ghost towns. Obviating the need for a cosmic military presence in Southeast Asia, the close of the Cold War dovetailed neatly with the rise of rancorous nationalism within the Philippine Senate and the end of the United States' lease agreement with the Filipino government. Despite overwhelming Filipino public support in favor of keeping the Americans, the military base leases were not renewed. America's permanent military presence in the P.I. ended when the last American warship, the helicopter carrier USS *Belleau Wood*, pulled out of Subic Bay on November 24, 1992. Amid a flood of tears and heartfelt speeches, the American flag was lowered. For the first time in four centuries, the Philippines were free of foreign military forces.

Three months later I was back in Olongapo doing interviews and gathering data for a project called "Filipino Relations at Home and Abroad," for which I'd received a grant from an Alaskan group with a connection to the National Endowment for the Humanities. The study was supposed to examine all manner of ties between the two countries, but the American military departure had left such a deep gash on the Filipino psyche that no one was able to talk about anything else. Its fallout quickly overwhelmed my project, turning it into a sort of social-impact study that flattered the Filipinos but which few Americans outside the Alaska Humanities Forum ended up caring about.

Walking down Magsaysay Boulevard in winter 1993 was like taking a tour through your worst hangover. Buildings were abandoned or gutted. The concert-strength sound systems were gone. Neon signs hung at crooked angles, their bulbs looted or punched out. In the few clubs trying to stick out the economic collapse, lone barmen waited for customers who never showed. Here and there a hostess stood in front of an empty restaurant. If the Philippines had tumbleweeds, they'd have been blowing down the street.

The most conspicuous legacy of the party were the Amerasian children—"souvenirs" they were called—left behind by American fathers. An estimated fifty thousand such kids were scattered around the country, at least three thousand in Olongapo. In more than a few pairs of the green and blue eyes juxtaposed against brown skin, one sensed the expectation of a future as bleak as the present.

Until recently the domain of navy officers and vacationers, upscale apartments and houses were renting for around ten or twenty dollars a day. Since I was going to be in the country for several months, I looked for one near the beach. The first place I checked out had a large banyan tree in front, new tile and counters in the kitchen, some decent leftover rattan furniture, and views of the gorgeous bay rimmed by brown and green hills. I was about to say, "I'll take it," when I stepped onto the balcony and tasted in my throat the sickly sweet effluvium of rotting flesh. I gagged reflexively and looked down to find the corpse of a headless pig decomposing in the grass below me.

From February to May I conducted interviews around the country, and although the military was gone, there was no shortage of trouble to get into. Traveling mostly by bus, I absorbed by osmosis the protocols of the country's intricate rural routes, a peculiarity of which led to one of my few uncomfortable encounters with locals in the P.I. Because control of commercial activity remains defiantly tribal in the Philippines, no single national bus line is allowed to service the entire country. Operating within strictly defined territories helps to protect minor corporate empires, but it can freight such simple acts as transferring buses with perilous consequences.

This I learned at three thirty on the blackest morning I've ever been awake for when my overnight bus from Ifugao to Olongapo stopped abruptly in the middle of the two-lane jungle track it had been speeding down for the past hour. The tough-looking ticket taker—in addition to the driver, P.I. buses have a guy who collects money and oversees the passengers—stood in front of me.

"You go Olongapo?"

I nodded.

"Get out here."

I looked out the window. It was as if we'd stopped inside a cave.

"Is there a bus station?"

"Not here," the ticket taker said. "Wait on side of road. Another bus come pick you up."

"How will I know which bus?"

"Is only one bus."

"How long till it comes?"

"Soon."

No one else was getting off. I looked outside again. No lights, no people, no buildings of any kind. The idling of the bus suggested comfort and safety to me, whereas the side of the road in the middle of what I was guessing was the Benguet province suggested a long, lonely wait.

"Here? Are you sure?" I was practically begging him to change his mind.

"You get off now or wind up in Ilocos."

I stood on the roadside watching the taillights of the bus being swallowed by the darkness. The chatter of the diesel engine disappeared. Not a sound from bird nor cricket moved into the dead calm to replace it.

Nothing is more tedious than waiting for a ride you're not sure is coming. For fifteen minutes I fought off a gnawing suspicion that I'd been dumped in the wrong spot. I walked up the road a hundred yards in both directions and found no sign of life.

And then something stirred in the bushes. Far ahead of me, a human outline, then another, emerged from the tall grass that lined the road. Two silhouettes began coming toward me. I squinted hard—two males, one carrying a long, narrow object that swayed from his hand. As they neared, two more men popped out from the bushes to my left, barely twenty yards away. There was something weird about their stiff posture. I knew right away they'd been in the high grass watching me since the moment the bus had driven off. Their appearance was followed by more rustling and more strangers.

With terrifying speed I went from being a guy waiting for a bus on the side of the road to a target surrounded by eight Filipino men in the middle of a deserted jungle highway. They wore loose-fitting jeans and old T-shirts with holes and stains, items most likely donated by American charities and picked up cheap at local markets. In Tagalog they spoke to each other, but not to me. Two of the men carried machetes—that was the long, narrow object I'd seen—which they swung slowly like pendulums, back and forth, back and forth, as the group appraised me. All farmers in the Philippines carry machetes, but these guys hadn't been out plowing the north forty in the middle of the night.

The leader was medium height, more round than angular, with wavy black hair, thick eyebrows, and what was, given the circumstances, a gracious smile. After a nerve-wracking moment of silence, he introduced himself, asked for my name, and, for whatever reason, told me that he was twenty-seven years old. I was so freaked out I couldn't recall his name, even the next day, but I've always thought of him as Rivera, because that was the name of a particularly breakneck member of the suicide-squad kickoff team at Oregon when I went to school there, and because I did remember the guy on the roadside rolling a couple of *r*'s in that distinctive staccato Filipino way.

"Is this the place to catch the bus for Olongapo?" I asked Rivera, trying to ignore the film of sweat crawling across my back.

"I think maybe. Why are you going to Olongapo, Chuck?"

Someone had taught Rivera the salesman's trick of establishing rapport by repeating the mark's name, but hadn't mentioned that overusing it was more creepy than congenial. I told him about the research project and my apartment in Olongapo.

"I don't like Olongapo, Chuck," he said. "The countryside is much nicer than the city. Don't you like my province?"

I told him his province was impressive. He said I should see it in the daylight when I could appreciate its beauty.

"You shouldn't travel alone at night," Rivera told me. "Foreigners are often kidnapped in these mountains."

As we spoke, Rivera edged within inches of my face. Rural Filipinos are generally as tough as bricks, and I'm generally not, but I did have size on Rivera, and to some extent, my back was against the wall. If the situation were going to be decided by desperate moves, I'd have taken my chances in a fight. Reading my mind, the posse tightened its ring around me.

"How much money are you carrying, Chuck?" Rivera asked me.

I strained my eyes down the road trying to will a pair of headlights into existence. It had been twenty minutes since the bus dropped me off, and not a single vehicle had passed.

"Not much money," I said. "Ten U.S." In fact, I had about two hundred, but ten bucks for a solo traveler was a believable figure in the province.

"You must carry credit cards. What kind do you have? Visa?"

"No cards, just a little cash."

"I don't think your bus will be coming soon." Rivera brushed my forearm with his fingertips. "Would you like to spend the night with us?"

I said I hadn't seen any houses nearby. He told me the name of his village and said it was along a trail just behind the road. It probably was. I'd heard of entire platoons walking within ten feet of villages in Vietnam and never seeing so much as a rooftop through the darkened jungle. Rivera feigned sadness when I declined his offer, but he kept after me about it, resting his hand on my shoulder while I tried to casually pivot away.

"Chuck, tell me something. Why are you insulting me?"

"I'm not insulting you. I'm waiting for my bus."

"For we Filipinos hospitality is a way of life. When you refuse our hospitality, it is seen by us as an insult."

"I'm sorry you feel that way, and I genuinely appreciate the offer. But I really need to get back to Olongapo."

It was still dark, but Rivera was so close I could see he was looking into my eyes.

"Chuck, tell me something," he said. "Have you ever had sex with a gay man?"

For the single male traveler, homosexual come-ons are, like delays at JFK and overpriced hotel food, a part of the process to which one grows accustomed. I've been pick-up quarry in the United States, Japan, Palau, and several other ports of call. In Lençóis, Brazil, a chatty American tourist sitting next to me at a hotel bar broached the sub-ject by saying, "Well, I guess you know why I've taken such an interest in talking with you." I told him I didn't, he explained, I said there had been some sort of misun-derstanding, he apologized, bought me a beer, and we ended up talking for another hour.

Rivera wasn't like that. For starters, no gay man I'd ever met had come with a retinue of machete-wielding bodyguards. You expect to see that kind of thing onstage with Madonna, not on the side of the road in Benguet province.

"You know what," I said to Rivera as confidently as I could, "I haven't had sex with a gay man, and I'm really not at all interested."

"Maybe I could change your mind, Chuck."

"I doubt it."

Rivera worked the how-do-you-know-you-won't-like-it-till-you've-tried-it angle as though arguing with a kid refusing to eat his lima beans. I told him I'd held out on smoking pot for my entire high school career, and after I'd broken down later I decided I didn't care for it any-way. This line of argument had a long history of failure with me.

If this was something beyond a very aggressive pickup, it had at least been fairly civilized, but by now we'd run out of things to say, and each of us sensed the time for action was at hand. Between fight, flight, or diplomacy, none of my options looked promising. And then, as if conjured by a magician, a pair of faint, yellow orbs blinked in the distance.

As kids roaming the Juneau streets late at night, we played a game called beady eyeballs. It was a straightforward sport that required the player to stand in the middle of the Loop Road—basically our highway—until a pair of headlights, or "beady eyeballs," appeared in the distance. The player then engaged in a game of chicken with the oncoming vehicle, holding his ground as the eyeballs became larger, leaping out of tragedy's way at the last possible instant, scaring the hell out of the driver and confirming his own bravado with the preadolescent peers laid out laughing and critiquing in the ditch. I was pretty good at beady eyeballs, and now for the first and only time in my adult life, I had a chance to revisit that glorious career. Nothing was going to get me out of the middle of the road.

Rivera knew what was on the way before I did. He and his gang backed toward the shoulder of the cracked asphalt. My feet might as well have been cast in concrete. When I heard the whine of the big engine and saw the boxy shape of the bus taking form, I began waving frantically.

No orchestra in the world ever hit a note as sweet as the pneumatic hiss of that Victory Liner bus door opening. I didn't ask which direction we were heading, just grabbed my bag, blew past the ticket taker, and found an empty seat next to a window. On the road outside, the Benguet gang shadowed my progress as I walked down the aisle.

"Nice meeting you, Chuck," Rivera said, raising his hand through the open window. "Please don't travel alone at night anymore. It is not always safe here in the province."

"Keep in touch," I said as the bus began rolling and our hands fell apart.

My brush with gay machete sex notwithstanding, I've never felt more at risk in the Philippines than in any other country. But it's true that strange things often happen in the Land of the Not Quite Right (as expats used to call it), and stories like mine from Benguet make the P.I. a staple of books such as Fielding's *The World's Most Dangerous Places*. It's a shame, but the fact stands that potential sodomy is more entertaining than clement weather, reliable public services, and obedient citizenry. After prostitution, "kidnapping" and "terrorism" are the words that many people associate with the P.I. Lured by such newsworthy qualities in the late '90s, *Escape* magazine offered to send me to Mindanao, the southernmost major island in the Philippines, center of Islamic culture, and home to its most notorious citizens.

Mindanao appealed to *Escape* for the same reason Colombia appealed to *Maxim*: danger. If Intrepid Reporter could walk into the P.I.'s treacherous Muslim-controlled rebel territory and come out with all his limbs attached, fabulous. If he managed to get himself taken hostage or simply disappeared in the forbidding territory, all the better.

Collectively called Moros, the Muslim peoples of Mindanao are by any standard among the toughest and most resilient in the world. While the rest of the P.I. was being subdued by four centuries of foreign colonization, the Moros never stopped fighting for their independence. The Moros are a case study in why you should never, ever expect Muslims to stop fighting any attempts to occupy or exploit lands they consider their own.

Early in the American attempt to pacify the Philippines' restive Islamic fundamentalists, Colonel Louis La Garde testified before an armaments board to the indomitable will of the Moros that had stunned U.S. forces. Telling of a relentless Moro who'd charged a group of Americans, La Garde described an entire squad opening fire on the man from a hundred yards away. Through a hail of bullets, the Filipino continued to charge. Just five yards from the firing party, he finally fell, but continued to struggle. It took a shot through the head with a .45-caliber Colt revolver to kill him and end the grisly incident.

"There were ten wounds in his body from the service rifle," said La Garde. "Three of the wounds were located in the chest, one in the abdomen, and the remainder had taken effect in the extremities. There were no broken bones." All that in addition, of course, to the bullet through the skull.

America is still fighting Muslims in Mindanao. A few weeks after 9/11, the Pentagon sent Special Forces and other troops to the island to deal with Abu Sayyaf, the Muslim separatist group charged with running terrorist camps there. Organizations such as the Moro Islamic Liberation Front—known by the unintentionally agreeable acronym MILF—also drew American attention. Before the Iraq invasion, Mindanao was for a brief time the "second front," after Afghanistan, in the war on terror. It remains today the focus of U.S. antiterrorism efforts in Southeast Asia.

Even Mindanaons are afraid of Mindanao. One of my duties for *Escape* in 1997 was to check out a medium-sized city in the interior of the island called Marawi, regarded as the burning and bloody heart of Muslim culture in the country. In the Philippines, taxis and eager drivers are as common as palm trees. But it took most of the morning in the coastal city of Cagayan de Oro to find someone daring enough to make the run to Marawi. The first two guys I asked laughed in my face.

"Marawi? Too dangerous," they said.

"What's dangerous?"

"For the foreigner, kidnappers, Muslims."

"What about for Filipinos?"

"This year, more than once, a taxi goes to Marawi from Cagayan and does not return. The driver is found in Lake Lanao. The car is never recovered."

"Marawi is a Muslim city," they concluded, laying the matter to rest in terms that even a dumbshit with a death wish should have grasped.

Eventually I came across a paunchy, fortyish guy with rheumy eyes named Carlos. He tripled his price, sucked on his teeth with disapproval, and agreed to take me on the condition that we return by nightfall. Two hours later, twenty miles from Marawi, Carlos's already stoic face had become a death mask.

"We are in Muslim territory now." He mumbled the words like an epitaph as veiled women, soldiers in jungle fatigues carrying M16s, and the distinctive onion shapes of mosque domes began to appear out of the sweltering jungle. We eased into town and soon got bogged down in a traffic snarl on a crowded street.

" '*Marumi*' means 'dirty' in Tagalog," Carlos said, pointing at a garbage can spilled across a sidewalk. "Sometimes we call Marawi City 'Marumi City' because it's so dirty."

For most of the drive, Carlos had been sociable and courteous—two virtues that define almost every Filipino I've ever known. But his Muslim paranoia was getting me down and, as this was my first overseas gig for *Escape*, I didn't want to miss any opportunity to get myself killed. I grabbed my camera and hopped out of the car, telling Carlos to circle the block a few times.

"Mr. Thompson, do not get out here!" he shouted. "Wait for a safer place!"

For a second it looked like Carlos's fears might be justified. I hadn't walked twenty yards from the car before a guy in a long, loose-fitting blue robe intercepted me in the street, grabbed my arm, and insisted I come with him. Since he was old and seemed more friendly than hostile, I followed him. He turned out to be a corn dealer who said he wanted to personally welcome me to Marawi. In his shop, hundreds of pounds of shucked corn were drying in the ninety-degree heat. He invited me to inspect his product and delivered a short speech about the importance of corn and coconuts as Mindanao cash crops. He introduced me to his three daughters—all wearing black veils over their heads, but not their faces— who helped him run the business. As I left the store, the old man forced a glass of water on me, shook my hand like he was mixing cookie batter, and smiled as if he were seeing off one of his five sons.

All over town the reception was the same. Two men

who sold furniture waved me in off the sidewalk and offered me food and water. At a busy intersection, a cop made a big show of stopping traffic and personally escorted me across his street while drivers hung out their windows praising Allah on my behalf. Instead of being threatened in Marawi, I felt like a long-lost nephew dropped into someone's family reunion, smothered by an endless stream of kissy aunts and sloshed uncles. I wandered for an hour chatting up the locals before finding Carlos parked in an alley, stewing in the front seat.

"Seems like a decent place," I said, trying to buck up the lump beside me. "Let's go grab some lunch."

Carlos stared through the windshield. He rebuked me for running off and reminded me of the fate of the cabbies who had been fished out of Lake Lanao. I said I understood his position but reminded him how much I was paying and that I hadn't come all the way to Marawi just to look out the windows.

"Frankly, I don't think you're giving these people a fair shake," I said. "I could've eaten ten free meals in the last hour if I'd wanted."

"It is true; most Muslims are good people," Carlos finally allowed. "But the Muslim problem is they have some very bad element. If they have problem, their solution is murder and kidnap. If Christian has problem, they are not murder and kidnap people."

"Maybe from the Muslim perspective the Christians have the national army and Americans to do their dirty work."

"There is truth in this. What you say is what we already know."

"So, there are problems on both sides. Maybe there's hope for us yet."

"Yes. As long as we are out of town by dark."

At Marawi's central mosque, people finally seemed more intent on their own business than mine. Carlos and I met a thin, middle-aged man named Ahmad.

"Perhaps it is an incongruous combination to you, these banana trees and mosques," Ahmad joked as best he could in his formal English.

"Maybe a little surprising," I said diplomatically. "But not necessarily out of place."

Carlos smiled politely but said nothing. After Ahmad went inside the mosque, I finally gave in to Carlos's simmering impatience and headed back toward the car. He smiled and said his wife and children would be relieved to see him. Like a stable horse turned around toward home, he drove twice as fast on the way back, and we made it to Cagayan de Oro in time for cocktails.

It wasn't the war on terror but a more romantic conflict that brought me back to the Philippines in 2002. Since it's impossible for anyone under thirty to recall a time when carrying an American passport abroad didn't make you the biggest douche bag in the room, it's only natural that the media has made a fetish of World War II, the crowning social, technical, and military achievement in American history. The site of some of the Pacific theater's most critical battles—names like Bataan, Corregidor, Leyte, and Manila still resonate with many Americans—the Philippines was the first stop on my twenty-five-site Asian tour for the World War II travel-guide project.

One of the poorest provinces in the Philippines, Leyte is a ninety-mile-long island where little has changed since the B-29 Superfortress ruled the skies and if you were American, your name was automatically "Hey, Joe!" When I was there, the airport used the same runway laid out by American Seabees during the war. Down the coast a plaque still marks the spot where in 1944 a stealthy former Boy Scout named Valeriano Abello used semaphore flags to alert American warships to the locations of entrenched Japanese defenders.

"Don't bomb beaches," he waved. "There are civilians. Let me direct the shellings."

After anxious debate aboard the ships, the American invaders gambled that Abello wasn't a Japanese plant. They flashed a reply: "Come immediately—awaiting."

Credited with risking his own life to save countless others, Abello became a local hero. He died on the island in 1999. World War II is full of these kinds of amazing stories, which is why its legacy will never die and the History Channel will never go off the air.

Leyte's pièce de résistance is a larger-than-life bronze sculpture near the village of Palo depicting the famous landing party led by General Douglas MacArthur. It was here in 1944 that MacArthur made good on his famous "I Shall Return" promise by wading ashore after the U.S. Navy had obliterated the Japanese fleet in the Battle of Leyte Gulf. MacArthur had been commander of all armed forces in the Philippines when the Japanese attacked in 1941. After his humiliating withdrawal from the islands, his subordinates were forced to surrender seventy-eight thousand Fil-Am troops to the Japanese, the largest capitulation of soldiers in American history. The ensuing Bataan Death March endured by many of those men remains the United States' most grievous battlefield disaster.

MacArthur's return was redemption not only for him but the entire Philippines, which suffered often inhuman brutality under Japanese military rule. Controversial among American veterans and historians, in the P.I., MacArthur is revered to this day with something approaching religious idolatry. His 1961 "sentimental journey" to the Philippines—his first visit since the end of the war—arguably marked the twentieth-century high point of American prestige throughout Asia, even if the general had to make the trip without "Dimples," his longtime Filipina mistress, whose existence proved that under the stars and chest decorations MacArthur had a heart and taste for Filipina babes like any other grunt.

"To the Filipinos, he was nothing less than superhuman," wrote journalist Stanley Karnow, who covered MacArthur's valedictory visit and later authored the best book yet written about the Philippines, *In Our Image*. Along Mac's parade route, thousands of admirers leaned from windows, climbed lampposts, waved signs proclaiming him "Our Savior," and surrounded his car for fleeting glimpses of the legend. Children sang to him. Girls threw flowers in his path.

Even if you don't care for bumpy runways and malaria-filled jungles, the Philippine provinces are great reminders that the world really did once love Americans. In Leyte, the goodwill remains. As I walked the shore in front of the MacArthur monument at Red Beach, a raspy "Hey, Joe" caught my attention. A short, wiry older guy with a few knocked-out teeth was walking my way with quick, tiny steps. He asked if I was American and invited me to his house a few minutes up the beach.

Three middle-aged guys sat outside the hut, smoking

cigarettes and, alarmingly it seemed to me, passing around an old plastic jug of Prestone antifreeze. The jug was filled with a nuclear orange fluid, which they poured into small glasses and guzzled. The old guy introduced me to his pals, and they introduced me to *tuba*, the P.I.'s famed homemade hooch made from the sap of a coconut tree. Once the fermenting process begins, the sap turns sour after a few days. Eight to twelve weeks later, it becomes pure vinegar. Somewhere in between it's pronounced *tuba* and declared ready for combat.

The boys offered me a taste. It went down like a rake through gravel. I shook my head and looked at the sediment in the bottom of the empty glass. The Prestone carafe suddenly made sense. Whatever dregs of radiator coolant were left over presumably made the *tuba* taste better.

I coughed and said, "Thank you, sir, may I have another?" The guys ate this up and poured me a second round. I threw it back and made a violent stab at my water bottle.

People who ridicule bottled water as the pinnacle of American consumer gullibility must not travel much. What those critics fail to realize is that we aren't buying the water, we're buying the bottle. More to the point, we're buying mobility. In places like Leyte, invaluable peace of mind comes from knowing there's always a clean rinse handy in the event you cut open your leg on a thorny plant or are called upon to pour rancid coconut sap down your throat. Make fun of bottled water all you like, it won't change the fact that it has opened obscure back roads and *tuba* socials to millions of travelers.

The boys and I sat outside doing *tuba* shots for an hour. Instead of drinking, the old guy talked. He'd been a kid during the war and had ended up working for twenty years in the ship-repair facilities at Subic Bay. All of his stories placed Americans in a supremely positive light, which I assumed was meant to put his somewhat *tuba*-wary American guest at ease. Given all the Philippines had been through, I told him I found his uncompromising support of the United States a little surprising.

"We still love you guys," he said through the cigarette smoke and *tuba* fumes. "See all those people back there?" He meant the MacArthur monument. "Leyte's shrine is a national treasure. At least once in their life, every Filipino will visit this place to pay their respects."

I asked him if he thought America was still the same country it had been in MacArthur's day. He waved his hand in front of his face.

"I've been talking to guys like you since 1944," he said. "Only the haircut changes. You know what I tell everyone who complains about the Americans? I was there in 1992 when all the guys shipped out to the Middle East. I supported them. I worked for them. Do you know why? Because they did the same job there that General MacArthur did here. You tell me something. What would the Middle East look like today if the Americans didn't kick Saddam Hussein's butt out of Kuwait?"

I told him I had no idea. Before he could reply, one of the guys leaned over with the Prestone jug and said, "Have some more *tuba* and maybe you'll be able to figure it out."

After photographing the MacArthur monument from every possible angle, inspecting the silent guns of

Corregidor, and walking and driving the length of the Bataan Death March, I finished my World War II research in Manila. Like Bangkok, Jakarta, and a handful of other festering, beggar-laden Third World megatropolises, Manila is one of the great sprawling shitholes of Asia, a reeking mess of poverty, traffic, smog, crime, corruption, and filth. Bursting with people who somehow maintain a bulletproof optimism in the face of decay, disorder, and daily tragedy, these are frenetic slum-cities where anything, from blow jobs to military coups, can happen at any time. Cities that you love just slightly more than you loathe.

For those unacquainted with the region, "sprawling Asian shithole" is employed as a term of endearment and does not apply, for instance, to cities such as Seoul, which are simply sprawling and Asian and shitty while lacking any sense of the epic or unexpected. Against my advice, Glasser once took a yearlong teaching job in Seoul, and the debriefings he sent as his tenure dragged on bore increasingly dark subject lines like "The Horror That Is South Korea."*

The first person I looked up in Manila was Helen Mendoza. A legend among the world's small community of Philippines scholars, Helen has a master's degree in English literature from Stanford and a PhD in American

---

* "Mine was primarily a prison story and maximum-security cells tend to look rather alike," he wrote me after he'd escaped. "The Penal Colony of Soong Schill Christian University, like Devil's Island, was not totally secure, but once out of the compound there was nowhere to go—unless you took particular pleasure in watching old women selling peppers on street corners or felt a sudden need to buy a fish-dog on a stick. Interestingly, the locals seemed to feel they were living in the Paris of the East and delighted in asking foreigners how they liked Korea, a question I was never able to answer to their complete satisfaction."

literature from the University of Minnesota. I mention her credentials because it's always worth reminding people that in spite of widespread perception, only a fraction of Filipina women, or Thai women for that matter, are engaged in the sex trade. (Not that half the stories in this book are going to tear down stereotypes.)

For years Helen has run a guesthouse and research office in Manila for visiting students and professors. She'd been a robust sixty-seven when I'd last seen her in 1993, and the intervening years hadn't aged her. We ate dinner at a Chinese restaurant, during which I asked if Bantai was still living at the house.

"Sadly, Bantai is no longer with us," Helen said.

I said I was sorry, and we told a few Bantai stories, laughing about the night I'd met him.

Enclosed within a high metal wall, Helen's guesthouse was actually a long, two-story dormitory with about ten rooms that faced the two-story home in which she lived. The space between the dorm and the house formed a courtyard where visitors socialized outside, house girls washed laundry by hand, and birds flitted in and out of wide shade trees.

When I was a guest in 1993, my room on the top floor of the dorm faced the courtyard. My first night, I was awakened in the early hours by the sound of a man wheezing and coughing at irregular intervals. My uncle Ralph had died from emphysema, and I imagined some similar respiratory affliction was behind this man's unnerving death rattle.

Though still weak, the coughing became heavier and steadier as the night wore on. When I heard frantic choking noises, I got out of bed and rushed to the window. The sound seemed to be coming from outside, so I stared down at the courtyard. The choking stopped. The courtyard was empty. A few minutes after I got back into bed, the coughing started up again and continued to wake me at intervals throughout the night.

This scenario repeated itself for the next two or three nights. An hour after lights-out, the wheezing and coughing would begin. I'd get up, look out the window, wander along the outer walkway, see nothing, go back to bed, and wake up sporadically till dawn to the sound of a man struggling to maintain his fragile hold on life.

Imagining the old man might be Helen's husband (I'd met her only a few days before) or some infirm resident, I decided not to risk offending anyone by asking about the coughing. During the day I kept an eye out for likely suspects, but aside from me the only other men around the place were Lauren, an expat student from Ohio, and a professor from Michigan who didn't look terribly fit but who I doubted was on the verge of a dirt nap. Able to stand the mystery no longer, I finally raised the subject of the sick old man as Helen and I sat outside one evening having iced tea.

"It's weird," I said. "I can hear this guy coughing and wheezing all night long, but I can't see him anywhere. I've looked all over the courtyard. I even opened the gate and walked around the block last night."

"You know we Filipinos are big believers in the supernatural," Helen said. "Maybe you are being visited by a ghost."

I told Helen that at this point I wasn't discounting anything. She laughed and shook her head.

"I am sorry to say you are not being haunted," she said. "Come this way."

Helen led me around the side of the courtyard to a

bushy spot where the fence formed a corner near the back of her house. Trash cans and cardboard boxes were stacked against the hedge and fence. She moved one of the garbage cans and pointed at the ground. Huddled against the fence, quivering as it slept, lay the body of a tiny, pitiful animal. Clumps of hair were missing from at least half its emaciated torso. Though it appeared to be a dog, perhaps some sort of mixed spaniel, the creature was so reduced and frail that discerning an actual breed was next to impossible. If it hadn't been for the shaking, I would have assumed the thing had flatlined earlier in the week and was being thrown out with the garbage.

"Say hello to Bantai," Helen said, reaching down to stroke the dog's eczema-ridden belly. Bantai stirred momentarily, then lapsed back into semiconsciousness.

"This poor animal," Helen said. "He has cataracts so he's almost blind. As you can see, all of his legs are still attached, but only three of them are in working order. He barely has the strength to eat. And he has liver flukes. That's what makes his barking sound like a person coughing."

"Barking?" I said. "You're telling me that the coughing I've been hearing all week has been this dog's idea of barking?"

"Of course," Helen said indignantly. "That is his job. In Tagalog, 'bantai' means 'protector.' He is our watchdog."

I burst out laughing.

"I don't see what's so hilarious," Helen said.

I told her I was laughing because it didn't look to me like "Bantai" was capable of protecting his own water dish, much less the house. Helen smiled at me, then looked down at the forlorn Bantai. She gave his repulsive belly another rub.

"That's all right," she said, ignoring my laughter. "Bantai's been around for a long time, and he's always done his job as well as he's needed to. The truth is, it's never been as dangerous around here as everybody would like to believe."

10

· · ·

Is It OK to Miss the Cold War?
The Philosophical Dilemma of
Eastern Europe

No one makes me feel older than Rick Steves. For those who haven't hit the downside of the demographic bell curve, Steves is the amiable and exhaustively informed über-goober of European travel who's built an empire by turning two millennia of Old World culture into half-hour packlettes of tourist vanilla for a PBS fan base that considers *60 Minutes* a bastion of youthful impertinence.

Because Steves has now introduced more Americans to European culture than Fellini, because lands of the former Eastern bloc have been crowned *the* up-and-coming Euro travel destination, and because I was prepping for a trip there, the Dufus King appeared unbidden one evening last year in my DVD player. Less jaded by industry puffery than I am, Joyce had brought into our home a pair of Steves videos covering Budapest, Slovenia, and Croatia, sites that comprised much of the itinerary for our own glorious expedition to Eastern and Central Europe.

Beyond the single-camera, boilerplate editing with the approximate production value of a local news field report, Steves's program depressed me for the same reasons almost all travel reporting depresses me. Everything the gushing host encountered was so relentlessly charming. Every description sounded as if it had been lifted from a feminine-hygiene-spray commercial. Seas glistened. Cities sparkled. Hungary was a "goulash" of influences. And, of course, the Croatian city of Split was the usual fascinating blend of the ancient and modern.

It was disappointing though not surprising that Steves had beaten me to the vacation republics of the former Yugoslavia. Shortly after the turn of the twenty-first century, the travel media began touting Eastern and Central Europe as a paradise of rock-bottom prices, undiscovered villages, and empty beaches. Even better, it was filled with local rustics as yet untainted by the Western economic blitz that would make spicy chicken-breast sandwiches slathered in chipotle barbecue sauce with a side of deep-fried tater nuggets available on every street corner in the world.

Like new inmates in prison, the appeal of emerging capitalist countries from the dismantled Soviet Union lies in their virginity. When travel writers and TV hosts brim lustily about "newly prosperous countries" where, paradoxically, hotel rooms go for only twenty bucks a night, it's not a celebration of a bustling economy or newfound political freedom. It's a clarion call for travelers to get their hands on the plunder before everyone else. Covering Bulgaria in 2006, Steves raved about three-dollar meals, reported on the Peace Corps' dutiful efforts to lay the groundwork for democracy, reassuringly noted the presence of a McDonald's just down the street from his hotel, and called the country "a capitalist puppy." (No offense, Bulgaria, but, seriously, you do make a really cute mascot!)

All of this raises a philosophical question that has long troubled thoughtful travelers: When we all know that tourism will destroy many of the exceptional qualities of a given culture, why do we rush to be part of the desecration?

Like our consumption of Middle East oil and hip-hop misogyny, the understanding that we're part of a corrosive, immoral practice doesn't stop us from partaking in it. In fact, that knowledge only seems to make our consumption more frenzied. We venerate what we destroy. But first we destroy. If you don't believe that, talk to a Native American. Or a Japanese samurai, if you can find one.

Prague is a prime example. Crammed with Romanesque, Baroque, and Gothic architecture dating to the twelfth century, Old Town Square in the Czech capital is a world treasure. It took less than a decade after the fall of Communism, however, for the area to be overrun by KFC, Pizza Hut, and those ridiculous European-brand boutiques that turn every historic site on the continent into outdoor malls for the most extravagant or clueless shoppers in the world. Prada. Fendi. Gucci. I could spend the rest of my life in Europe and still not understand why anyone goes to St. Mark's Square in Venice or Váci Utca in Budapest to shop at places that consider 600 percent a fair markup.

In the West, we take for granted the material prizes available to the most industrious, intelligent, or financially fortunate among us. Hermès handbags and chrome-plated Ferrari stick shifts are the carrots that keep the capitalist mule groaning along. Across the old

Soviet bloc, however, the uneven economic transformation has brought swarms of Westerners looking for deals on everything from cheap property and antiques to sex with minors—Romania being just one well-known target of pedophiles—leading to a curious kind of nostalgia for the days when the Western market economy somehow seemed more benign as an enemy than it does now as a friend.

Among the more fascinating products of *Ostalgia* (German slang for the country's omnipresent nostalgia for the goods, services, and symbols of the former East Germany) is the return of the Trabant or, affectionately, the Trabi. Following the fall of the Berlin Wall in 1989, the flimsy, two-stroke, plastic-and-fiberglass car that once dominated East German roads quickly became a symbol of disgraced Soviet-style market controls. In recent years, however, Trabi clubs around Germany helped return the stubby little vehicle to view. Hans Q. Public loved it. A modified version of the car went back into manufacture. Today, companies such as Trabi-Safari offer rides around Berlin and Dresden in the phoenix of the East German auto industry.

"A few years ago only a few enthusiasts dared show themselves in public with their Trabis," says the company. "Now the cult vehicle of the East is back."

The resurgence of perhaps the crappiest car ever put into mass production reflects a three-tiered wave of Iron Curtain nostalgia in Europe that begins with wistful old proles who pine for the more prosperous lives they enjoyed under the former economy. Their maudlin Slavic outlook trickles down to Eastern Europe's perpetually unemployed or underemployed younger generation who never even had the chance to work in the system their parents romanticize. Finally, there are the foreign hipsters and countrymen wealthy enough to indulge an interest in Communist kitsch.

Once considered gloomy and socially frigid, life with the Russian bear now seems almost quaint in comparison with the troubles of today, leading a number of Easterners as well as Westerners to consider what was once unimaginable: Is it possible that the days of the Rosenbergs, Sputnik, classroom air-raid drills, Cuban Missile Crisis, Khrushchev pounding his shoe on a desk at the U.N., mutually assured destruction, and Olympic boycotts were in fact better times? In simpler terms, is it wrong to miss the Cold War?

In 1999, *Sports Illustrated* named the Miracle on Ice, the 1980 U.S. Olympic hockey victory over the Soviet Union, the greatest sports moment of the twentieth century. The selection surprised no one. The now-mythic triumph of the ragtag crew of blue-collar, college hockey amateurs over the professional Communist juggernaut at Lake Placid routinely shows up on lists devoted not simply to sports milestones but to American history. The U.S. hockey-team defeat of the evil empire is still viewed as a defining political moment, a sorely needed American victory during a time of social disillusionment, economic recession, humiliation in Iran, and perceived military weakness.

A contrarian by nature, I tend to dismiss hyperbole that expands the importance of ordinary events. The world is too complicated a place to anoint any single incident a "turning point" upon which all pivots. In the case of the Miracle on Ice, I make an exception.

The Miracle on Ice occurred during my junior year of high school. No other happening from that era lives in my mind with greater clarity; more than two decades on, I recognize that game as the zenith of my feelings of patriotism and unbridled zeal for sports. The coke train at the Alaska legislature, Iran-Contra, and 1981 baseball strike were just around the corner.

Like the Cold War, the Miracle on Ice was a multi-layered affair, and the extraordinary circumstances in which I saw the game no doubt contribute to my abiding nostalgia for its mythology. Alongside perhaps a hundred high school kids from around Southeast Alaska, I experienced the greatest moment in twentieth-century sports in a double room at the old Marine View Hotel in Ketchikan. The occasion for this massive gathering of youth was not the soon-to-be-historic hockey game but something considered at the time even more sacred: the annual Southeast Alaska High School Basketball Tournament.

Held in a different town each year, "Southeast" was the culmination of the region's high school sports and social calendar. Separated by ocean and mountains throughout the year, kids who traveled to the tournament on state ferries as part of school organizations (band geek, in my case) were housed over the long weekend with local families of area kids. Students who traveled independent of official school groups, such as my enterprising pal Randy, arranged their own ferry tickets and accommodations. Unburdened by curfews or other school regulations, these freelancers stayed where they pleased and hosted the kinds of parties that might be thrown beyond the reach of parents, teachers, preachers, and other enemies of adolescent freedom.

Which is how I came to spend the night of February 22, 1980, bumping shoulders with a crowd of high school kids crammed into a seventh-floor hotel room rented out by Randy and two other Juneau guys.

Sometime around four in the afternoon on game day, my buddy Tom* and I walked from the Ketchikan High School gym to Randy's room and found that he and his pals had filled their bathtub with the largest batch of P.J. we'd ever seen. Harder to swallow than a North Korean election result, P.J. (aka Purple Jesus) was an Alaska party tradition that consisted of a large vessel filled with whatever fruit juices and alcohol high school kids could round up on short notice—frozen grape juice, Hawaiian Punch, vodka, rum, beer, anything else that wouldn't be missed from parents' liquor cabinets. The critical ingredient, however, was Everclear, the lethal 190-proof grain alcohol that can also be used as a solvent, hand cleanser, disinfectant, and fuel in lightweight backpacker stoves. In other parts of the country, P.J. goes by names like Rat Poison, Jungle Juice, and Sex Mix.

As afternoon faded into night and kids dipped their cups for the tenth and twentieth times into the makeshift bathtub tureen, the P.J. level slowly went down, leaving soapy purple rings around the tub, a nauseating record of the party's progress. In addition to a general aroma of fermentation, the room was redolent of Matanuska Thunderfuck and other sublime weed vintages. Kids in letterman's jackets—giant *P*'s for Petersburg, *W*'s for

---

* As a member of the U.S. Army band stationed in Germany, Tom and several buddies were in Berlin, high on hash, when the wall came down: "There were hammers and chisels laying all around, and I got to knock out two pieces of rock from the actual Berlin Wall! I still have them in storage with all my other stuff," he later wrote me.

Wrangell, *M*'s for Metlakatla, and so on—moved through the crowd. The Haines Glacier Bears cheerleader whom every guy wanted to meet had reportedly been called by someone with connections to Haines High and was on her way over. Lynyrd Skynyrd, Foghat, and Van Halen roared out of an oversized portable tape deck.

Needless to say, we were ready for a hockey game.

What people remember most about the Miracle on Ice is the game-winning goal scored by captain Mike Eruzione, and Al Michaels screaming, "Do you believe in miracles?" More than just the final minutes, however, the entire game was played under the weight of an almost unbearable tension. The machinelike Soviets controlled the puck for virtually every tick of the clock. They outshot the gutsy young Americans thirty-nine to sixteen. Against the four-time defending champions, however, something about the Americans' body language—and in goalie Jim Craig's supernatural night of netminding— kept you believing that the impossible might happen.

The Soviets led three to two going into the final period. With hope fading and twelve minutes remaining, Mark Johnson scored the tying goal. Just ninety seconds later, while our celebration of Johnson's goal was still vibrating the rafters, Eruzione flicked his game-winning twenty-five-footer into the back of the net. The Marine View seemed to teeter on its foundation. The final ten minutes of the game was the most indescribable "Please, God, let us hang on" agony I've ever endured. I watched most of it with my hands folded and eyes closed. I don't know this for certain, but the beating applied to the Marine View by a packed house of euphoric high school drunks who stomped in triumph for three straight hours after the United States skated off the ice had to have contributed to the venerable hotel's closure a few years later.

The win over the robotic titans from the USSR was indeed a political as well as an athletic statement. I've always been surprised, however, that one of the most satisfying elements of the victory has been overlooked by academics seeking to imbue it with larger meaning. As much as anything, and this was particularly true for genuine sports fans, the Miracle on Ice was payback for the Soviet theft of the basketball gold medal at the 1972 Olympics in Munich, when referees twice put time back on the clock of a completed game, allowing the Russians to win with a Hail Stalin play as the clock expired for a third time.

Ever since I was eight years old, I've associated cheating at sports with pagan Communism and still consider that Olympic abomination the most painful and corrupt sports defeat I've ever witnessed. The visceral satisfaction of seeing justice meted out on the ice at Lake Placid exorcised eight years of pent-up rage. In the Marine View, we weren't just celebrating a shocking upset, a political coup, or even the late-night arrival of more Everclear and (finally!) the cheerleader from Haines. We were celebrating the fulfillment of that most precious and seldom realized human emotion: revenge.

As a kid, other than the "From Russia with Love" pictorials that *Playboy* and *Penthouse* reliably cranked out every few years in the name of forbidden temptation, nothing about the Union of Soviet Socialist Republics struck me as attractive or enticing. Any appreciation I had of the nuance that existed behind the Iron Curtain was limited to whether the grim-faced Muscovites we saw on the news were waiting in lines for toilet paper or spoiled cabbage. I grew up with no interest or expectation of ever visiting Eastern Europe.

That changed in 1994 when a group of guys I barely knew asked if I wanted to go with them to Germany. As I had no other prospects at the time, and they promised to pay my expenses, I said, "Why not?" The group was called the Surf Trio.

In the early nineties, when I wasn't in Asia or Juneau, I was in Portland, Oregon, playing music in plywood practice rooms and occasionally in the type of smoky bars where, if songs like Motörhead's "Ace of Spades" didn't blast out of the jukebox at least twice an hour, it wasn't considered a good crowd. The music of the day would soon make international stars of the flannel-and-thrift-store musicians who played the same humble stages I did. After bailing out of a band called Mood Paint that would go on to become Pond (dedicated grunge-era fans will recognize the group founded by my Juneau pals Charlie Campbell and Chris Brady), I hooked on with Portland's Surf Trio, an established band who had recently lost their drummer and needed a new one in a hurry.

The Surf Trio was neither a trio nor a traditional surf band. Despite the unfortunate name and tedious explanations about its pseudo-ironic origins, the band's distortion-heavy, four-four rock, catchy two-minute tunes—almost every song began "Onetwothreefour!"— melodic lead guitars, and energetic front man Jeff had earned it a decent regional following. More scruffy than pretty, the only groupies our guitarists Ron and Pete attracted were the grizzled guys at the bar who'd stagger backstage after shows to tell us how great we were, but how you couldn't hear the rhythm guitar for shit in the mix, and, at any rate, how the Dandy Warhols or Candlebox or Sweaty Nipples or Death Midget or Completely Grocery show the night before had drawn a way bigger crowd.

In that strange "big in Japan" way, the Surf Trio also had a name and small record deal in Germany. While I was in the band, the label twice flew the Surf Trio to Germany for concert tours, the second of which we made with a Swedish bubblegum-punk outfit called Psychotic Youth. In this way, crammed in a van with seven other unshowered and temperamental rock-and-roll hopefuls, led by a gentle yet absentminded tour manager named Gerd, I managed to beat the capitalist masses to Eastern Europe. Or at least what had until recently been East Germany.

With one exception, Psychotic Youth weren't as scary as their name implied. They were in some respects the Surf Trio's European doppelgängers—four garrulous guys from Gothenburg whose knowledge of music trivia and useless pop culture was as extensive as our own. Such information is valuable on long rides in a tour van if you're the type, as I am, who prides himself on being able to answer the question, "Who is the only lead singer to reach the American Top 40 charts as part of four different acts?" The answer is Paul Carrack* ("How Long" with Ace in 1975; "Tempted" with Squeeze in 1981; "I Need You" as a solo artist in 1982; "The Living Years" with Mike and the Mechanics in 1988). The

---

* If you count his duets with Stevie Wonder and Michael Jackson as separate from his solo work, Paul McCartney can also *technically* make this claim.

kicker, however, is knowing that the former front man for alleged cheese-merchants Mike and the Mechanics was also the man who played the tinkling piano line on the Smiths' landmark "Reel Around the Fountain." Psychotic Youth appreciated this type of banter, and the Surf Trio appreciated them for appreciating it. We got along like IKEA and Allen wrenches.

The aforementioned exception was Alex, Psychotic Youth's drummer, a man with no patience for trivial chatter and whose Eric the Red tresses, beer breakfasts, and perpetually clenched fists were constant reminders that bloodthirsty Vikings came from all over Scandinavia, not just Norway. Alex was unhappy about a lot of things—the cramped tour van, the sweltering heat, the lousy food provided each night by the clubs and halls where we played. But mostly what he didn't like were Germans. As Gerd was for the better part of the day the only German within striking distance, and as Gerd was, this side of Sergeant Schultz, the most incompetent manager the Germans ever put in charge of anything, he quickly became the target of Alex's intimidating harassment.

With Gerd behind the wheel, even two-block trips down the street couldn't be completed without a complicated series of U-turns, three-point maneuvers, and extended map consultations. After a few days of this, Gerd couldn't pull over to take a leak without his intelligence being questioned by Alex, who made matters worse by screaming "Imbecile!" and comparing everything the poor guy did to some atrocity committed by the Third Reich. Europe will probably have to burn itself to the ground once again before it completely gets over World War II.

Near the end of the tour, Gerd announced that we would once more be heading into the former East Germany, this time to headline an all-day music festival in a city called Magdeburg. We'd already played a semi-dreary former East German city called Freiberg, where the terrain of mountains and valleys had made it impossible during the Cold War for residents to pick up radio and television transmissions from the West. Cut off for decades from virtually all outside news, music, and entertainment, Freiberg had been part of an area known as Dark Germany, or the Valley of the Ignorants.

"Magdeburg wasn't in the Valley of the Ignorants," Gerd told us as we motored down a stretch of autobahn that for once wasn't clogged with vehicles. "But it was known as a backward part of the country. Maybe you will find it has not improved at the same rate as other places in the old GDR."

Gerd's warning turned out to be the understatement of the trip. What Godzilla did to Tokyo, what Mount St. Helens did to Mount St. Helens, Communism, or maybe post-Communism, had done to Magdeburg. The entire city had the burned-out look of a condemned block in the Bronx. Rows of drab Soviet-era apartment buildings stood like crumbling boxes, hoary relics of an irrelevant civilization. Concrete walls were eroded to the rebar. Windows were broken out. Front doors were missing.

And people were living inside these wrecks. This we could tell only by the furtive heads that poked in and out of the spaces where windows should have been as we drove slowly through the narrow, deserted streets. Glares of suspicion followed us around every turn. No one spoke, smiled, or waved; they just stared with that discomfiting Eastern European mixture of curiosity, resentment, and muted hostility. Magdeburg was a time warp, a garbage-strewn *Star Trek* episode freakish enough to silence even Alex.

Our destination was a venue called Knast, which turned out to be an imposing structure of soot-covered red bricks that during the Cold War had served as a Stasi prison—Stasi being the East German secret police as fearsome as the KGB. Once a center for interrogation and torture of political prisoners, the facility had been recast somewhat ironically as a youth center. In the case of Knast, "youth center" was a definition loose enough to make a presidential press secretary weep with pride. Far from a boys or girls club, much less a concert venue, Knast was essentially a former jail now functioning as a flophouse and dealing station for a small army of half-dressed homeless kids whose ragged appearance conjured images of postapocalyptic desolation.

Excepting a Psychotic Youth/Surf Trio tour poster someone had hung on the front gate, no one appeared to be prepping for an afternoon music festival. Gerd parked the van, and we wandered tentatively through the old prison, literally stumbling over slow-moving or immobile figures passed out on dirt and concrete floors amid empty beer cans, vodka bottles, hypodermic needles, burnt spoons, crack pipes, trash, puddles of piss, roaches, and mice. The oldest kid in the place was maybe nineteen, the youngest no more than seven or eight. Occasionally a sluggish form would roll over and shoot us a menacing stare. Mostly we were ignored.

Though no one appeared to be in charge, Gerd eventually found a weedy-haired blond kid who looked about thirty-five but who was actually thirteen. The kid took us around to the back of the prison to show us where bands sometimes set up. A sad little concrete stage stood in a corner of the large yard overgrown with grass and weeds; it was easy to imagine a prison commandant standing on it and addressing rows of ashen-faced Communist inmates. Graffiti covered every hard surface. Mongrel dogs patrolled the yard like hyenas, teeth bared, tongues lolling. If you squinted hard enough, you'd swear you could still see police snipers posted in the original brick watchtowers that loomed over the entire milieu in an accusatory fashion.

"Where are the other bands?" Gerd asked the scraggly-haired kid.

"What bands?" said the kid.

"We are here to play the music festival," Gerd replied. "There are supposed to be four other bands on the lineup."

"I know nothing of this," said the kid.

"Where is Cristoph?" Christoph was the guy who'd booked us into Knast.

"Cristoph has gone. He left Magdeburg last month. Maybe Berlin." Without another word, the kid turned and walked away.

As the French author Michel Houellebecq has noted, "One cannot say that communism particularly fostered sentimentality in human relations."

Across Germany, I'd been documenting the Surf Trio's adventures on film, but in Magdeburg I decided it might be wise to keep my camera as inconspicuous as possible. I did get in a few snaps—though, as with places like the Grand Canyon, the results proved the difficulty of doing photographic justice to nature's most spectacular scenes—but we were surrounded by a desperate bunch, and I knew that, even fenced, my new Canon

EOS was probably worth ten times the collective liquid holdings of the Knast crowd. I'm not a jittery traveler, but my grandfather had a famous story about meeting strangers on the road and being at Knast did everything but summon his ghost for the retelling.

Bop's story took place during the Great Depression. He was seventeen or eighteen at the time, driving his father's truck somewhere in Ohio when he picked up a hitchhiker. The hitcher was a young man, not much older than Bop. He tossed his duffel bag in the back, hopped in front, and immediately began reciting a dreadful tale of woe.

The guy had been discharged from the army six months earlier and hadn't been able to find work since. The government still owed him back pay. His parents had recently lost their house to the bank. Now the whole family was broke, hungry, and wandering the Midwest in search of jobs and shelter. He finished his bleak yarn by looking across the cab at Bop and saying, "You know, I believe I'd kill a man for five dollars if the opportunity presented itself."

My grandfather hadn't yet been around the world, but he knew he didn't like the way the hitchhiker's eyes darted around the cab. He also knew that even if the truck he was driving wasn't worth five dollars, the sawbuck in his pocket was. Bop continued making small talk, asking about the army and so forth, before suggesting the two of them pull over for a cup of coffee.

"On me," Bop said. "I've got a little extra change in my pocket."

A few miles up the road, Bop spotted a diner and pulled over. The two men settled into a table, but before the waitress could come over, Bop feigned a look of surprise.

"Son of a bitch," he said, patting his coat pockets. "I left my wallet out in the truck. Be right back."

Leaving his new friend at the table, Bop hustled out to the parking lot, lifted the guy's duffel bag from the back of the truck, and tossed it next to the front door of the diner. Then he got in the truck and roared off.

"It's not that I thought he was a bad guy," Bop said. "But an empty belly can lead even the best people to do bad things."

In a rain that had been threatening since dawn, the Surf Trio and Psychotic Youth rocked the Magdeburg "music festival." Not that anyone cared. Though most of Knast's homeless tribe stirred at the first sounds of power chords in the prison yard, only a few wraithlike figures hung around the stage for more than two or three songs. The Surf Trio went on first, and we ended up playing most of our set in front of four half-naked ten-year-olds, who, to their credit, pressed close to the stage and seemed to enjoy themselves. Though since they were drinking beer the whole time, we tried not to give ourselves too much credit, even when they shyly asked for our autographs after the show.

Psychotic Youth fared worse. Their power-pop harmonies and more polished sound didn't sit well with the ten or fifteen hard-core derelicts who wandered out to see the headliners. From their opening number, the Swedes were jeered by a gang of rough-boy Germans dressed like seventies London punks, sending Alex into a blind rage as he pounded away on his drum kit. Mercifully, the hecklers retreated after a few songs to the far end of the yard, where a picnic table and decaying snack kiosk filled with beer kept the rabble occupied while the orchestra fiddled onstage.

Knast broke the tour. Unleashing a fury that had been building from the moment Gerd had taken his first wrong turn out of the Frankfurt airport, Alex channeled Al Pacino in *Dog Day Afternoon*. After the humiliation of the show, he jumped into Gerd's face and demanded we be taken at once to a four-star hotel, fed properly, and given a day off from the van, the tour, and, most especially, from Gerd. He followed the verbal onslaught by shoving into Gerd's chest a written list of terms dictating the way the rest of the tour would proceed. Alex presented his manifesto along with the information that he and the other members of the bands were from this point onward in charge of the tour. To hell with the record label. If he wished, Gerd could stay on with the new title of "driver." Otherwise, we were taking the van.

Gerd put up no fight. It's possible he'd been even more shocked by the conditions in Magdeburg than we were. By nightfall, we were ensconced in a business hotel far from Knast. The crisp white sheets felt good, but the hellish day had left us all too drained to enjoy them. The entry I made in my journal that night suggested that there was more than one drama-queen drummer on the tour:

One of the most miserable days of my life. East Germany is a post-Orwellian nightmare. All is dour, gray, abandoned, defeated. Highlight of day was dinner of potato chips and soda purchased and consumed at a gas station, the only sign of working commerce Jeff, Jörgen, Ulf, Johannes, and I could find after thirty minutes of walking following Alex's meltdown. Awful show. Fights between rival packs of mangy dogs received more attention than the bands. Magdeburg is seediest, scuzziest, most squalid disaster I've ever seen. Memory has a way of injecting a golden hue on hardship—I won't forget the wretched truth of this day. Those who survive epic adversity become members of an infamous fraternity whose suffering becomes associated with a single name. Pompeii. Bataan. Chernobyl. Add Magdeburg to that notorious list. This might seem hysterical, but there are in my midst at least seven musicians and one ruined manager who wouldn't argue the point.

By morning, Alex had calmed down, and so had I, but the chatty, jocular atmosphere in the van was never restored. Gerd continued driving, but he barely spoke the rest of the trip. The agony was short-lived. We had only two shows to go; then it was time for relieved handshakes and flights back to Sweden and the States. I sat next to Ron and Pete on the way home, and we agreed that none of us had any desire or intention of ever witnessing more of life behind the old Iron Curtain. Though I know for a fact that Ron and Pete have kept their end of the bargain, for me, it was just another resolution I'd eventually end up breaking.

One of my most satisfying Soviet-style encounters came seven years later on a winter train trip from Moscow to Berlin. The memory of Magdeburg hadn't faded, but work is work, and I was traveling once more through post-Communist lands, this time doing research for the European edition of my World War II guidebooks.

Well aware of the rules against carrying contraband across international borders, I'd nonetheless hidden in the bottom of my suitcase a massive Russian Navy flag that had once flown above the deck on a Soviet submarine. Sifting through a junk shop in Moscow, I'd become infatuated with the maritime flag, its white field, blue stripe across the bottom, ominous red star in the left corner, and hammer and sickle in the right. My brother had spent much of his U.S. Navy career inside P-3 aircraft dropping sonar buoys on Soviet subs in the Pacific, and I was taken by the idea that he couldn't possibly receive a more unexpected Christmas present than this rare and historic trophy.

Although they're widely available from dealers across the country, it's illegal to take Communist military artifacts out of Russia. Being caught with the flag, however, didn't concern me until the moment my overnight train to Germany jerked to a violent halt in the middle of a dead-black night somewhere west of Moscow. I awoke to a commotion of angry Russian voices. I pulled back the flimsy curtain on the window. Heavy snow was falling at a forty-five-degree angle. We weren't in a station or for that matter near any signs of civilization or electricity. I checked the clock. 2:45 AM. For a moment I wondered if a group of Russia's famed gangsters had hijacked the train.

Sets of steel-toed boots clattered along the corridor, and a moment later an insistent pounding shook the door of my compartment. Before I could answer, the door swung open. Two husky, uniformed men wearing tight frowns and comically high green and red military hats dusted with snow stood in the hallway. I immediately thought, "Why the hell did I buy that goddamn flag?"

"Passport."

The taller of the officials held out his hand while the shorter one cast fishy looks around the tiny compartment. Apparently we'd arrived at a border crossing. The men were Belarusian customs agents. Belarus had been a province within the USSR. Now it's an independent nation between Russia and Poland.

"American?"

It said so on the little blue booklet, but the guys wanted a second opinion. Generally fearful of European border officials and preoccupied with the flag, I was in no frame of mind to offer a snappy comeback.

"What is the purpose of your trip to Belarus?"

"Just transit to Berlin," I said.

The two agents squeezed into the compartment. The tall one stood in front of my bunk turning over blankets and pillows. The short one picked up the green plastic tube on the sink, opened it, found my toothbrush, pulled it out of the container, inspected the bristles, and put it away. This wasn't going to be like sneaking an extra gallon of Kahlua through Tijuana.

"Your suitcase?"

"Yes."

"Open."

I tried to simulate the composure of a man who'd opened thousands of suitcases in the middle of the night for impatient ex–Soviet officials. The top layer was dirty underwear and old socks. Joyce once told me this would discourage inspections. The short guard dug in without hesitation. Within twenty seconds he'd found one of the Red Army medals I'd rolled up in a pair of socks. His nose twitched like a hound dog's in a prison cell. A minute later he was holding up my flag and nodding to his buddy, obviously pleased with his work. Stretched out, the flag reached nearly from one side of the compartment to the other.

"You are American military?" the tall one asked, though it didn't sound exactly like a question.

"No, no. Not military. Civilian."

"Then why you carry Soviet Navy flag?"

Despite having plenty of time to prepare for this very fair and clearly inevitable question, I didn't have an answer that I thought might satisfy the type of people likely to ask it. Since I figured the flag was probably a goner—these guys could've been pissed-off ex–Soviet Navy for all I knew—I told the truth. I said it was a souvenir for my Cold Warrior brother. Now retired, mind you, and utterly respectful of the determined, resourceful, and noble enemy against whom he operated as a mere pawn in a superpower game fueled by inexorable forces beyond the control of rational men such as ourselves, who . . .

"You may not take this flag out of Russia," the tall one said.

I shrugged, but my insides were churning at the thought of what the punishment for such a crime might be. The guard looked me in the face once more, held my eyes for an uncomfortably long time, then handed back my passport.

"But you are in Belarus now, not Russia."

With that, the short guard carefully refolded the flag, military style, placed it back in my suitcase, and closed the top. He very nearly smiled as he turned and shut the door behind him.

My stories about Magdeburg junkie-orphans and Belarusian border officials might give the impression that Eastern Europe hasn't changed much since Yeltsin left the Kremlin liquor cabinet empty. For better or worse, though, the truth is that these experiences grow more infrequent with each passing year. With few exceptions, what traces of the Iron Curtain that remain are now, like pie 'n' mash shops in London, subject to tourist-driven preservation without which they'd quickly go the way of Yakov Smirnoff. Just as you can imagine the Revolutionary War while walking the Freedom Trail in Boston, it's easy enough to find evidence of the Cold War in Eastern Europe but usually only in places where it's been shot, stuffed, tagged, and sealed in a glass case: the Checkpoint Charlie Museum in Berlin, Josip Tito's birthplace in Croatia, the secret police House of Terror in Budapest, the Central Armed Forces Museum in Moscow. The latter displays a piece of Francis Gary Powers's U-2 spy plane, on exhibit since being shot down in 1960, an event that dashed American hopes for success at an upcoming superpower conference and some years later provided a quartet of Irish rockers with both a name and early muse.

The Moscow museum is among the finest military museums in the world, but other sites dedicated strictly to Cold War history often aren't very good. The Museum of Communism in Prague, designed primarily to dance on the Soviet grave by spreading procapitalist ideology, sells cards and T-shirts that make an ironic joke of the fact that it shares building space with a McDonald's.

It's a clever shtick that sells lots of merchandise, though I found it discouraging that no one at the museum seemed aware of, much less bothered by, what a sad fucking fact it is that the Big Mac has emerged as the ultimate symbol of Western conquest.

I'm not saying I won't shove a Quarter Pounder in my face from time to time when I'm overseas. Nor that I want to see a leader get off Air Force One in Berlin and shout, "Mr. Putin, rebuild that wall!" In significant ways, Eastern Europe is much better off now than it was fifteen years ago.

What I am saying is that it's not just lonely at the top; it's boring. The spread of Western ideology might be good for big business, but speaking strictly from the perspective of an individual traveler who values the exotic, capitalism sucks. Countries that function with outlandish economic or political systems may not be as comfortable or easy to get to, and may not have very good shopping, but being different and difficult is precisely what makes them rewarding for many visitors. It's a funny line, but there are plenty of people like me who disagree with Stephen Colbert when he says, "There's nothing American tourists like more than the things they can get at home."

The U.S. government's campaign to remake the international map in its own image, or at the very least make it conform to American corporate rules and standards, makes the world a duller place. What's the point of a planet where vive la différence refers simply to the distances that can be measured between S, M, L, and XL? For me, getting to Red Square in 2003 might have felt more like an achievement had we not eaten Sbarro pizza in a mall immediately afterward.

Ruminating over these general themes last year in a beach restaurant on the Croatian island of Vis while enjoying a gorgonzola-and-pepperoni pizza as George Benson's "Breezin' " played in the background, I arrived at a somewhat surprising conclusion. There was only one way for me to come to grips with my ambivalent feelings about missing the Cold War. I needed to return to Magdeburg.

From Croatia, Joyce and I had made the two-day overland trip to Berlin, where I sprang the news of the idea that had been boiling inside me since Vis. Given that over the years she'd heard numerous versions of my story about Knast and Gerd and Psychotic Youth, it was not altogether surprising that the levelheaded Joyce disapproved of the plan and declared that she would not be joining me on any quixotic voyages into my murky past. I told her about the tree of personal questing growing inside of me. She told me Berlin was filled with excellent museums and restaurants. The next morning, I made the two-hour train trip to Magdeburg alone.

As I've mentioned before, one sneaky thing about travel stories are the phony raisons d'être writers often invent to justify their travels. Rather than just admit that they're hang gliding over the Argentine pampas because some magazine or book publisher paid them to, they fabricate a steaming pile about their urgent desire to follow the footsteps of Che Guevara or some other nonsense that makes them sound both appealingly adventuresome and introspective. This is why I want to stress that I didn't have any good reason to return to Magdeburg. Nobody was paying me to go there—and, believe me, travel writers *hate* paying for trips with their own money—and

Joyce and I were in Germany only because I wanted to visit my old *Maxim* pal Dave Malley, who had moved there.

What I wanted from Magdeburg a decade after surviving my initial trauma, I wasn't sure. Having traveled through Germany often in the intervening years, however, I knew what I was likely going to find: change. Specifically, the kind that blurs the lines that once solidly separated East and West.

Change in Magdeburg was evident in more than just the bright autumn sunshine and new "Fan American Sports Bar" across the street from the station where I disembarked. Despair had been replaced by vitality. And chain stores. People sat outside drinking coffee and tilting their faces back to catch the sun. Couples pushed babies in strollers down tree-lined sidewalks. Downtown's historic walking route looked mildly interesting, but rather than delay the inevitable, I hailed a cab and told the driver, "Knast."

At least one beat-up GDR apartment house was as neglected as the entire neighborhood had been when I'd walked through it with Jeff, Jörgen, Ulf, and Johannes, but, for the most part, the buildings were new or renovated. All of them had doors. Flower boxes hung beneath new vinyl window frames. Not exactly McMansion suburbia, Magdeburg nonetheless looked like a perfectly functional mid-major city, a German San Antonio or Charlotte. It's mind-boggling how fast an entire city can be rebuilt once proud, defiant people get organized. In less than a decade virtually all of Magdeburg had rebounded. Six-plus years later, the scorched hole in the earth at Ground Zero in New York remains a national disgrace.

Aside from the odd apartment building, about the only thing that had escaped the extreme-makeover treatment was Knast itself. I immediately recognized the graffiti-covered metal gate where Gerd had parked the van and we'd unloaded our gear in gloomy silence. Still plastered with tour posters—alas, not a trace of the old Psychotic Youth/Surf Trio handbill remained—the gate was locked. Between the hinges I could see the yard had been mowed and the piles of broken bricks and cinder blocks hauled away. Otherwise, the same.

In front, a large sign with white block letters hung across the imposing prison facade: "Gedenkstätte Moritzplatz Megdberg für die Opfer politischer Gewaltherrschaft 1945–1989." I couldn't read the German, but anything commemorating the dark years of 1945–1989 didn't suggest a party inside. I pushed the door beneath the sign and found it open.

Since no one seemed to be around, I gave myself a tour, stepping tentatively at first, then marching through the eerily empty hallways like I owned the place. Last time I'd been here, the rooms, cells, and basement closets had been teeming with underage squatters and sundry vermin. Now they were cleaned up, painted, and decorated with black-and-white historical photo enlargements and interpretive signage.

"Yes, can I help you?"

A lean woman with short, straight brown hair was calling from the far end of a darkened corridor. I looked up to find her moving toward me with brisk, officious strides. She was dressed in wide black pants, and her shoes clacked across the tile floor. Not the type, I guessed, who'd consider my sentimental journey just cause for trespassing.

"Ah, yes, well," I said. "Do you work here?"

I'm not, as a rule, what's known as a "charmer" with the ladies. But I hadn't come all the way to Knast just to get kicked out five minutes after I'd breached the door. Calling on all of my JET cross-cultural training and foreign diplomacy skills, I smiled, offered a handshake, and introduced myself.

Her name was Kirsa. She'd grown up on the outskirts of Magdeburg under GDR rule, and she was now the chief fund-raiser for and caretaker of this former Stasi prison, since converted into a museum. At forty-three, she was older than me, though not by much, meaning that while I'd been in Ketchikan watching the U.S. hockey team thrash the Soviets, she'd been in an East German university writing a paper or studying for an exam or partying in whatever way they did in the GDR.

Kirsa was thus a potential fountain of information, and though she was obviously anxious for both of us to leave—it was Sunday, the museum was officially closed, and she'd just stopped by to collect some things, which explained the open door and empty halls—I pressed her into conversation. The first thing I told her was that I'd been to Magdeburg a decade earlier and that the city now not only looked completely different, it felt different.

"As in most of East Germany, a number of programs have been undertaken to rebuild the city," she told me in slow, concise English. "Naturally, the city looks much nicer than before. But the situation with jobs is still not good for many people, so maybe looks can be deceiving."

I told Kirsa that in ten years I'd yet to meet an Eastern European who hadn't bemoaned the false promises of democracy, a betrayal that had annihilated the pillars of the education and social-welfare system that once held their societies intact. She looked at me as if I'd just pointed out that the sun was a star around which our spherical earth orbited and rotated.

"Of course, many necessary aspects of life have been degraded in recent years," she said. "There is much more a sense of hopelessness about these things."

"Yet clearly things are better now than they were before," I said. "Magdeburg looked like a war zone when I was here in the midnineties."

Kirsa shrugged and looked at me with hard, icy blue eyes. It occurred to me that twenty years ago she'd have been exactly the type of mirthless East German hard-ass I wouldn't have had a chance in hell of beating in the hundred-meter freestyle.

"I have a good job, so for me and my children, the situation is much better than before," she said. "For those people without jobs, maybe you have to ask them this question for yourself."

I asked Kirsa if she could let me into the prison yard where the Surf Trio had played. She told me she didn't have the key and, anyway, that part of the facility still belonged to the youth center, not the museum. I told her what type of "youth center" it had been a decade earlier.

"I think you will find it is much better now," she said, "but perhaps the young people there are not so different as you describe. It is still a hard life here for many people."

We talked some more—employment, education, politics—but she was getting fidgety, and I didn't want to lose her without addressing what I was gradually beginning to understand as the point of my visit. Coming to Magdeburg with all the advantages available to the average white, college-educated American male, I didn't want to sound like a naïve or entitled dick. I was going to have to put this as delicately as possible. I smiled and cleared my throat.

"Given that I never lived under Communist rule, and given how oppressive I know it was, and not wanting to trivialize any of that, I'm embarrassed saying this," I began, "but I can't help feeling a little regret whenever I visit Eastern Europe. In an abstract way, I hated you, or at least your government and country, for a good portion of my life. But now, the militaristic statuary and Social Realism art and threatening totalitarian uniforms? They look sort of stylish. The straightforward morality of a Cold War struggle against a professional and worthy foe dedicated to science and economic equality, at least as they interpreted it? I sort of miss it."

Kirsa thought about this strange confession for a long time. Then she nodded without smiling.

"Many *Ossi* (East Germans) can understand this feeling," she said, and nothing more.

Kirsa walked me to the door and locked it behind me. In front of the building, a stocky man in a black leather coat was parking his BMW. I waited until he'd shut the door, then held out my Canon. "Take my picture?" I asked.

The guy said, "No problem." I stood in front of Knast looking over the photographer's shoulder at a nicely manicured park across the street. While he lined me up in the frame, I thought, "Not only can you not go home again; you can't even go back to Magdeburg."

I ate lunch in a café and took a late train to Berlin. Back at the hotel, I flopped on the bed, turned on the TV, and stopped flicking channels when I hit a basketball game. The NBA season was getting under way with a series of exhibition games in Cologne and the Philadelphia 76ers were playing CSKA Moscow, the outfit formerly known as the Red Army team. Three Americans were on the Moscow roster, one of whom, I was surprised to see, was Trajan Langdon.

Trajan Langdon was once the most famous man in Alaska. Born in May 1976, he was three years old at the time of the Miracle on Ice, too young to remember anything of the day beyond perhaps the twenty-foot Nerf shots I'm sure he was already draining in his parents' living room. He hadn't even been alive when the original evildoers had stolen the 1972 Olympic basketball gold medal.

The first basketball player from the state to achieve national recognition, Langdon had been heavily recruited out of Anchorage Christian High in 1994 and played for coach Mike Krzyzewski at Duke. There, as one of the best outside shooters in the country, he became known as the "Alaskan Assassin." Langdon went on to play for the Cleveland Cavaliers, but as a medium-sized guard with below-average ball-handling skills, he never established his groove in the NBA. He washed out of the league after three seasons.

Expat ballplayers in Russia don't get many chances to perform in front of NBA coaches—against Philadelphia, Langdon was playing his ass off, chesting up much bigger guys on D, scrambling for loose balls, fighting through picks, jacking up shots every time he touched the rock. Even as a small figure on TV, he showed the intensity of a man desperate to work his way back to the States, a desire no one who's spent time in Moscow could hold against him. Langdon wasn't the team's first offensive option on the floor, and he wasn't surrounded by great players, but if CSKA Moscow lost, it wasn't going to be his fault.

Despite his hard-nosed effort, the Alaskan Assassin didn't score much in the first half. Allen Iverson was lighting up Moscow; no one would ever mistake this for a larger-than-life duel between East and West. Then in the third quarter Langdon flashed some of his old form, stopping a Philly run by popping behind the arc and burying a clutch three-pointer.

For a moment it looked like a game-changing bucket. As he ran down court sharing high fives with his Russian teammates, the camera zoomed in on Langdon's smiling face, and all at once I wondered if I'd been wrong about him wanting to go back to the States. Far from looking at a homesick baller, I was watching a man in a red jersey unambiguously interested in nothing more than beating the Americans. I was looking, with a mixture of envy and pity, at a man who even if he wanted to would never be able to find his way back in a world in which war had become peace, freedom had become slavery, ignorance had become strength, and East had become West.

11

. . .

Not-So-Ugly Americans and
the Road of Good Intentions

The principal figure in each of the four scenarios below
is either (a) Indian, (b) German, (c) French, or (d) American. Test your knowledge of international stereotypes
by matching the behavior of the traveler with his or her
nationality.

1. A ferry is scheduled to depart the Croatian island of
   Rab for the mainland at 5:30 AM. Because the ship is
   small and vehicle space limited, tourists and locals
   have been gathering at the pier since four o'clock in
   the morning. By the time the tiny, wooden ticket
   booth opens at five, approximately thirty parties are
   lined up in as cooperative a manner as Europeans of
   varying nationalities, all of them high on caffeine and
   nicotine, are capable of in the hours before dawn.
       At precisely 4:58 AM, a sporty, two-door Saab
   pulls up across from the ticket booth. As the wooden
   window slides up and the ferry office readies for

business, the door of the Saab opens. A broad-shouldered man in a suede jacket leaps from the vehicle and sprints to the window. Using his elbows like an NFL fullback breaking through a pile at the end zone, the man muscles to the front of the line. Unaware of this minor ruckus, the clerk in the booth looks up, assumes the man in the suede jacket is first in line (which, technically, he is), and sells him a ticket. In response to the murmur of protest that spreads through the crowd, the blatant line-cutter offers a grunt of aristocratic entitlement and returns to his car, which he proceeds to maneuver in front of all the other vehicles waiting to drive onto the ship.

2. A train leaves Bangkok for the three-and-a-half-hour trip to Kanchanaburi, site of the Bridge on the River Kwai, made infamous by the Academy Award–winning World War II film of the same name. Thirty minutes before Kanchanaburi, the train stops in a small town. Among the large group of tourists who pile on is a middle-aged couple with wide-brimmed hats, cameras slung like silver bricks around their necks, and the scent of mosquito repellant and body odor thick in their clothes and hair. The woman and man—who is bald and several inches shorter than his wife—quickly move to the row with the last vacant seat, a window spot next to a man in a blue T-shirt who occupies the aisle seat. The woman motions to the blue T-shirt man that she would like to sit by the window. He nods politely, stands, and steps into the aisle to make room for her to slide past. This she does, but when the man in the T-shirt sits back down, he's startled to find himself in the lap of the

bald man. Using the momentary diversion created by his wife, baldie has violated a number of widely accepted rules of public civility and stolen the other man's seat.

The chump on the losing end of this bit of shameless chicanery smiles icily and shoves his ticket in front of the bald man's face. This shows beyond any doubt that the man in the T-shirt holds a reservation for the seat, which he makes clear he wants back. Instead of rising with an embarrassed apology, the bald man simply ignores the complaints. With the dead eyes of a shark, he fixes his gaze out the window and keeps his lips pursed until the man in the T-shirt finally accepts the fact that although it's humiliating to lose his seat to a complete and utter asshole, standing for the next thirty minutes is preferable to engaging in a physical confrontation on a train rumbling through countryside already notorious for the spilled blood of foreigners.

3. On a flight from Melbourne, Australia, to Fiji, a man is seated next to a middle-aged woman in a loose-fitting, multihued dress. Ten minutes into the flight, the woman removes a glitter-covered shoe, folds her right foot onto her left thigh, and begins furiously picking at a thick scab that covers the side of her foot with an impressionistic pattern of purplish bubbles. After puncturing and removing parts of the scab, the woman begins carelessly flicking away bits of skin, many of which land on the pant leg of the man seated next to her.

Next, the woman removes from her enormous bag (which takes up most of the space beneath both seats) a long pick, something resembling a blunt fondue sword, and starts scraping off layers of dried and cracked toe skin with a scooping motion that sends more flaky particles in the direction of her seatmate. By the time the flight is over, the entire scab and other sections of unwanted skin have been removed like endless layers of moist filo dough. The woman's foot is a throbbing red stump, a signal of either recovery or advancing infection. Impressively, her labor has been completed with virtually no pause despite the increasingly insistent complaints from the unfortunate man forced to endure this revolting exhibition of DIY surgery.

4. A solo male tourist arrives on Malaysia's Tioman Island, a paradise of swaying palms, soft beaches, and volcanic peaks that rise straight from the sea, the kind of place where one walks around all day humming "Bali Hai," half expecting Bloody Mary to pop out from behind a thatch hut spitting betel nut and offering a good price on her daughter. Naturally, Tioman has been discovered by backpackers who come to the island in clumps to do the usual backpacker things—get high, wander around in Bob Marley T-shirts, make ill-tempered demands of the local help as though they were staying in a four-star resort, and complain about the United States. For whatever positive traits they might possess, backpackers aren't renowned as tidy people, and since neither are most Asians, islands like Tioman have acquired the patina of magnificent garbage dumps.

On the first day of his visit, the aforementioned tourist checks into a cheap bungalow, throws his bag on the bamboo-frame bed, takes a walk along a length of garbage-strewn beach, and gets an idea. Back in the village, he scares up a large, plastic garbage bag and returns to the beach, this time picking up all the trash in his path and putting it in the bag. He makes it a hundred yards before the bag is full, at which point he returns to the village for another sack.

"What you doing?" In the village, the man is pelted with questions. There's no Sierra Club in Asia, not even a legacy of TV ads featuring tearful Indian chiefs mourning Big Mac wrappers on the side of the road, so the man's selfless behavior has aroused suspicion.

"I'm cleaning your beach," the man answers his mystified inquisitors. "It's filthy."

During his short stay on the island, the man fills ten or fifteen bags. Not one person, local or tourist, lifts a hand to help him. In a place like Tioman, it's likely the bags will be "thrown away" by being hauled fifty yards out to sea and dumped overboard. Still, the man feels good about the fact that the beach is cleaner when he leaves than it was when he arrived.

The answers are:
1. b (German)
2. c (French)
3. a (Indian)
4. d (American)

The man in the Saab was actually driving a Mercedes-Benz, but since that detail seemed like a dead German giveaway, I changed it. Otherwise, all of the stories are completely true. The hapless victim of foreign abuse in each of the first three examples was I. The heroic beach cleaner in the fourth anecdote was my brother-in-law, Matt, a man also admirable for being the rare white guy who speaks decent Cantonese yet almost never whips it out when ordering in a Chinese restaurant.

Given the setup and my predictably contrarian point of view, it probably wasn't hard to guess where I was going with those anecdotes. But that doesn't make their point—that Americans aren't the worst travelers in the world, and that oftentimes they're the best—any less valid. Or difficult to prove.

Choosing to illuminate my encounters with a nasty German, a French couple, and an Indian lady was tough because it meant ignoring the two Dutch girls who clogged the toilet, flooded the floor, and, only after someone else cleaned the mess, kept themselves locked in the shared bathroom of a guesthouse in Dubrovnik; the freeloading Austrian who arrived in the Philippines woefully unprepared to hike ninety-five-hundred-foot Mount Apo and subsequently demanded and received from me and everyone else on the hill loans of dry clothing, gloves, water, food, and money, without so much as a thank-you; the legion of Middle Eastern satyrs who feast on young boys and girls in Southeast Asian brothels yet treat the rest of the population as though it were beneath contempt; and the Koreans who erected a sign on Tinian Island in the Western Pacific attesting to the "eternal grudge" they swore on behalf of their ancestors to bear out against the despised Japanese.*

None of these stories are meant to imply that *all* foreigners are line-cutting, seat-stealing, scab-picking, litter-bugging, bathroom-hogging, boy-screwing, hate-mongering jackoffs. On the American-Canadian Chilkoot Trail, Randy and I were befriended by an immensely likable German hiker named Eckhard Holler with whom I retain hope of someday reconnecting. In predigital days, a French photographer on a sailboat from Scotland to Norway saved my ass by generously sharing his film. In this book, I've thrown a few good-natured shots at Australians (believe me, they can take it), but without the friendship of a pair of Aussies named Dean Robson and Donella Johnston, to say nothing of a timely introduction to legendary Aussie bar band Cold Chisel, I very likely would have lost my mind in Gifu, Japan. An Indian guy in . . . well, for whatever reason I haven't had much interaction with Indian tourists beyond the foot-scraping lady on the plane to Fiji, but the Indians I know in the States are all good people, so I have faith that the vast majority of their home-country brethren, like the vast majority of all humans, are all right.

They just haven't been drilled in the new art of cultural accommodation the way twenty-first-century Americans have. Molded by two decades of politically correct boot camp—in what we like to call the world's most free-speaking country, it's worth noting that your professional career can be ruined by any number of random

---

* Bone up on the twentieth-century history between Korea and Japan and you can kind of see the Koreans' point.

remarks less offensive than those heard daily on school playgrounds—an entire generation of Americans has been browbeaten into becoming, after Buddhist monks, the most considerate, polite, and nonjudgmental travelers in the world. Whereas writers like Paul Theroux once became famous for bringing their unyielding value systems in contact with distant cultures and describing the inevitable conflict, today's inbred terror of criticism based on cultural differences hamstrings all but the most fearless or pompous of modern American travelers. Compared with the stereotype that gained universal recognition with the 1958 publication of *The Ugly American*, U.S. tourists today move across international territory like neurotic kittens, apologizing ad nauseam for everything from their inability to speak foreign languages (and unless you work at the United Nations, this is nothing to be made to feel guilty about) to their country's habit of electing a nonstop parade of opportunistic slimeballs to political office, as though politicians in every country weren't a nonstop parade of opportunistic slimeballs.

There remain, of course, plenty of asshole Yanks with passports. I once watched an American, a friend no less, entertain himself in Tijuana by throwing pennies on the sidewalk so that he could laugh at the street urchins who kicked and shoved each other out of the way as they scrambled for the loot. No nationality has a monopoly on, or scarcity of, ugly.

There's just one problem with this rosy view of Americans as enlightened, beach-cleaning priests of tolerance. No one believes it. If indeed Americans are the least objectionable tourists in the world, they sure don't get treated like it. As anyone who's been abroad before and after the U.S. invasion of Iraq can tell you, the reception desks overseas have become chillier, the locals a little less friendly, the political debates a lot more spittle filled. Explaining this paradox—good people/bad reputation—requires a brief digression into current events.

First the bad news: Americans are the new Germans. Around the planet, "America" has become a byword for the kind of pushy, greedy, arrogant, ignorant, scheming, intolerant, hypocritical, violent, militaristic, goose-stepping, blood-gulping, Limbaugh-worshipping bullies that civilized people since time eternal have despised and occasionally battled to the death. We're no longer the Rick Blaines of the world, romantic rogues just trying to lie low and mend a broken heart with a little gin and jazz. We're the Major Strassers, dickhead rulers of the new order practically begging the world for comeuppance. All you 82 million Germans can start thanking the United States anytime now for taking those goat horns off your heads.

No matter how many beaches we pick up, no matter how many schools we build amid the rubble of villages we bomb, the world will judge Americans not as well-meaning individuals but as faceless supporters of a fascist regime drunk with military power and an unslakable thirst for oil. In the way Americans once held all citizens of the Soviet Union in contempt, in the way the world's 1 billion baptized Catholics are somehow held accountable for every impetuous decree from a geriatric pontiff whose native language the majority of them don't even speak, the world now judges Americans as an evil herd.

Unfair, maybe, but this makes a kind of sense. Universal scorn is what results from willingly paying taxes to a government that sends soldiers around the globe to secure oil fields and flatten ancient civilizations before trying to rebuild them according to its own shabby blueprints. More than voting, demonstrating, righteous sermonizing at cocktail parties, or forwarding Cheney-bashing e-mails, it's April 15, not the first Tuesday in November, that reveals the depth of your political convictions. It doesn't matter whom you voted for or who's in the White House, if you pay the taxes that foot the bills, you're complicit in the big picture. And you're hated for it.

Not that this gives the Europeans, in particular, the right to complain about the American government, given the fact that it wasn't Americans but Europeans who introduced land theft, African slavery, gunpowder, religious intolerance, and genocide of natives to North America. Since the entirety of American civilization is based upon European civilization—language, religion, education, military, politics, banking, architecture, farming, industry, transportation, all copied from Europe, the continent that never met a dictator it didn't line up to salute—the progression of American history shouldn't come as a surprise to anyone in the Old World. In the Middle East today, the United States is only acting in the manner that virtually all of its European fathers did whenever they enjoyed military, technological, and economic superiority over a foreign country—that is to say, using a dominant army to overthrow a foreign regime and shuttle in private enterprise beneath the security of a semipermanent military presence to extract resources and amass wealth. Long ago these quasi-governmental commercial operations had names like the Hudson's Bay Company and Dutch East India Company. Today they're called Halliburton and Bechtel. Nothing bums out America-bashing Euros like having their own reflection held up in a mirror. I've spun the beret off the head of more than one smug citizen of the EU Corporation with that argument.

On the other hand, let's all stop being so naïve about who runs the U.S. government and remember, particularly if you're a hater of Herr Bush, that it was that great peacenik Jimmy Carter who in 1980 signed the Carter Doctrine, making it official U.S. policy to employ "any means necessary" to protect the flow of oil from the Middle East, a document used by both Bushes to justify military actions in the region. Democrat or Republican, the U.S. government always operates in the interest of corporate profit. And when it yaps about protecting your freedom and the "American way of life," that expressly means the inalienable right to burn Middle Eastern oil so that we can be warm in winter, cool in summer, and travel anywhere we want, whenever we want, whether it's to a beach in Tahiti or the beer cooler at the Quickie Mart down the street.

Over the next two decades, the way and frequency with which Americans travel abroad will likely proceed down one of two very different paths. The optimistic forecast, shared by most of the large companies whose business it is to make bankers and stockholders optimistic about these things, is that travel will grow exponentially in the next twenty years, turning the global village into a global metropolis. Boeing and Airbus, the world's only important manufacturers of large commercial aircraft, each project an annual 5 percent increase in air travel, which they say will cause world air traffic to triple by 2030. Imagine New York to L.A., only with three times more screaming babies and three times as many wankers in the middle seat battling you for armrest hegemony.

In this scenario, as in everything else, Asia will lead the boom. The three most traveled air routes in the world are already in Japan (Tokyo/Haneda-Sapporo, Tokyo/Haneda-Fukuoka, Tokyo/Haneda-Osaka). Within two decades, Chinese airlines are expected to add twenty-three hundred aircraft worth $200 billion to their fleets. To accommodate increased traffic, Boeing will introduce its 787 Dreamliner. Boeing calls the plane, which is capable of carrying 350 passengers, "the biggest step we have taken in fifty years." The 787 is expected to enter service in time for the 2008 Beijing Olympics, the People's Republic of China's glorious coming-out party.

All of this growth is predicated on one decisive variable: the uninterrupted supply of affordable oil. Boeing likes to call its new 787 a "game changing" aircraft, but the real game changer on the horizon is the possible disruption of the global fuel supply. And even a secure and peaceful Middle East might not be enough to guard against it, bringing the discussion to future-travel model number two.

Conceived in the 1950s but gaining widespread acceptance only recently, the concept of "peak oil" is the recognition that oil and gas are finite resources subject to depletion. This might not sound like a groundbreaking idea, but it sort of is. For most of the twentieth century, the petrochemical industry operated on the assumption that oil and gas reserves were governed by the inelastic laws of supply-and-demand economics. As long as there was a demand for oil, so went the thinking, there would be oil. Which is like saying as long as people want to keep illuminating streetlamps with whale oil, there will always be a supply of whale oil. Strictly speaking, true, but not necessarily practical in the twenty-first century.

The arrival of peak oil—the date, one to twenty-five years in the future, when global oil production begins to decline—is expected in some quarters to lead to rapid societal disintegration. This will be kicked into high gear by the collapse of the international banking system, the totality of which is dependent upon the increasing prosperity of an oil-based economy, and end with you guarding your family and meager supply of canned vegetables from packs of bandits with whatever primitive weapons you were able to fashion from the trees and houses in your neighborhood before they were all burned for warmth. In this context, your winter trip to Costa Rica to commune with macaws and howler monkeys will appear slightly frivolous, if not impossible. You'll be lucky to make it to the Ration Center and back each month with your stick of lard and four ounces of sugar.

This might or might not be farce, but even the oil-glutted Saudis have a well-known saying: "My father rode a camel. I drive a car. My son rides in a jet. His son will ride a camel." Even if peak oil is dystopian fallacy, oil prices might still reach the stratosphere, turning recreational travel into an activity restricted solely to the truly elite. Mass tourism as we know it could cease to exist.

Given this grave potential sequence of events, it's not unreasonable to suggest that we're living at the end of a golden age of travel. The period that began with the jet age in the 1950s and got a boost from deregulation of the airline industry in the 1980s has moved more people to more parts of the planet over the last half century than in all the years of human history that preceded it. Today, almost anybody armed with plastic can buy a ticket and, within a day or two, land him- or herself in just about any place in the world.

You can take a week off work and be in Dakar or Tashkent or Borneo in less time than it took Ben Franklin to get from Boston to Philadelphia. Largely taken for granted, this revolutionary ability to go anywhere on a whim has altered our perception of the world in ways we probably don't fully comprehend. If that instant mobility is taken away, our worldview will be drastically reshaped again. The planet could once more become a forbidding place, expensive to see and scary to traverse, one that forces us to reexamine the basic lessons about the world collective that travel used to teach. This might not be a bad thing.

As I've alluded to more than once, a few months after I turned seventeen, I bought a 1973 Ford Torino for four hundred dollars and announced a plan to spend the summer driving to New York City and back, catching as many Major League Baseball games along the way as I could. The Torino was the color of day-old guacamole, and its rear quarter panel on the passenger side so weakened by rust that it flapped in the wind. Otherwise I believed this machine to be among the last credible products of the American muscle-car era (Starsky and Hutch drove the slightly sportier and, let it be said here,

ridiculously painted Gran Torino). Running away with
the circus always seemed like an idiotic idea to me; a
summer behind the wheel of an uninsured, decade-old
Ford was the type of adventure that held real promise.

The cross-country extravaganza was originally to
have included Randy, alongside whom the Alaska–to–
New York idea was hatched. Like Morgan with Thailand, however, Randy wound up bailing on the trip. In
the end, this proved to be a good move, since the baseball players went on strike in June, I got hit by a drunk
driver in South Bend, Indiana, made it only as far as
Grove City, Ohio, ran out of money on the way home,
and spent three weeks stranded in a one-bedroom apartment with two other guys in Salt Lake City. With no
idea that any of these events were on the horizon, I quit
my job at Juneau's KINY AM-TV and put the Torino on
the ferry to Prince Rupert, British Columbia, a day and
a half away by ship, and the nearest road entry to the
Lower Forty-eight.

I spent the first night on board amid the colorful ny-
lon village of freestanding tents and sleeping bags that
turn the upper decks of Alaska state ferries into floating
hippie festivals each summer. Snagging a plastic lounge
chair, I laid out my sleeping bag next to a pair of guys
with greasy gray ponytails who, as the entire ship would
soon discover, made up a pretty mean guitar-and-fiddle
duo. Aging though by no means over-the-hill folkies, the
guys broke out their instruments sometime after dinner
and used them to earn applause and gratis bong hits
from the mob of like-minded sprout munchers who par-
tied deep into the starry Alaskan night.

As I was young and talkative and one of the few locals
slumming it on the top deck, I became a sort of pet for

the friendly dopers from Down South. It felt good to be taken into their adult fold, get to play a few songs on guitar, and, most important, share in their never-ending supply of Canadian Club whiskey, a fresh bottle of which somehow materialized each time another was finished. You'd never imagine how pleasant a fiddle screeching in your ear at two in the morning can be until you've experienced it with your tenth cup of CC and Coke resting just next to your head as you black out.

The morning sun rose like an angry red meatball. Shortly after sunrise, I crept out of my sleeping bag, clutched my throbbing skull, staggered to the head, took a terrifyingly long and out-of-control piss during which I had to brace myself with both hands against the wall, somehow made it back outside in time to spray several gallons of vomit over the railing, and returned to my deck chair, where I remained paralyzed inside my fart sack for the rest of the morning, unable to answer my body's ferocious demands for more water and urination.

Sometime around noon, one of the ponytailed guys sauntered across the deck (sans fiddle, praise Christ) and tactfully informed me that it was time to man up and clean the mess from beneath my deck chair. I lifted an eyelid, rolled on my side, and looked under the chair. Despite the agonizing rush of blood to my forehead, I could plainly see that directly beneath me was a sizable lake of puke that I'd apparently discharged the night before.

With the sun now high in the sky, the aroma of festering chunder was starting to bum out the tie-dye crowd. A dustpan and spatula were presented to me. Scraping up my own walrus call in front of fifty or sixty strangers and pitching it over the side of the ship was brutal—getting the dried bits out of the Brillo fibers of the deck's outdoor turf took prodigious effort—but with the job done the hippies rallied round, forced some organic beet juice down my throat, and made me feel like part of the gang again. The fiddle player even offered me a pick-me-up toke.

"Just brush your teeth first," he said, and for the first time I noticed the gums along his bottom row of teeth were almost entirely black.

I didn't touch his soggy one-hitter and didn't go near the Canadian Club again either, so it was with a clear head, bright eyes, and more or less purified body that on the following morning I said farewell to my new pals, inched the Torino onto land at Prince Rupert, and found the terminus of the famed Yellowhead Highway: 1,002 miles of narrow, two-lane asphalt through Canada and across the border to Seattle.

Particularly along the 450 miles between Prince Rupert and the first major town of Prince George, the Yellowhead travels through a desolate wilderness of dense forests, empty meadows, rushing rivers, and misty, glacier-covered mountainsides. As the Torino's after-market sound system blared and wild Canadian splendor flew past my window, I spent the morning congratulating myself on leaving home and driving to New York in a four-hundred-dollar automobile, a move that, at this early stage of the trip, was looking like the wisest decision I'd ever made in my life.

Like all perfect things, this wasn't meant to last. At some point between microscopic settlements with names like Telkwa and Endako, a dark presence began shadowing my path. On the downhill side of a long slope, I glanced behind me and was startled to see a metallic black Pontiac GTO, which only a moment before had appeared in my rearview mirror as an indistinguishable dot. The GTO had the model's famous hood scoop, squared front end, stacked headlights, and split chrome grill, but within seconds, its front end was so far up my ass I couldn't even read its B.C. plates.

Around corners, up hills, on straightaways, the black GTO stuck to my bumper like an alien parasite. When I accelerated, the GTO accelerated, never leaving more than a body length between us. After five or six miles of this unnerving intimidation, the GTO's engine finally opened into a full-throated roar, overwhelming Sweet's *Desolation Boulevard* blasting from the Torino's tape deck, and the maniac behind the wheel swerved into the opposite lane and pulled alongside me. There he remained until we careened into a tight curve, waiting until we were about halfway through before completing his pass.

As he sped by, the guy in the driver's seat flashed a sly smile, causing me to instantly make two observations. One, this guy was a tremendous douche bag. And, two, despite his crew cut and chiseled jaw, he didn't look much older than me. This surprising discovery released a bit of my fear and stimulated a competitive nerve. Soon I found myself punching the Torino's gas pedal and jamming my front bumper as close to the rear end of the GTO as I could manage. Keeping the heat on high boil, I waited for an opportune spot to pass—plenty of flat, straight blacktop for me—and slammed my foot to the floor as though squashing an insect.

A couple of times in Juneau, I'd coaxed the Torino above the hundred-mile-per-hour mark, a feat that required a small hill, fifteen or twenty seconds to gather momentum, and Randy in the passenger seat watching the speedometer while I kept my eyes glued to the pavement. Getting from ninety to a hundred in the Torino was a labor of love, but between eighty and ninety, the car had always demonstrated good pickup, so I was able to blast past the GTO and in the process flash the same shit-eating grin at the Canuck he'd thrown me a few miles back.

With my heart racing like a hummingbird's, we continued our precarious duel for twenty or thirty minutes, passing and repassing as the grades became steeper, the curves sharper, the speeds more daring, and the late-afternoon sky darker; our through-the-windows smiles turned to snarls, the kind you see just before the first punch is thrown. On a piece of cliff-side road, the GTO pulled alongside me. I was used to this trick by now, except this time a pickup truck coming from the opposite direction loomed in the near distance. Even steven at ninety miles per hour, the GTO had forced one of three choices upon me: I could accept defeat, hit my brakes, and let him slide in front me; hope that he'd chicken out, hit his own brakes, and fall behind; or maintain speed and force a fiery three-car collision in approximately ten seconds.

The oncoming truck began flashing its lights. Its driver's panic and confusion were palpable. So were mine. With maybe three seconds till showtime, my front bumper deadlocked with the GTO's, I mashed both of my feet into the brake pedal hard enough to give myself blisters, fishtailed into the oncoming lane with a high-pitched scream of smoking rubber, miraculously righted myself at seventy miles per hour, watched the GTO dart ahead of me, and heard the Doppler whine of the pickup's horn as it passed safely by.

A hand emerged from the GTO and waved at me as it shot away, leaving me beaten and choking on the smell of exhaust and alpha wolf. Only then did it occur to me that a 1973 Ford Torino with a factory Windsor 351 under the hood never stood a prayer against a customized GTO. The son of a bitch behind the wheel had been cat and mousing me from the start. In terms a later generation would understand, I'd been playing Dick Trickle to his Dale Earnhardt.

He'd also been toying with a primary fear on the Yellowhead Highway: fuel. Drivers crossed central British Columbia in those days much the way the Afrika Korps crossed the Libyan desert, constantly reassessing the relationship between the petrol in their tanks and the distance to the next filling station. With the GTO out of sight, I had time to review my dashboard and saw to my alarm that the needle on the gas gauge was hovering directly over the big red *E*.

I slowed to forty, agonizing after the high-speed dogfight, and continued on in silent terror as the needle actually dropped below *E*, something I'd not known was possible. My scrotum tightened like a frozen walnut as I obsessed over the gas situation. Even on the flat track in Detroit, the Torino had never been celebrated for its fuel efficiency. At the nerve-splintering speed I'd been traveling up and down mountains for the past half hour, it had been sucking down juice faster than a team of six-year-old soccer players.

When the car finally sputtered to its inevitable death on the side of the road, I remained in the front seat for a full five minutes, demeaning myself with a healthy session of self-loathing. Then, like an estate attorney opening the will in front of the family for the first time, I gingerly unfolded the enormous B.C. map my dad had given me for the trip. With forty-four panels, the map took up half the cabin, and it was tough to tell exactly where I was. No matter what, the next town was easily miles away and getting to one was no guarantee of salvation. Half the "towns" marked along the route didn't seem to have a gas station, much less any permanent residents.

A dozen or more cars ignored my outstretched thumb as they screamed by on their ways to whatever oh-so-goddamn-important appointments they possibly could have had in the sphincter of British Columbia on a Tuesday evening. I offered each of them a piece of my anger as they passed until, after two miles of walking, I heard the sweet crunch of tires slowing on a gravel shoulder. I turned around to see a blond guy with a scraggly beard and embroidered headband sticking his head out of the passenger-side window of a sky blue VW Microbus.

"Need a leeft?"

I ran to the van before whoever was inside could change their mind.

"Get een back," the blond guy said.

The side door jerked open on a set of rusty tracks, and for a moment I could only stare in bewilderment as several pairs of hands beckoned me into the Marrakech Express. Surrounded by red tapestries, paisley pillows, beaded curtains, and assorted orange and saffron accoutrements, two guys, one girl, and a filthy long-haired baby dressed only in a stained little white tank top were splayed in the back of the van like Nepalese monarchs on feast day. Up front were the driver, one of those balding-on-top-but-long-hair-down-the-back dudes, and the blond guy in the passenger seat. I've never cared for the mixed aroma of hummus, ganja, and dirty feet, but I had Brother Torino to think about. The door rattled shut behind me, the van crawled off the shoulder at a solid five miles per hour, and my old pal Eric Clapton started up through a set of blown-out Pioneer speakers.

"*Es r oto bahine?*"

This was the driver saying something I couldn't catch.

"Eh?" I said.

"The green car," explained the blond guy in the passenger seat. "We saw the car on the side of road. Have you lost your gas?"

I acknowledged my immense shame. "No problems," said the blond, scratching his beard. "We take you to gas."

They were six Germans, counting the baby, who'd been traveling the west coasts of Canada and the States in this van they'd purchased in California.

"You have very beautiful country," the blond guy told me.

"It's not mine," I said. "I'm American, not Canadian."

"Well, we have been to United States and you also have very beautiful country."

The rest of the van bobbed their heads in agreement, and I settled into an old beanbag missing half its beans. Tabouleh and hookah smoke flowed, but I was too agitated to take a puff or accept the vile-looking plate of fecal-y organics the woman put together for me. My up-

tight vibe quickly infected the van. I felt lousy about
this, but at seventeen the Torino was pretty much everything I had in life and until I got to a gas station and
back to my car, I wasn't emotionally ready to get started
on the happy hour. Getting high and chilling with a
hairy-pitted German chick while she breast-fed a pants-
less baby wasn't going to get me back on the road any
faster.

"*Käse?*" The woman thrust a sweaty white lump at me.

"Eet es cheese," said the guy in an orange blouse
next to her. "Bery goot. Try."

I tore off a hunk of bread and ate the cheese, hoping
this might appease my hosts. Mistaking this sacrifice for
conviviality, one of the guys passed me a bottle of red
wine with the cork out. Christ. I don't even like drinking out of the same bottle as my wife, let alone Euro
stoners who appeared not to have showered in weeks.
In certain situations, however, the kindness of strangers
is impossible to snub. I took a mighty swig from the bottle just as the van hit a pothole and a quarter cup or so
of dark red wine dribbled down the front of my jacket.

The Germans were nice, but I never found a rhythm
in the van. Despite my artful attempt at discretion, they'd
all seen me wipe the rim of the wine bottle with my shirt
sleeve before touching it to my lips. Worse, although I'm
generally good around babies, this one smelled like the
bottom of a bag of beef jerky, and I did what I could to
discourage its advances on me. Even the blond guy up
front exhaled with relief when a gas station and restaurant finally appeared in the distance.

I offered money for the lift, a gesture they refused
with such violence that I wondered if they thought I was
trying to purchase their baby. We traded good-byes, and

I hopped out of the van in front of the gas station, which, I noticed after the VW had creaked away, was burning only a dim security light. I walked to the pumps. Both were padlocked. A handwritten sign on a piece of cardboard hung from one of the nozzles: "Closed."

I stared without expression at the pumps, then jiggled the handles to make sure the locks were secure. They were. With the weary, self-pitying moan of the defeated, I turned and faced the small clapboard restaurant across the empty parking lot. A lamp glowed weakly in a corner window. At the very least, there must be a phone inside. Hunching against a gathering wind and steadily dropping temperature, I trudged across the pavement, turned a corner around the side of the building, and felt my stomach rise into my mouth. Parked in front of the restaurant was the metallic black GTO.

Aside from an old couple eating silently in the middle of the room, the restaurant was empty. Nobody appeared to be working. The oldsters ignoring me, I rattled the bells on the front door for a second time and shouted, "Hello!" This brought a muted conversation from the back. A door opened behind the bar and out stepped, unmistakably, the lantern-jawed, crew-cut driver of the GTO. He looked across the room, instantly recognized me, and flashed his cock-of-the-walk grin.

"Didn't see you drive up," he said, pulling back the curtain on the front window. "Where's the Torino?"

Such tender irony, bowing your head to the prick who just ran you off the road. I might as well have been on the USS *Midway*, pushing choppers off the deck on the way out of Saigon. I mumbled something noncommittal, the way you do when you creep in at two in the morning and your mother asks what you've been doing all night.

"Ran out of gas?" he guessed. "Don't worry about it. Happens all the time along this stretch." He extended his hand and gave a friendly shake.

Shanghai Bob once confided that his first impression of me was that I was a tremendous horse's ass, exactly the type of neophyte gaijin that old Asia hands such as himself loathed on principle. It was not an uncommon confession. Many of the people I now count as friends apparently had to overcome some initial repugnance toward my supposedly radioactive personality. Though I've never completely understood it, over the years I've come up with a few theories to explain this intriguing phenomenon. People are thin-skinned. They get offended when you refuse to slurp out of wine bottles with them. Or point out that no matter how many times they voted Democrat, voluntarily coughing up federal taxes means they've got Iraqi blood on their hands. Or insist that since two remakes ("Cocaine" and "I Shot the Sheriff") represent the pinnacle of Eric Clapton's career, and since "Layla" is memorable mostly for Duane Allman's slide guitar and the Jim Gordon–composed piano coda, the allegedly masterful Slowhand belongs atop the compost heap of rock's most overrated stars. It takes a while to get used to some people, I guess.

Despite the rocky first impression, the GTO driver didn't seem like a bad guy, and I sensed he was thinking the same about me. His name was Gary; he was nineteen, from Nova Scotia, working that summer for his aunt and uncle, running the gas station and tending bar six days a week and not getting paid squat, but at least his room and board were taken care of.

"It's not bad out here," Gary said, comparing B.C. to his home in the east. "Boring as shit, though. Running into you was the most exciting thing all week. Got a gas can?"

Gary yelled at someone in the kitchen, grabbed a loop of about fifty keys from a wooden peg by the door, and led us outside. On the outer wall of the restaurant, he flipped a switch and the fueling bay lit up like Christmas morning. He unlocked one of the pumps and filled a large red fuel can, talking nonstop while the burning ember of his cigarette dangled within the mirage of blurry vapors escaping the pump.

"Canadians out west are a dim bunch," he said. "Can't even get a fucking beer after ten o' clock in most places. Sunday's the worst. How's Alaska? I was supposed to work on a·fishing boat out of Sitka, but it fell through. Got offered a cannery job instead. Fuck that shit. I'll stick it out till winter, then go home. Pretty nice here, but between the best-looking girls and the best-looking cows, there isn't much difference. Slower than algebra class most nights. How far back's your car?"

We got in the GTO. Gary turned the ignition, and a pair of afterburners he must have stolen from an F-16 shook the car to life. We sat idling for a while, the expression on Gary's face indicating that I should be taking this moment to drink in the stirring howl of his motor. He leaned on the gas until the car began vibrating on its chassis like a rocket trembling on the launchpad. Gary talked about things like engine displacement and torque-induced gyroscopic precession, and I nodded in a way that suggested these were precisely the types of conversations my grease-monkey buddies and I sat around having all the time. Then he shoved the beast into gear, and we peeled out shooting twin rooster tails of gravel behind us.

On the highway, Gary weaved through dark corners and mountain inclines averaging eighty. I got the feeling he could've managed every hairpin with his eyes closed. While he drove and smoked, he gave me the specs on the GTO and bitched some more about Western Canada's backward ways. I'd grown up far enough from New York and the East Coast to both be in awe of them and have a chip on my shoulder about their influence. It had never occurred to me that a similar regional rivalry existed in Canada.

"Found On Road Dead," Gary smirked when the Torino came into view. "That's what Ford stands for. Also, Fix Or Repair Daily."

When we got to the car, Gary showed me the neatest trick I'd seen since my dad had fixed my stalling carburetor by clipping open its check valve with a wooden clothespin. The gas tank on the Torino was located behind the rear license plate, which flipped down on a little spring, revealing the fuel pipe. When Gary saw this, he grunted and toed out his cigarette on the road.

"Fucking nozzle is never going to reach that tank," he said, and I immediately saw the problem. The stubby nozzle on the gas can poked out only a few inches, not nearly far enough to reach the Torino's recessed gas tank. We tried to bridge the gap by pouring gas on an arc through the air, but it spilled all over the back bumper and onto the ground.

"Got a newspaper or magazine or something?" Gary asked.

I shook my head. Nothing.

Gary opened the door of the Torino and fished through the debris under my seats.

"This should work." He held up a crumpled Alaska Marine Highway summer schedule newspaper insert. Pressing it out flat on the trunk, he tore the schedule in half and creased the pages in the middle as though making a paper airplane. Then he crimped one end into the shape of a funnel and ran his cupped hand up and down the crease until it formed the approximate shape of a half-pipe. He jammed the funnel end of the paper pipe into the gas tank and told me to hold it in place while he poured gas from the can down the paper. It took about ten minutes, and my hands were marinated with gasoline and newsprint by the time we were finished, but most of the fifteen liters made it into the tank. There wasn't any good place to throw a section of gas-soaked newspaper, so Gary dropped it on the ground and tossed a match on it, and we watched it crinkle into a little black fist and disappear in the wind.

"You can fill up at our place if you want, but this'll get you seventy or eighty kilometers," Gary said. "About twenty kilometers past the restaurant, there's all-night gas. It's cheaper than ours. Good pizza, too."

Gary stuck around to make sure the Torino fired up. It took a few pumps on the gas pedal, then the engine purred to life. I left it idling and walked over to the GTO.

"I really need to pay you something." This was the third time I'd offered. Gary waved me off for a third time.

"You'll do the same for someone down the road," he said, sticking his hand through the window. "It evens out in the end."

I thanked him again, and we shook hands and said

good-bye. Gary whipped the GTO around with a theatrical squeal of tires and gave his horn a short blast as he crested a small hill and disappeared.

Standing on the side of the road, waiting for the cry of afterburners to fade away, I had no way of knowing that someday I'd be writing about this moment. Nor could I have been aware that some distant corner of my mind was already banking lessons that would reach far into a future I barely recognized as reality. Growing up in an isolated town, I already knew I was going to end up traveling as much as I could. And as an occasionally snakebit traveler, I'd soon be accepting more Good Samaritan charity, like the loan from the Kiwi in Thailand; I'd also be passing it on, like the food, clothing, and cash I gave to the Austrian in the Philippines. But as a fundamentally skeptical kid, it would have seemed laughable to me that I'd ever move beyond sheer recreational travel and end up devoting a substantial portion of my life to an industry in which snakebites and other reality checks are kept hidden away like back hair and incarcerated cousins.

As the years drifted by, however, and my life became one of delayed flights, middle seats, bad hotels, cold buffets, awkward property tours, pushy PR flacks, off-season travel, miserly budgets, butchered copy, kill fees, and every other indignity visited upon the itinerant travel writer, my unexpected blizzard of experiences led to a growing collection of ideas. These I made a goal of one day stepping outside of the system to share with an audience perpetually cheated out of the truth. In time, my stacks of Mead spiral notebooks filled an entire file cabinet. My catalog of untold stories, impertinent observations, and verboten opinions added up to miles of material, the first section of which, I eventually came to realize, had been laid by the small list of rules that started me down this road in the first place:

Clean up your own mess, no matter how tough a job it is.

Foreigners are almost never as bad as you think they'll be.

A lot of interesting things can happen when you run out of gas.

If the world can forgive the Germans, it can forgive anybody.

Just when you think you've seen the best the world has to offer, there'll always be Canada.

Acknowledgments

• • •

Because for the writer it's the most meaningful and easiest to screw up, the acknowledgments page is the most daunting of any book. Given the many locations covered here, the best way to begin is with an apology for inevitable omissions from the literal cast of thousands of family, friends, coworkers, and strangers who have assisted me along the way. I regret that I can't thank them all, but each is fondly remembered and appreciated. I'll let Kevin Hiestand—who gallantly devoured the world's worst fish dinner in Honduras so that I didn't have to—stand as the symbol for all of those not mentioned.

I'm grateful to every editor who ever sent me anywhere to work. Special thanks are extended to Don Campbell in Portland, Joe Robinson in Los Angeles, Dana Joseph in Dallas, James Heidenry in New York, and Ed Needham in London. Also, publishers Rick Morrison and Alan Davis.

The quote from John Butrovich in the Alaska chapter

comes from *Alaska Agonistes: The Age of Petroleum (How Big Oil Bought Alaska)* by Joe LaRocca, the definitive account of the topic by the legendary reporter I had the privilege of working with briefly at KINY AM-TV in Juneau.

Randal Davis; Jayne Kuchac; Bill, John, and Margaret May; Dave Malley; and David Swanson provided invaluable assistance to various chapters. Jack Boulware, Kinky Friedman, Andrew Krystal, Candida Mannozzi, and Joe Queenan were of great help from the beginning. My cousin Michelle Thompson helped me survive the most harrowing, and oddly entertaining, Russian commuter flight that ever safely returned to earth.

In significant ways this book owes its existence to John DeVore's openhearted generosity and the reliable guidance of my agent, Joëlle Delbourgo.

Some might argue that I don't have the broad experience to know, but I believe Sarah Knight may be the finest editor in the book business and am prepared to provide endless red-ink examples to prove the point. It's humbling to imagine the mess this book would have been without her. The support of John Sterling, Patrick Clark, Richard Rhorer, Maggie Richards, Dana Trombley, and everyone at Holt has been tremendous.

Thanks and love to Mike, Carlene, Amy, and especially Mom and Dad, whose parenting skills and epic generosity I appreciate more with each passing year.

Without Joyce, none of the names above would appear, for without her nothing would be possible, much less worth doing.

• • •

About the Author

CHUCK THOMPSON is a former features editor for *Maxim* and was the first editor in chief of *Travelocity* magazine. His writing and photography have appeared in *The Atlantic, Esquire, National Geographic Adventure, Playboy, Spy, Escape, WWE Magazine,* MTV's *The Jenny McCarthy Show,* and the *Los Angeles Times.* He has traveled on assignment in more than thirty-five countries, and is the author of two guidebooks, *The 25 Best World War II Sites: European Theater* and *The 25 Best World War II Sites: Pacific Theater.* He's played in a variety of professional musical groups, and worked as an ESL instructor, radio DJ, deckhand, and assistant sergeant at arms in the Alaska House of Representatives. He lives in the Pacific Northwest.